RACE RIOT

D0167876

Blacks in the New World

Edited by August Meier and John H. Bracey

A list of books in the series appears at the back of this book.

RACE RIOT

Chicago in the Red Summer
of 1919

WILLIAM M. TUTTLE, JR.

University of Illinois Press
Urbana and Chicago

University of Illinois Press
1325 South Oak Street
Champaign, IL 61820-6903
www.press.uillinois.edu

First Illinois paperback, 1996
© 1970 by William M. Tuttle, Jr.
Manufactured in the United States of America
P 9 8 7

⊚ This book is printed on acid-free paper.

Library of Congress Cataloging-in-Publication Data
Tuttle, William M., 1937–
    Race riot : Chicago in the Red Summer of 1919 / William M.
Tuttle, Jr.
        p.   cm. — (Blacks in the New World)
    Originally published: New York, Atheneum, 1970.
    Includes bibliographical references and index.
    ISBN 0-252-06586-7 (alk. paper)
    1. Riots—Illinois—Chicago—History—20th century. 2. Afro-
Americans—Illinois—Chicago—History—20th century. 3. Chicago
(Ill.)—History, 1875– . I. Title. II. Series.
F548.9.N4T88   1996
977.3'1100496073—dc20   96-7602
                                                    CIP
ISBN 978-0-252-06586-6

Preface

So MUCH has been written about the squalor of life in America's black ghettos that white Americans, and especially guilt-ridden whites sympathetic to the economic, political, and social advancement of black citizens, tend to overlook or at least minimize the healthy, positive, and indeed dynamic aspects of life in the black community. What have we done to them? white liberals ask. How can we help them to share in "our way of life"? Whether justified or not, such a feeling of guilt can result in an attitude of condescension, and, in the hands of historians, can produce distortion of the past. Writing in reply to one liberal who had urged integration into white society as a way of elevating black people, Ralph Ellison noted that his foe in debate "ignores the fact that we love our Harlems, love to be with other Negroes, marry mostly Negroes, and would consider the loss of such churches as Harlem's Abyssinia a national calamity, just as we consider the destruction of the Savoy Ballroom a cultural disaster of international dimensions." He explained his belief that white liberals along with white segregationists flatter themselves by exaggerating and misrepresenting "the Negro American thrust for an equal share of the prizes of democracy." It was not that black Americans aspired to be just like whites. Both liberals and segregationists, Ellison wrote, "completely ignore the obvious fact that Negroes find their own variant of the American culture . . . and their own communities just as dear to them as other groups find theirs." Why, he added, there were even "Negro fathers with adolescent daughters who . . . would view intermarriage as a disaster." No, it was simply that black people, knowing only too well "that most privilege in this society has been supported by the inequality of opportunity of some groups of outsiders," wanted an equal chance and "a fairer share of what has been created by their suppression and exploitation. . . ." [1]

Unfortunately, much that has been written about black Americans by whites has been written from the point of view of Ellison's liberal antagonist. This is true, for example, of much of the literature on racial violence. Moreover, to add to this propensity for distortion, scholars writing from a white middle-class perspective have often referred to their subjects collectively as "the Negro" or "the black American"; in their group analyses there was thus little investigation of the immense possibilities for individual variation from the norm. Race, of course, is the badge separating blacks from whites— but what of the variations within the black community in social and economic level, education, regional background, sex, shade of skin color, physical health, and temperament? What of the "exceptions"? What of a black family, for example, with a history of generations of patrifocal family stability? For scholars, white and black alike, such a family obviously has not commanded the same degree of consideration as has

[1] *Harper's,* CCXXXV (July 1967), 14, 16.

been devoted to disintegrating family structure with its "pathology" of illegitimacy, unemployment, illiteracy, and disease. In surveying black America the focus has been on failure, not success; on group statistics, not on individual human beings; on passive recipients of injustice, not on people capable of adjusting to and ordering their own lives within a caste society.

Race Riot, as is evident from the title, has little to say about the healthy and positive aspects of life in the nation's black communities. To most observers, of course, urban riots represent the ultimate failure in a city's race relations. Unfortunately, too, the treatment of racial, ethnic, religious, economic, political, and social groups *as* groups is, to a high degree, unavoidable. But whenever possible in this study, an effort has been made to write of individuals and, as race riots are occurrences of the streets, to write history "from the bottom up." Of all the scholarly disciplines, history at least should honor the commitment to study the individual as well as the unique in the past; and this should be a commitment to study more than just the educated, articulate, quotable individuals representative of the governing elite. It should be to study members of the bottom and middle strata of society as well.

The recorded voice of the masses, both black and white, has been barely audible; the masses have not bequeathed much to historians in the way of spoken evidence. Yet this obstacle does not have to be insurmountable; valuable records do exist, and historians working with the recent past can also interview the "common people" who witnessed and suffered racial violence at first hand. Difficulty in ferreting out evidence, however, is but one of the obstacles. Another is the narrow conceptualization of the processes of race relations and especially of racial violence. Too often historians and other scholars have surveyed race relations in the United States, not on the basis of the black people and the white people who were or were not relating to each other, but on the basis of policy statements by special-interest groups. The historian can glean helpful information from policy statements, but there is frequently a large gap separating an organization's views from those of its members, especially on matters of race; and it is unlikely that many riot participants took their prompting from the NAACP, AFL, or Urban League before hurling rocks at their racial enemies.

The origins of the Chicago race riot of 1919 are to be found, not in high-level policy, but in gut-level animosities between black and white people who were generally inarticulate and presentist-oriented, and who did not record their motivations or feelings for posterity. The tensions that eventually erupted in bloodshed in Chicago were born in attitudes of racial superiority and inferiority ("white racism," as the Kerner Commission would eventually label it), and nurtured on the killing floors in the stockyards, on all-white blocks threatened with black occupancy, and in parks and on beaches that were racially contested. The truly bitter and functional animosities were thus not at the top, but at the bottom, at the common denominators at which races coexisted—at the shop level in industry, at the block level, at the neighborhood recreational level. To explain the Chicago riot, this evidence has to be found; and though such evidence is not abundant by any means, it does exist.[2] Recorded in typescript copy and hidden away at a federal records center, for example, is the verbatim testimony of workers in the stockyards, angry, volatile men like "Heavy" Williams, "Tubs," and Joseph Hodge. If a black worker shouted "Fuck the union, fuck you in the [union] button" to a white organizer, as many did in 1919, the historian should quote this expression of heated bitterness, for this angry outburst—far more, for example, than the AFL's rather meaningless action in June 1919 of welcoming blacks to unionize when its exclusionist affiliates had no intention of lowering their color bars —illuminates why black men and white men tried to kill each

[2] See "Essay on Sources."

other. Also that summer, light-skinned blacks who could "pass" sneaked into the meetings of hostile white property owners; "niggers," or the euphemism "undesirables," were the subject of debate. "If we can't get them out any other way," a speaker warned, "we are going to . . . bomb them out." "Let them step on my corns," declared another, "and I'll show them what I'll do." The reports of these spies help to make explicable the bomber mentality of people who were probably never quoted again in their lives. Speaking from archives and manuscript collections are the voices of black men and women known only to their families and friends—to mention two, men like Shot Pinckney, who told his story of escaping from the peonage of a Mississippi plantation and migrating to Chicago in 1916, and Stanley Norvell, an ex-AEF officer and "New Negro," who expressed his determination to fight on in Chicago for the equal rights he thought he had earned on the battlefield in France. Finally, there are interviews, such as that with John Turner Harris, who in 1919, at the age of fourteen, was enjoying the waters of Lake Michigan when a friend floating next to him was struck on the forehead with a rock and drowned, thereby immediately precipitating the race riot.

The author hopes that he has succeeded, at least in part, in explaining the race riot and its causes in terms of individuals as well as of groups. This, at any rate, is what he has tried to do with the historical resources he could uncover.

Many people and many institutions have aided me in my research and writing. Without fail, the staffs of libraries and archives have been both cordial and helpful. I should like to express my appreciation to the staffs of the National Archives, especially its Social and Economic Records Division; the Federal Records Center, Suitland, Maryland; the Library of Congress; the Chicago *Daily News-Sun Times* Library; Harper Library, University of Chicago; the Chicago Historical Society and especially its chief of manuscripts, Archie

Motley; Newberry Library; Chicago Municipal Reference Library; George Cleveland Hall Branch, Chicago Public Library; University of Illinois, Chicago Circle; State Historical Society of Wisconsin; Memorial Library, University of Wisconsin; Watson Library, University of Kansas; State Historical Society of Kansas; State Archives of Illinois; Milton S. Eisenhower Library, Johns Hopkins University; Soper Library, Morgan State College; Moorland Collection, Howard University; New York Public Library; Middle Atlantic Youth Division, NAACP; and the Amistad Research Center, Fisk University. Financial assistance has been invaluable to the furtherance of this project. I wish to thank both the University of Kansas for awarding me funds for research expenses for 1967–1970 as well as summer salary for 1968 and a Watkins Summer Faculty Fellowship for 1969, and the Kansas City Association of Trusts and Foundations for graciously aiding my work in black history with a grant-in-aid. Finally, my appointment for 1969–1970 as a Senior Fellow in Southern and Negro History in the Institute of Southern History, Johns Hopkins University, has enabled me to devote ten months of uninterrupted attention to research and writing. For this opportunity I am especially grateful to Professors David Donald and Hugh Davis Graham.

Many people have helped me over the past few years, so many in fact that I am afraid I shall overlook some of them. Several people read all or parts of the several drafts of this book; others sent word of untapped historical materials; and still others granted me interviews and in other ways shared their insights into black history with me. Individual suggestions I have acknowledged in footnotes, and I have listed interviewees and described the nature of our interviews in the "Essay on Sources." Although this is inadequate repayment indeed, I should also like to acknowledge my indebtedness to Professor John M. Allswang, California State College at Los Angeles; Mr. Jacob E. Alschuler, Aurora, Illinois; President Leslie H. Fishel, Jr., Heidelberg College; Professor Allen D.

Grimshaw, Indiana University; Mr. Hilton E. Hanna, Amalgamated Meat Cutters and Butcher Workmen; Mr. Irwin E. Klass, Chicago Federation of Labor; Dean David A. Shannon, University of Virginia; and Professor Arvarh E. Strickland, University of Missouri. Professor Allan H. Spear and the University of Chicago Press have granted permission to have maps reprinted from Spear's perceptive study of *Black Chicago*. I am grateful to Mrs. Joe Akerman for typing the manuscript. The men with whom I have worked at Atheneum Publishers and Professor August Meier of Kent State University have prodded me along with just the right combination of encouragement, patience, and understanding. I owe a special debt of gratitude to my major professor at the University of Wisconsin, E. David Cronon, who not only shepherded me through my graduate work but taught me a great deal along the way. Finally, I want to thank my wife. Being both my most sympathetic sustainer and my toughest critic, she kept me on an even keel, not too depressed and yet, I hope, not too pompous.

William M. Tuttle, Jr.

Baltimore, Maryland
March 12, 1970

Contents

Illustrations

Maps

RACE RIOT

The Red Summer and the Red Scare

THE PARKS AND BATHING BEACHES," Chicago's leading black newspaper, the *Defender,* reminded its readers in July 1919, "are much more inviting these warm days than State Street. A hint to the wise should be sufficient." Specifically, the *Defender* recommended Lake Michigan's 25th Street beach, where there were free towels and lockers and where "every precaution is being taken to safeguard the interests of the bathers. The *Whip,* another of the city's black newspapers, also boosted the attractions to be found at the 25th Street beach. There were not only bathing beauties there but even a black lifeguard, who, unlike some of his white counterparts, was courteous and helpful. So come to 25th Street, the *Whip* urged, and help Chicago's black people "make this beach [their] Atlantic City." [1]

[1] *Chicago Defender,* July 5, 1919; *Chicago Whip,* July 5, 19, 1919. Some people called the beach the 26th Street beach, others the 25th Street beach.

For teenage boys, however, such advice was superfluous, especially as the temperature on Sunday, July 27, soared into the nineties. Fourteen-year-old John Harris was an energetic teenager, as were his companions that day, four boys named Williams.[2] Charles and Lawrence Williams were brothers, who with Harris and Paul Williams, unrelated, all lived on Chicago's South Side in the vicinity of Harris' house at 53rd and State, while Eugene Williams lived in another neighborhood, about fifteen blocks to the north. The four lads from farther south in the city had met Eugene at the beach.

The heat was already stifling by early afternoon when the boys hopped onto a produce truck driving north on Wabash Avenue. It was an Autocar, "a real speed wagon." At 26th Street, the truck slowed down again, this time to cross the streetcar tracks, and the boys alighted. They walked east and they walked fast, practically jogging the seven blocks to the lake. Perspiring freely and carrying their rolled-up swimming trunks, they were naturally eager to get to the cooling water and to the homemade raft that awaited them at the beach. But they also moved hurriedly because the territory through which they were passing was the domain of an Irish gang that had attacked them several times before with rocks.

The boys were not headed for the black-patronized 25th Street beach; nor did they intend to try to swim at the white beach at 29th Street, behind the Michael Reese Hospital. They were going to their own, very private spot, which was located just in between. Familiar landmarks loomed up as they walked east on 26th Street—the Burnham Park Police Station, the Hydrox Ice Cream Company, the tracks of the Illinois Central, and finally, at the lake front, a little island which the boys called the "hot and cold." Located behind the

[2] Interview with Mr. John Turner Harris, Chicago, June 26, 1969. Now a social worker in Chicago, Mr. Harris spent the better part of a day describing the events of July 27, 1919. Fearing punishment by his mother for swimming on a Sunday, Mr. Harris never told the police what he saw that day; in fact, the only person he told was Eugene Williams' mother, at Eugene's funeral.

Keeley Brewery and Consumers Ice, the "hot and cold" got its name from the effluence discharged by these companies. The waters of Lake Michigan could be as cold as the melting ice from Consumers, yet the run-off from the vats at the brewery was not only hot but chemically potent as well. It could even temporarily bleach a black person white. "It was hot," John Harris recalled, "and Jesus, I would be as white [as a white man] when I got done—so actually no women or nothing ever come through, so we [often] didn't even wear a suit, just take our clothes off and go down to the bank. . . ."

Tied up at the "hot and cold" was the raft. The product of several weeks of work by a dozen-and-a-half teenagers, the raft was "a tremendous thing," fully fourteen by nine feet, with a "big chain with a hook on one of the big logs, and we'd put a rope through it and tie it." Harris and his friends were far from being expert swimmers, but they could hang onto the raft and propel it forward by kicking; and, occasionally, "we could swim under water and dive under water and come up," always making sure, however, that they were within easy distance of the raft. "As long as the raft was there," Harris noted, "we were safe." The goal of the youths that Sunday was a marker nailed on a post several hundred yards from shore. At about two o'clock, the boys pushed off, angling their raft south toward the post—and toward 29th Street.

Meanwhile, at the 29th Street beach, the fury of racial hatred had just erupted. Defying the unwritten law which designated that beach as exclusively white, several black men and women had strolled to 29th Street determined to enter the water. Curses, threatening gestures, and rocks had frightened the intruders away. Minutes later, however, their numbers reinforced, the blacks reappeared, this time hurling rocks. The white bathers fled. But the blacks' possession of the beach was only temporary; behind a barrage of stones white bathers and numerous sympathizers returned. The battle that ensued was frightening in its violence but it merely anticipated Chicago's long-feared race war. Sparked by the conflict at the beach, all the racial fears and hates of the past months and years in Chicago would explode in bloody warfare.[3]

Innocently unaware of the savage exchange of projectiles and angry words at 29th Street, the five boys continued to "swim, kick, dive, and play around." Passing by the breakwater near 26th Street, the youths noticed a white man. He was standing on the end of the breakwater about seventy-five feet from the raft, and he was hurling rocks at them. It was simply "a little game," the boys thought. "We were watching him," said Harris. "He'd take a rock and throw it, and we would duck it—this sort of thing. . . . As long as we could see him, he never could hit us, because after all a guy throwing that far is not a likely shot. And you could see the brick coming. . . ." For several minutes he hurled rocks; and "one fellow would say, 'Look out, here comes one,' and we would duck. It was a game that we would play." It is not clear whether the rock thrower was playing the same game as the boys, or whether he was acting in angry retaliation against the black intrusion at 29th Street. One thing is certain, though: the next act in this drama brought pure tragedy.

Eugene Williams' head had just bobbed out of the water when one of the other boys diverted his attention. "And just as he turned his head this fellow threw [the rock] and it struck him . . . on the . . . forehead." John Harris could tell that Eugene was injured, for he slid back into the water; not diving, "he just sort of relaxed." Harris dived down to try to help, but, as he remembered, Eugene "grabbed my right ankle, and, hell, I got scared. I shook him off." By that time the boys were in about fifteen feet of water. Gasping for breath and panic-stricken, Harris surfaced and "began to shudder." "I shook away from him to come back up, and you

[3] Peter M. Hoffman (comp.), *The Race Riots: Biennial* [Cook County Coroner's] *Report, 1918–1919* (Chicago: n.pub., n.d.), 20, 27–28; *Chicago Daily Tribune,* July 28, 1919; *Chicago Defender,* August 2, 1919; Joseph A. Logsdon, "The Rev. Archibald J. Carey and the Negro in Chicago Politics" (unpublished M.A. thesis, University of Chicago, 1961), 71.

6

could see the blood coming up, and the fellows were all excited. . . ." Groaning something like "Oh, my God," the man on the breakwater then ran toward 29th Street.

"Let's get the lifeguard," shouted Harris as he pushed off from the raft. Dog-paddling and swimming under water, Harris finally reached shore. Then he dashed to the 25th Street beach to tell the head lifeguard, Butch, who "blew a whistle and sent a boat around." But by that time there was nothing that anybody could do. Thirty minutes later, divers recovered Eugene's body.[4]

Also by that time, anger had begun to replace the panic and the awe of the black boys. With the black policeman from 25th Street, they marched to 29th Street and pointed out the man they believed to be the rock thrower to the white policeman on duty, Officer Daniel Callahan. But Callahan would not only not arrest the man; he even refused to permit the black policeman to arrest him. As the policemen argued, Harris and his friends ran back to 25th Street and "told the colored people what was happening, and they started running this way," to 29th Street.[5]

[4] Harris interview; *Chicago Herald-Examiner*, August 3, 1919; Hoffman, *Coroner's Report*, 27–28. It should be pointed out that Mr. Harris' relating of the events of July 27, 1919, conflicts at times with the coroner's version. The coroner contended, for example, that Williams was an excellent swimmer, but there is no indication of his source for this information, and the evidence seems to be to the contrary. He also held that "a superficial abrasion" on the decedent's body could not of itself have caused death; true, but a rock hitting one's body, however slightly, could cause panic and result in drowning. It is possible, too, that had the coroner had an opportunity to interview Mr. Harris, his findings might have been quite different.

[5] Walter White, "Notes on Chicago of WFW," September 17, 1919, in NAACP Papers (NAACP-2), in the possession of the Middle Atlantic Youth Division of the NAACP, Washington, D.C,; Juvenile Protective Association, *18th Annual Report, 1918–1919* (Chicago: n.pub., *ca.* 1920), 23–25; Chicago Commission on Race Relations, *The Negro in Chicago* (Chicago: University of Chicago Press, 1922), 4–5, 11, 24, 34, 596–97; *New York Times*, July 28, 1919; *Chicago Daily Tribune*, July 28, 1919; *Chicago Herald-Examiner*, July 28, 1919; *Chicago Defender*, August 2, 1919; *Chicago Broad Ax*, August 2, 1919.

Panic had again overtaken the black youths. Hastily gathering up their clothes, they sprinted along 26th Street "all the way to Wabash." "We were putting our clothes on as fast as we were running." Boarding the first bus that appeared, they rode to the 55th Street beach, where they collapsed on the sand, thoroughly shaken and still panting. "I wasn't going home [right away]," said Harris, "because I knew I had better cool myself down. . . ." Also, he had left his cap and shoes at 26th Street, and he had to think of a way to explain their disappearance to his mother.[6]

The argument at 29th Street raged on. And in the midst of it, Officer Callahan, while continuing to ignore the exhortations of blacks to arrest the alleged murderer, arrested a black man on the complaint of a white. In the meantime, distorted rumors of the drowning and the brawl had assumed exaggerated proportions on the South Side. Whites told each other in alarmed voices that a white swimmer had drowned after being struck with a rock thrown by a black. A rumor in the nearby "black belt" was that Officer Callahan had not only caused Williams' death by preventing expert swimmers from rescuing him, but that he had even "held [his] gun on [the] colored crowd and permitted white rioters to throw bricks and stones at [the] colored." Hundreds of angry blacks and whites swarmed to the beach. The crowd was tumultuous when a patrol wagon pulled up at 29th Street to put the arrested black man in custody. Volleys of bricks and rocks were exchanged. Then a black man, James Crawford, drew a revolver and fired into a cluster of policemen, wounding one of them. A black officer returned the fire, fatally injuring Crawford. Suddenly other pistol shots reverberated. The restless onlookers, many of them armed, had their cue. The gunfire had signaled the start of a race war.[7]

Once ignited on July 27, the rioting raged virtually uncon-

---

[6] Harris interview.
[7] See footnote 5; and interview with Mr. A. L. Jackson, Chicago, June 27, 1969.

Beginning of a race riot—blacks and whites leaving Chicago's 29th Street beach after the drowning of Eugene Williams

trolled for the greater part of five days. Day and night white toughs assaulted isolated blacks, and teenage black mobsters beat white peddlers and merchants in the black belt. As rumors of atrocities circulated throughout the city, members of both races craved vengeance. White gunmen in automobiles sped through the black belt shooting indiscriminately as they passed, and black snipers fired back. Roaming mobs shot, beat, and stabbed to death their victims. The undermanned police force was an ineffectual deterrent to the waves of violence which soon overflowed the environs of the black belt and flooded the North and West Sides and the Loop, Chicago's downtown business district. Only several regiments of state militiamen and a cooling rain finally quenched the passions of the rioters, and even then sporadic outbursts punctuated the atmosphere for another week. The toll was awesome. Police officers had fatally wounded seven black men during the riot. Vicious mobs and lone gunmen had brutally murdered an additional sixteen blacks and fifteen whites, and well over 500 Chicagoans of both races had sustained injuries.[8]

The bloodshed inflicted an ineradicable scar on the city's reputation, and it outraged the sensibilities of countless Americans, black and white. But the Chicago race riot of 1919 should not have been altogether surprising to men and women who had read the chronicle of America's past, with its history, if not its tradition, of racial violence. Racial bloodshed struck New York City in the 1830's and in 1863; race riots erupted in Cincinnati in 1829 and 1841; in Utica and Palmyra, New York, in the 1830's; in Philadelphia in 1819 and at least five separate times in the 1830's and 1840's; various northern cities experienced interracial labor conflict during the Civil War; the races clashed in numerous places during Reconstruction, and at Wilmington, North Carolina, in 1898.[9] Add to these outbreaks the violence of the traffic in

[8] For a detailed description of the riot, see Chapter II.
[9] See, for example, Sam Bass Warner, *The Private City: Philadel-*

slaves and of oppressive slaveholders, revolts by slaves, vigilante tactics of the Ku Klux Klan, election riots in various Southern states in the 1880's and 1890's, and thousands of lynchings, and one can begin to understand this history.

The advent of the twentieth century brought no surcease to racial bloodshed in America. The North as well as the South saw a burgeoning of racial violence in the first decades of the new century. Monuments to this fact were the riots in New York City in 1900, Springfield, Ohio, in 1904, Atlanta, Georgia, and Greensburg, Indiana, in 1906, and Springfield, Illinois, in 1908.[10]

Clearly, urban racial violence was a national problem. White Northerners could no longer scoff at the barbarity of their Southern countrymen. "I'm not sure," the well-known satirist Mr. Dooley wrote at the turn of the century, "that I'd not as lave be gently lynched in Mississippi as baten to death in New York." The North had no corner on racial justice, he added; quite the contrary. "I'm not so much throubled about th' naygur whim he lives among his opprissors as I am whin he falls into the hands iv his liberators. Whin he's in th' south he can make up his mind to be lynched soon or late an' give his

phia in Three Periods of Its Growth (Philadelphia: University of Pennsylvania Press, 1968), 125–57; James McCague, *The Second Rebellion: The Story of the New York City Draft Riots of 1863* (N.Y.: Dial, 1968); W. H. Lofton, "Northern Labor and the Negro during the Civil War," *Journal of Negro History*, XXXIV (July 1949), 251–273; Henry L. West, "The Race War in North Carolina," *The Forum*, XXVI (January 1899), 578–91; John Hope Franklin, *From Slavery to Freedom* (N.Y.: Knopf, 1967), 234–37, 278–79, 330, 337, 341, 439.

[10] Gilbert Osofsky, *Harlem: The Making of a Ghetto* (N.Y.: Harper Torchbooks, 1968), 46–52; Ray Stannard Baker, *Following the Color Line* (N.Y.: Harper Torchbooks, 1964), 124–29, 160–61, 201 ff.; Ray Stannard Baker, "The Color Line in the North," *American Magazine*, LXV (February 1908), 345–57; Charles Crowe, "Racial Violence and Social Reform—Origins of the Atlanta Riot of 1906," *Journal of Negro History*, LIII (July 1968), 234–56; Crowe, "Racial Massacre in Atlanta, September 22, 1906," *Journal of Negro History*, LIV (April 1969), 150–73; James L. Crouthamel, "The Springfield Race Riot of 1908," *Journal of Negro History*, XLV (July 1960), 164–81; William English Walling, "The Race War in the North," *Independent*, LXV (September 3, 1908), 529–34.

attintion to his other pleasures iv . . . wurrukin' f'r th' man that used to own him an' now on'y owes him his wages. But 'tis th' divvle's own hardship f'r a coon to . . . be pursooed be a mob iv abolitionists till he's dhriven to seek polis protection, which . . . is th' polite name f'r fracture iv th' skull." [11]

East St. Louis, Illinois, stands as corroboration of Mr. Dooley's observation. Fueled by bigoted and alarmist trade unionists, self-centered corporate managers, strikebreaking black migrants from the South, corrupt white politicians, inflammatory news reporters, and biased and lax police officials, the smoldering fires of antagonism between blacks and whites exploded into furious rioting in July 1917. When the smoke from burning boxcars and houses lifted, nine whites and about forty blacks were dead, many of them the victims of unspeakable horror. A white reporter counted six black corpses lying near the corner of Fourth and Broadway. "I think every one I saw killed had both hands above his head begging for mercy." He had heard one moan, "My God, don't kill me, white man." Whites put torches to the homes of black people, leaving them with the choice of burning alive or fleeing to risk death by gunfire. Black women and children died along with their men; clubbed, shot, and stabbed, wounded and dying blacks lay in the streets. Others were lynched, including some who were already practically dead from other injuries. One black man had suffered severe head wounds; but, as he was not dead yet, the mob decided to hang him. "To put the rope around the negro's neck," noted a reporter, "one of the lynchers stuck his fingers inside the gaping scalp and lifted the negro's head by it, literally bathing his hand in the man's blood." Whites did not allow their black victims "to die easily"; when "flies settled on their terrible wounds the dying blacks [were warned not] to brush them off." Law enforcement was worse than nonexistent. Many police and militiamen, rather than try to quell the violence, worked in collusion with the white mobs in their quest to "get a nigger." State

[11] Finley Peter Dunne, "The Negro Problem," in *Mr. Dooley's Philosophy* (N.Y.: R. H. Russell, 1902), 217–22.

troops fraternized and joked with lawbreaking whites, and many were seen helping in the murders and arson.[12]

Disgust and anger stirred many people in the nation after East St. Louis, though some whites in the Deep South praised the riot as just one more example of the "dauntless spirit of the white man" who would not bow before a "congenitally inferior race." Some blacks, on the other hand, called for revenge and retaliatory violence; and disconsolate words marked the conversations of black people regarding their future in America. Some asked how white America, in good conscience, could tolerate the enormous gulf between its professed ideals and the reality of race relations in its native land. Such was the import of a cartoon in the *New York Evening Mail* showing a black woman kneeling before President Woodrow Wilson, pleading for mercy. Huddling next to the woman were her two young children. In the background, East St. Louis was on fire. Wilson held a document asserting that "The World Must be Made Safe for Democracy." The simple entreaty of the black woman was, "Mr. President, Why Not Make America Safe for Democracy?" [13]

The factors that had caused East St. Louis to explode were evident in varying degrees in other American cities in 1919, two years later.[14] It seemed, in fact, that the atmosphere during the first year of peace after World War I was even more

[12] See the excellent study by Elliott M. Rudwick, *Race Riot at East St. Louis, July 2, 1917* (Carbondale, Illinois: Southern Illinois University Press, 1964), 41–57; Martha Gruening, "The White Hand in Illinois," in NAACP-2; Oscar Leonard, "The East St. Louis Pogrom," *Survey*, XXXVIII (July 14, 1917), 331–33; U. S. House of Representatives, 65th Cong., 2nd Sess., *Report of the Special Committee Authorized by Congress to Investigate the East St. Louis Riots* (Washington: Government Printing Office, 1918); State of Illinois, Council of Defense, Committee on Labor, *The Race Riots at East St. Louis* (Chicago: n.pub., 1917); Chicago Commission, *Negro in Chicago*, 71–78.

[13] Rudwick, *East St. Louis*, 58–71. Although it was by far the most spectacular, East St. Louis was not the only wartime riot; there were others, for example, in Philadelphia and Chester, Pennsylvania, and Houston, Texas.

[14] For a more detailed statement regarding causes of race riots, see Chapter VIII.

conducive to racial violence than that during the war itself. When black intellectual and civil rights leader James Weldon Johnson spoke of "the Red Summer," he was talking about the race riots that bloodied the streets of twenty-five towns and cities in the six-month period from April to early October 1919. One of these riots was a massacre, with an undetermined number of people slaughtered in rural Arkansas, and it is impossible to know exactly how many died in race riots that summer. But the number of blacks and whites killed must exceed 120.[15]

The Red Summer was obviously consistent with the nation's history of racial violence. Yet the accentuated climate of violence in 1919 helps to account for the exorbitant number of race riots that year. It is not coincidental that the summer of 1919 also marked the beginning of the xenophobic and hysterically antiradical "Red Scare." Both phenomena were the ugly offspring of some of the same unrest, anxieties, and dislocations that plagued the United States and, indeed, most of the world in the immediate postwar years. Mankind's values, attitudes, and expectations were in disarray in 1919, and the resultant violence was worldwide.

In Europe, for example, the new states that had emerged from the dismantled Hapsburg Empire or had seceded from Russia clashed in the various regions of mixed nationality to

[15] U. S. House of Representatives, 66th Cong., 2nd Sess., Committee on the Judiciary, *Hearings on H.J. Res. 75; H.R. 259, 4123, 11873* (Washington: Government Printing Office, 1920), 58; hereafter cited as *Antilynching Hearings;* James Weldon Johnson, *Along This Way* (N.Y.: Viking Press, 1935), 341; *New York Times*, October 5, 1919. The estimates of people killed in the Elaine, Arkansas, riots in October range from a dozen to several hundred. The Army claimed that one soldier, four whites, and fourteen blacks were killed: Major Eugene E. Barton to Acting Intelligence Officer, Chicago, October 9, 1919, in Justice Department Papers, National Archives. In NAACP-2, however, there is a statement by George Washington Davis, a black man from Pine City, Arkansas, who claimed that 103 black Masons had died, and that he, as acting grand secretary, had paid their death benefits; in addition, he said, seventy-three blacks who were not Masons died along with "fully 250 white men."

14

which two or more laid claim. The Poles waged pitched battles with the Lithuanians over the Jewish city of Vilna and with the Czechs over the Teschen district; while Hungary clashed with Austria over Burgenland and with Rumania over Transylvania. Yugoslavia and Italy contended for Fiume; Rumania and Czechoslavakia vied for Bukovina; and Italy and Turkey wanted part of Anatolia. Greece and Turkey and Ireland and England vented their ancient hatred for each other. Nationalists in India and Egypt rebelled against British rule. In addition to these and other disputes, there was the Great Civil War, with the Bolshevik Red Army struggling to reconquer the territories that had proclaimed their independence from Russia, and with Allied armies intervening to contain Bolshevism. Despite these efforts, revolution swept briefly into Germany and Hungary in 1919. In January, the Spartacists in Germany sought to duplicate the events of 1917 in Russia. Although the Spartacists failed in Germany, Communists in Hungary established a short-lived government in March. But the Bolshevik undertaking which provoked widespread anxiety in the United States was the formation in March of the Third International, or Comintern. The Comintern's manifesto urged the workers to arm and seize governmental power. People in the United States looked around suspiciously. Even the most innocuous events began to suggest class revolution.

The world unrest was not confined to territorial disputes or the specter of revolutionary communism. Indeed, Hannah Arendt has written, the "magnitude of the violence let loose in the First World War," certainly one of the bloodiest conflicts in history, might "have been enough to cause revolutions in its aftermath even without any revolutionary tradition and even if no revolution had ever occurred before." [16] Much of the distress was economic. The war had disjointed the pre-

[16] Hannah Arendt, *On Revolution* (N.Y.: Viking Press, 1963), 9; as quoted in Arthur I. Waskow, *From Race Riot to Sit-In* (Garden City, N.Y.: Anchor Books of Doubleday, 1967), 1.

war economy in which industrial Western Europe had prospered by trading with Eastern Europe and overseas nations. The value of many currencies in 1919 was uncertain, and several nations faced bankruptcy. In addition, demobilization had dumped millions of soldiers and war workers on the labor market. Unemployment was widespread, and the unemployed were hungry and restless. General strikes paralyzed Winnipeg and Havana, while riots and hunger strikes broke out in Spain, Germany, and Italy. "Bread and Peace" was the strikers' angry protest slogan.

A final manifestation of the acute disorder that plagued the world in 1919 was racial violence. Riots between black and white workers disrupted Johannesburg, South Africa; and in London and Liverpool, in Cardiff and Barry, Wales, demobilized soldiers bitterly assaulted blacks imported from Jamaica during the war.

The United States' isolation from this unrest did not immunize it against similar domestic disorders. Indeed, in one field of violence, race riots and lynchings, America set the pattern. In the United States, as elsewhere in the world, 1919 was a year of transition. The Germans had been vanquished, yet the immediate fruits of victory disappointed those Americans who were unwilling to relinquish the moral idealism that the war had exuded, or whose desire for unified national purpose had gone unfulfilled. The nation was in transit between the passions of war and "normalcy"; in the meantime, it was also a battlefield for domestic conflict.[17]

The nation had faced a common foe in April 1917, and Americans of diverse national origins, races, economic strata, and religions had united to defeat it. They did so not only by answering the appeal for troops, but also by flocking to factories to turn out the tools of war, purchasing Liberty Bonds,

[17] See H. O. Dahlke, "Race and Minority Riots—A Study in the Typology of Violence," *Social Forces,* XXX (May 1952), 419–25; John Higham, *Strangers in the Land: Patterns of American Nativism, 1860–1925* (N.Y.: Atheneum edition, 1963), 222–24, 255.

adhering to meatless days and breadless meals, and contributing services and funds to the YMCA and Red Cross. The singular purpose of these enterprises established intense national unity. Such unity demanded an unquestioning loyalty, intolerant of nonconforming ideas and behavior or even of suspected nonconformity. Yet in a significant way the wartime cohesion also served to restrain aggression. Heterogeneous elements of the population had united, and involvement in the war effort accorded to even the lowest strata of society a degree of status. With the Armistice, however, this national unity dissolved, and with it the restraint emanating from common purpose. But the wartime zeal survived, and social schisms proliferated. One offspring of this environment was the Red Scare.[18]

The Red Scare was an extension of the atmosphere of the war, with its cult of patriotism, its generalized climate of violence, and its need of an enemy. In fact, the anti-German and antiradical agitation of late 1918 and the early months of 1919 so overlapped that, as John Higham has noted, "no date marks the end of one or the beginning of the other." [19] Yet, by midyear, the emotional opposition to the external threat had blurred into indiscriminate hatred of the "inner enemy," aliens and dissenters. So widespread had become this inability to discriminate that *The Fleet Review* could

[18] Georg Simmel has observed: ". . . groups in any sort of war situation are not tolerant. They cannot afford individual deviations from the unity of the coordinating principle beyond a definitely limited degree": *Conflict and The Web of Group-Affiliations* (Glencoe, Illinois: Free Press, 1955), 93. See also Lewis A. Coser, *The Functions of Social Conflict* (Glencoe, Illinois: Free Press, 1956), 33–38, 85–97; Allen D. Grimshaw, "A Study of Social Violence: Urban Race Riots in the United States" (unpublished Ph.D. dissertation, University of Pennsylvania, 1959), 48–49.

[19] Higham, *Strangers in the Land,* 223. Sociologists and social psychologists have also noted that "it is not farfetched to suggest that an entire political entity may become a culture of violence when engaging in war": Marvin E. Wolfgang, "A Preface to Violence," *The Annals of the American Academy of Political and Social Science* (hereafter, simply *Annals*), CCCLXIV (March 1966), 5–6.

ask: "Wonder if Berlin Bill is raising a scrubby beard so as to join the Bolsheviki? He'd doubtless feel at home with his friends Trotsky and Lenin." [20]

Although subversion and sabotage did crop up spectacularly in 1919, such as the springtime bombings of government officials' residences, critics of the radicals ascribed every sort of disorder to them, including the social and industrial unrest that trailed in the wake of the federal government's amorphous demobilization program. "The moment we knew the armistice to have been signed," President Wilson told Congress in December 1918, "we took the harness off." [21] With few controls and little planning, armies dispersed, wartime regulations expired, and industries either shut down or underwent the task of retooling for peacetime consumption. By July, while government agencies had abruptly terminated war contracts, the army had issued 2,600,000 discharges, at the rate of 15,000 per day.[22] Veterans thus glutted the labor market in the very months of decreasing employment.

Unemployment rose sharply in April and May, and with it the nation's industrial unrest. As a consequence, the United States suffered one of its worst years of labor strife since the 1890's. As the 181 strikes and lockouts in March soared to 262 in April and 413 in May, employers and politicians, some of them genuinely frightened, others perceiving advantage in allegations of radicalism, blamed these disruptions on radicals and traitors.[23] Probably more than any other labor dispute of that year, the Seattle general strike of February reinforced the dread of a workers' revolution. Although con-

[20] *The Fleet Review*, X (July 1919), 17.
[21] R. S. Baker and W. E. Dodd (eds.), *War and Peace: Presidential Messages, Addresses, and Public Papers (1917–1924) by Woodrow Wilson* (N.Y.: Harper, 1927), I, 313; Frederic L. Paxson, *The Great Demobilization and Other Essays* (Madison: University of Wisconsin Press, 1941), 7.
[22] *Chicago Daily News,* July 3, 5, 1919.
[23] Edson L. Whitney (comp.), "Strikes and Lockouts in the United States, 1916, 1917, 1918, and 1919," *Monthly Labor Review,* X (June 1920), 200.

ducted by craft unionists who were hardly revolutionaries, the strike helped to transform the anxiety of countless people into panic. It was not a labor dispute at all, claimed Seattle's Mayor Ole Hanson. It was an attempt by revolutionaries "to establish a Soviet Government and control and operate all enterprises and industries." Hanson and other publicists of the threat of radicalism also asserted that alien agitators were the masterminds behind the strike, thus linking the fear of revolution to the distrust and hatred of the foreign-born and accentuating the apprehension that immigrant laborers were inherently dangerous to internal security.[24]

Politicians and industrialists were not alone in embracing the emotionalism of antiradicalism and xenophobia. Overzealous soldiers, sailors, and Marines continued to act according to the militant aims that had guided them during the war. The fear of a proletarian uprising evoked responses similar to those elicited earlier by the "Huns." When radical union members circumvented a red flag ordinance by sporting red neckties at a rally protesting the conviction of Tom Mooney, a fellow unionist sentenced to death for murder, the organ of the enlisted men of the Navy declared resolutely: "If regulated authority fails in its mission to suppress the 'Reds,' there is some hope in the prospect that there will be enough of the Navy and Marine Corps and Army in the vicinity of these revolutionary meetings to deal properly with the enemies of the country." [25] On May Day, soldiers invaded the Russian People's House in New York City, confiscated radical literature, and forced the aliens there to sing the "Star Spangled Banner." Later that day, more soldiers and sailors stormed the offices of the New York *Call,* a Socialist newspaper, assaulting several May Day celebrants. Vigilante war veterans also disrupted demonstrations in Boston and Cleveland, and

[24] See Robert K. Murray, *The Red Scare: A Study in National Hysteria, 1919–1920* (Minneapolis: University of Minnesota Press, 1955), 3–17, 58–66.

[25] "The Navy and the 'Reds,'" *The Fleet Review,* X (January 1919), 21.

in each of these cities one person was mortally wounded.

By midyear, the balmy spring of 1919 had become a torrid summer, and the antiradical and xenophobic mania had clearly risen with the heat. In the hands of employers, politicians, and much of the press, the epithet "Bolshevism" had become an increasingly effective instrument for damning all sorts of opposition and contrary beliefs; Communism was a phantom that conjured up a myriad of demonic images, and these images inspired a host of aggressive impulses.[26] By midyear, moreover, government at all levels had succumbed to this emotional tide. Several states had enacted red flag, criminal anarchy, syndicalist, and sedition laws; and the federal police powers, led by Attorney General A. Mitchell Palmer, were mounting the onslaught that would yield the grossest indignities of the Red Scare.

The Red Scare was functioning without reserve by late summer and early autumn. A visitor to the United States at that time, A. G. Gardiner, editor of *The London Daily News,* was dismayed by the irrationality he witnessed. He could not forget, he wrote a half-dozen years later, "the feverish condition of the public mind at that time. It was hag-ridden by the spectre of Bolshevism. It was like a sleeper in a nightmare, enveloped by a thousand phantoms of destruction. Property was in an agony of fear"; and dissent, and indeed most any kind of nonconformity, was in danger of being denounced as "radical." " 'Radical' covered the most innocent departure from conventional thought with a suspicion of desperate purpose. 'America,' as a wit of the time said, 'is the land of liberty—liberty to keep in step.' " [27]

The structure of society in 1919 was thus as conducive to the Red Scare as to the Red Summer. Bolstered by the force

[26] To obtain some appreciation of the temper of this hysteria, see Edmund Vance Cook's poem "Bolshevik" in *Public,* XXII (July 19, 1919), 772.

[27] Gardiner, *Portraits and Portents* (N.Y.: Harper, 1926), 13; quoted in Murray, *Red Scare,* 17.

of law and the nation's mores, the "search for the 'inner enemy,' " as the sociologist Georg Simmel observed, "became institutionalized after World War I; and then instead of being disapproved by members of one's group for being prejudiced, one was punished for not being prejudiced." Although the motives for and the manifestations of race prejudice in 1919 were somewhat different, this statement was as true of race relations as it was of antiradicalism and the treatment of the foreign-born. For the most highly susceptible objects of prejudice in postwar America were its black men and women, not because they were radicals, but because they threatened the accommodative race system of white superordination and black subordination. The white populace had long been inimical to the strivings of black people, and during World War I this hostility became markedly more intense as over 450,000 Southern blacks migrated to the North. There, in crowded cities, they met in bitter competition with whites over jobs, housing, political power, and facilities for education, transportation, and relaxation. Moreover, black people, visibly distinct and with behavior patterns ostensibly alien to whites, were convenient scapegoats, especially for whites who feared that their social status had dropped because of the influx of blacks from the South. The employment of a new black worker in a shop or the arrival of a black family on a block only heightened anxieties of status deprivation, often prompting whites to revive the ancient shibboleth that blacks were grasping, not for material improvement, but for "social equality." White hostility to individual black people became generalized into a categorical hatred of an entire race.

For their part, black men and women, North and South, entered 1919 with aspirations for a larger share of both the nation's democracy and its wealth. Tension mounted as these aspirations collided with a general white determination to reaffirm the black people's prewar status on the bottom rung of the nation's racial and economic ladder. In 1919 racial uneasiness was evident in cities and towns throughout the country.[28] And there seemed to be a threshold of tension above which racial violence was almost bound to occur, if spurred by a precipitating incident and in the absence of external controls of law enforcement. These various factors coalesced time and time again in 1919, to provoke an unparalleled outburst of racial violence.[29]

Lynch mobs murdered seventy-eight black people in 1919, an increase of fifteen over 1918 and thirty over 1917. Ten of the victims were war veterans, several of them still in uniform. Throughout the South the hangings, shootings, and burnings multiplied in frequency and brutality as summer followed spring. March and April each saw four outrages, while nine blacks were lynched in May and nine more in June. The National Association for the Advancement of Colored People had expressed shock in 1918 when lynch mobs had murdered two black men by fire; in 1919, eleven men were burned alive at the stake.[30]

Perhaps the most monstrous lynching of the summer oc-

[28] Leonard Berkowitz, *Aggression: A Social Psychological Analysis* (N.Y.: McGraw-Hill, 1962), 136–64, 184–85; Grimshaw, "Study of Social Violence," 180–83; Dahlke, "Race and Minority Riots," 419–25; Grimshaw, "Lawlessness and Violence in America and Their Special Manifestations in Changing Negro-White Relationships," *Journal of Negro History,* XLIV (January 1959), 52 ff.; Grimshaw, "Urban Racial Violence in the United States: Changing Ecological Considerations," *American Journal of Sociology,* LXVI (September 1960), 107, 118–19; Grimshaw, "Negro-White Relations in the Urban North: Two Areas of High Conflict Potential," *Journal of Intergroup Relations,* III (Spring 1962), 146–58.

[29] Neil J. Smelser, *Theory of Collective Behavior* (N.Y.: Free Press, 1962), 3, 6, 8–9, 12–21, 101–9, 222–69; Stanley Lieberson and Arnold R. Silverman, "The Precipitants and Underlying Conditions of Race Riots," *Amercian Sociological Review,* XXX (December 1965), 887–98.

[30] NAACP, *Thirty Years of Lynching in the United States, 1889–1918* (N.Y.: NAACP, 1919), *passim;* U. S. House of Representatives, 66th Cong., 2nd Sess., *Antilynching Bill,* Report No. 1027 (Washington: Government Printing Office, 1920), 9–17; "For July Crisis," June 20, 1919, in NAACP Papers (NAACP-1), Library of Congress (F-1); *Chicago Daily Journal,* July 5, 1919; Herbert J. Seligmann, "Protecting Southern Womanhood," *Nation,* CVIII (June 14, 1919), 938–39; *Antilynching Hearings,* 52–60; NAACP, *Tenth Annual Report* (N.Y.: NAACP, 1920), 14–15, 18–20, 21–25.

curred in Mississippi in late June. The day before the lynching, a mob had severely wounded an accused black rapist, John Hartfield, in the canebrakes near Ellisville. Fearing that Hartfield might expire before the hanging and burning scheduled for the next day at "the big gum tree," a doctor prolonged his life. In the meantime, newspapers in Jackson and New Orleans advertised the forthcoming event. "3,000 WILL BURN NEGRO," proclaimed the *New Orleans States* in bold red type across the top of the front page. Thousands of curiosity seekers flocked to Ellisville, and Mississippi's Governor Theodore G. Bilbo gave the lynching his official sanction. When asked if he planned to prevent it, Bilbo replied: "I am utterly powerless. The State has no troops, and if the civil authorities at Ellisville are helpless, the State is equally so." Moreover, he added, "excitement is at such a high pitch throughout South Mississippi that any attempt to interfere with the mob would doubtless result in the death of hundreds of persons. The negro has confessed, says he is ready to die, and nobody can keep the inevitable from happening." White Mississippians evidently disagreed only about the method of executing Hartfield. The *New Orleans States* reported that "some of the angry citizens . . . wanted Hartfield lynched, while others wanted him burned." He was both hanged and burned, and also shot.[31]

While the lynchings of the Red Summer were usually confined to the South, practically half of the epidemic of race riots burst forth in Northern and border states. Several proposed hangings, moreover, soon developed into riots when blacks retaliated.[32]

Charleston, South Carolina, suffered the first of the major

[31] *Antilynching Hearings*, 47; *New York Times*, June 27, 1919; *Chicago Defender*, July 5, 1919; NAACP, *Tenth Annual Report*, 21, 24. In the 1920's, Ho Chi Minh also wrote about the Hartfield and other lynchings in the United States; see his *Selected Works* (Hanoi: Foreign Languages Publishing House, 1960), I, 99–105, 127–32.

[32] For example, read about the riot in Millen, Georgia, in *Antilynching Hearings*, 58; *New York Times*, April 15, 1919; *Chicago Defender*, April 19, 1919; *Memphis Commercial Appeal*, April 15, 1919.

riots of the Red Summer. It was Saturday night, May 10, when the black man doubled up in pain and slumped to the street. There had been an argument, and the bullet wound inflicted by a white sailor had been fatal. Hundreds of other sailors were also on liberty that night; hearing rumors of a racial altercation involving a Navy man, they began to swarm angrily into the city's black district. Augustus Bonaparte was having his hair cut at the time. Looking out the barbershop window, he saw a mob of sailors dash into the nearby shooting gallery, which they proceeded to loot for rifles. Automobiles filled with sailors, many of them armed with rifles, clubs, and hammers, soon crowded the streets. "Get a nigger," was their cry. James Frayer, a black cobbler, saw frightened black men and boys running toward his shop, shouting that the sailors were coming. Quickly, Frayer shut his door and latched it. He hid behind the counter with three customers. "Open the door," yelled a voice. When nobody moved, the sailor outside fired his weapon at random through the door, wounding Frayer's apprentice in the lower part of his back. Unable to subdue the rioters, the city police asked for help from Navy officials, who promptly ordered sailors to return to ship and dispatched Marines with fixed bayonets to occupy the streets. Although the presence of Marines aided in restoring calm, certain of the troops continued the terror that the sailors had begun. T. B. Nelson, for example, darted from his house upon hearing moaning in the street. Lying there wounded was a black youth, who pleaded with the Marines who hovered over him. "What are you shooting me for? I was not doing anything." "Why didn't you halt when we told you to?" demanded one of the troops. The boy gasped that he had not been ordered to stop. "Hush your mouth or we'll give you some more." When Isaac Moses also told Marines that he had not heard their command to halt, they responded by calling him a "damned liar," knocking him in the head with a gun butt, stealing five dollars, and stabbing him through the left leg with a bayonet. The death toll from that night of rioting in

Charleston was two black men. Wounded were seventeen blacks, seven sailors, and a white policeman.[33]

Longview, the center of population of Gregg County, an east Texas county of 8,500 whites and 8,200 blacks, had been uneasy with racial tension during the spring and summer months of 1919. Members of the local chapter of the Negro Business League had established black cooperative stores that sold products at lower prices than the white merchants. Black leaders—men such as Dr. C. P. Davis, a physician, and S. L. Jones, a high school teacher—had urged black farmers to avoid the white cotton brokers in Longview by selling direct to the buyers in Galveston. On June 16, Lemuel Walters was discovered in a white woman's bedroom. The next day his nude body was found lying near the railroad tracks at a desolate spot known as Foote's Switch, four miles south of Longview. Fear and apprehension swept the black community, and a delegation of eleven men led by Davis and Jones made a call on the county judge, Erskine H. Bramlette. The judge advised silence, saying that "there [should] be no talking as talking would interfere with locating the culprits." Days passed, but no arrests were made, and it appeared to the men of the Negro Business League that law officials not only were not investigating the lynching but that they were even using this time to destroy evidence which would prove the guilt of the perpetrators of the crime. The black men returned to Judge Bramlette, who told them that he had informed the district attorney of their suspicions. Again the judge advised "no talking." [34]

[33] Affidavits by witnesses and victims of the riot, in NAACP-2; and, in *ibid.*, clippings from *Charleston News and Courier*, May 11, 12, 16, 1919; *New Orleans Times-Picayune*, May 12, 1919; *Cleveland Advocate*, May 17, 1919; *Chicago Defender*, May 17, 1919; Waskow, *From Race Riot to Sit-In*, 12–16, 210.

[34] Most of the Longview information is from "Confidential" interview with S. L. Jones and C. P. Davis, Chicago, August 18, 1919, in Arthur B. Spingarn Papers, Library of Congress; and from newspapers. See "The Riot at Longview, Texas," *Crisis*, XVIII (October, 1919), 297–98; *Dallas Morning News*, July 12–15, 1919; *San Antonio Express*,

A Saturday morning event in Longview's black district, as in black sections in towns across the South, was the arrival on the train of the weekly *Chicago Defender*. That July 5 issue of the newspaper was of special interest, for it had a story about Longview. Lemuel Walters, read the article on page two, "was taken from the Longview jail by a crowd of white men when a prominent white woman declared she loved him, and if she were in the North would obtain a divorce and marry him." His only offense, the *Defender* added, was having had a white woman love him, and the penalty he had paid was death. No formal charges had been preferred against Walters, and the sheriff had "gladly welcomed the mob" that had dragged the black man from jail and "shot [him] to pieces."

Jones, who was also the local *Defender* agent, drove his automobile to the downtown business district the following Thursday, July 10. But when he returned to his car, he encountered three white men who brusquely demanded that he come with them. Jones refused and tried to pull away from one of the men who had seized him. Another of the men pulled a wrench out of his coat and struck Jones a heavy blow on the head. Other blows followed. Jones fell to the pavement, struggled to get up, but fell again. He had written the *Defender* article, his attackers charged, and it would be much easier if he simply admitted it. When Jones denied that he had, they beat him again. Finally, the pummeling stopped, and Jones dragged himself to Dr. Davis' office. Later, at home, Jones asked that J. J. Ross, secretary of the Chamber of Commerce, be brought to him. He told Ross what he had

July 12–17, 1919; *New York Times*, July 12, 14, 1919; *Topeka Plaindealer*, July 25, 1919; *Chicago Herald-Examiner*, July 12, 14, 23, 1919; *Chicago Defender*, July 5, 1919; *Kansas City Advocate*, July 25, 1919; Waskow, *From Race Riot to Sit-In*, 16–20, 180, 193, 209, 212; in NAACP-1, W. E. B. Du Bois to George A. Towns, July 18, 1919 (C-3); and in NAACP-2, P. A. Williams to J. R. Shilladay, August 11, 1919; Williams to Mary White Ovington, August 16, 1919; and newspaper clippings from *Shreveport Times*, July 12–13, 15, 17, 23, 27, 1919.

told his assailants—that he was not the author of the article; and if Ross did not believe him, Jones said, he should wire the *Defender* for confirmation. Ross said he would.

Meanwhile, there was talk in town of impending "trouble that night." If Jones were still in Longview by midnight, according to one rumor, he would be lynched. Mayor G. A. Bodenheim sent a messenger to Davis to warn him and Jones to leave town at once. But Davis sent word back that he was staying. Davis also learned that the mayor and other city officials were meeting in emergency session at city hall, and he decided to join them. When he arrived at city hall, however, all that the white authorities would tell him was to take off his hat. "Yes!" Davis replied heatedly. "That's all you all say to a colored man who comes to talk serious business to you: 'Take off your hat.' I am not going to do it. I want to know what protection we colored citizens are going to have tonight." "You will have to take your chances," the mayor replied.

As darkness settled on Longview, black volunteers met at Davis' house, "pledging their lives in his defense." The doctor assumed command of the men, posting them "where they could safeguard every side from which an attack could be made," and instructing them not to fire before he did and "under no circumstances to shoot into white people's houses." At about 11:00, Dr. Davis sneaked through alleys and dark streets to within eyeshot of the city hall. It was just as he had feared. There he saw armed men gathering, using the fire department as their command post. Returning to Jones' house, he told his troops what the prospects were, and "offered to allow any of them who did not feel like risking his life . . . to retire. . . . Every man stayed and said he was prepared to take what might come." "Soon afterward and approaching midnight," Davis and Jones recalled, "the mob came down through a back street." The black men crouched quietly, waiting in ambush until Jones' house was "approached or attacked. Four white men came on the back

27

porch of the house and called to Jones to come out." There was no answer. "When it became evident that they intended to force their way in, Davis fired the first shot and the melee began." Between 100 and 150 shots were fired in a half hour, and four whites fell with fatal wounds. The rest of the mob of about a dozen whites retreated to the town square. Minutes later, and one at a time, automobiles sped down the street leading to Jones' house, white men hopped out, picked up the dead and wounded, and sped away.

Throughout the night, a fire bell was sounded, eventually summoning about 1,000 white men to the town square. The mayor, Judge Bramlette, and other town leaders also arrived, however, to make speeches urging the men to disperse and go home. Until almost daybreak the leaderless crowd simply milled around. Then, as if suddenly energized by the first shafts of daylight, men began smashing their way into the hardware store and helping themselves to rifles, pistols, and ammunition. Thus armed, a mob headed back to Jones' house. But by then Jones and Davis were in hiding, so the mob occupied itself by dousing their homes with kerosene and igniting them, along with the homes of four other of the "principal" black residents. The next day, police officers, aided by bloodhounds, tracked down Marion Bush, the 60-year-old father-in-law of Davis, and shot him dead in a corn field three miles south of town.

Davis and Jones succeeded in escaping from Longview. Dressed in a soldier's uniform and improvised leggings, Davis boarded a train a few miles from town. Knowing that authorities searching for him would be looking for a doctor, he "bought some popcorn, some red pop and some other refreshment and walked around . . . throwing the bottle in the air, drinking from it ostentatiously and eating and singing, like a simple 'darky.' " He also talked a white boy into shooting craps with him, and after making a special effort to lose fifteen cents, he muttered, "That cleans me. I ain't done got no more money. . . ." Fearing worse violence, the governor of Texas declared martial law in Longview and ordered the state militia and Texas Rangers into the town. Yet there was no more bloodshed. Certain white citizens of the community even adopted a resolution deploring the vigilante actions of the white mob, after also deploring the "scurrilous [*Defender*] article" about "a respectable white lady." That day and night of rioting, however, had left five dead, a score wounded, and many homeless.

After Charleston and Longview, the third major riot of the Red Summer erupted in Washington, D.C., a city where lurid tales of black rapists had been rampant for weeks.[35] In June and July, four women allegedly were assaulted in Washington, and three in the portion of Maryland contiguous to the District of Columbia. The press featured emotional accounts of these attacks, imputing them all, without substantive evidence, to blacks. One alleged victim claimed that she had been sexually assaulted by "two young negroes . . . wearing white shirts, no coats, tan or yellow hats." Two weeks later she admitted that she had not been attacked by black youths, or indeed attacked at all. But the denial received miniscule coverage compared to the initial accusation. Such inflammatory journalism aroused the ire of whites, especially of military personnel stationed in or near the Capital, and racial tension mounted. On Saturday, July 19, the *Washington Post* ran headlines telling of another sexual assault: "NEGROES ATTACK GIRL . . . WHITE MEN VAINLY PURSUE." The next night Washington exploded. Racial tempers flared after a minor dispute on Pennsylvania Avenue in the midst of the capital city. Roaming bands of soldiers, sailors, and Ma-

[35] The most extensive account is in Waskow, *From Race Riot to Sit-In,* 21–37; but see also *Washington Bee,* July 19, 1919; *Washington Post,* July 19–24, August 5, 1919; *Chicago Daily Tribune,* July 7, 22, 1919; William G. Haan to Brigadier General C. R. Boardman, August 5, 1919, Haan Papers, State Historical Society of Wisconsin; "Racial Tension and Race Riot," *Outlook,* CXXII (August 6, 1919), 533; Constance McLaughlin Green, *The Secret City: A History of Race Relations in the Nation's Capital* (Princeton: Princeton University Press, 1967), 190–97.

rines began to molest any black person in sight, hauling them off streetcars and out of restaurants, chasing them up alleys, and beating them mercilessly on street corners. With ineffectual police restraint, violence reigned for three days as white mobs ran amuck through the streets. Blacks retaliated on the fourth day when the whites threatened to burn their homes.

During the riot, further irresponsible journalism, by both the white and the black press, heightened the anger of the mobs. On the first day of bloodshed, for example, the *Bee,* a black newspaper, declared: "A RIOT IS ALMOST CREATED: A Texan in the War Risk Bureau Assaults a Colored Female." The article beneath the headline told that the "assault" was actually a verbal insult. Two days later the *Washington Post* notified the aroused armed servicemen of a "Mobilization for Tonight." "It was learned," the *Post* noted, "that a mobilization of every available service man . . . has been ordered for tomorrow evening near the Knights of Columbus hut. . . . The hour of assembly is 9 o'clock and the purpose is a 'clean-up' that will cause the events of the last two evenings to pale into insignificance." Thus the *Post* had not only inflamed the passions of the rioters, it had even furnished them with a battle plan.

The helplessness of the Washington police compelled Secretary of War Newton D. Baker to order in 2,000 regular Army soldiers. On the evening of July 22, with federal troops and a downpour of rain deterring would-be rioters, the violence finally subsided, having left six dead in the streets and upwards of 100 injured.

After the bloodshed in Washington, the *New York Times* consoled itself by noting that, "painful as it is to say," a race riot such as the one in the Capital "could not have arisen in any Northern city where the police had been trained to expect riot duty." [36] The *Times* displayed little prescience on this occasion, however. For in a Northern city, just four days later, John Harris and his four young black friends hopped onto the

[36] *New York Times,* July 23, 1919.

back of a produce truck, dreaming about the Lake Michigan beach at the foot of Chicago's 26th Street, and about their homemade raft and all the excitement that awaited them in the water.

Race Riot at Chicago

NOT LONG after Eugene Williams' body had been raised to the surface of Lake Michigan, Chicago's "athletic clubs" had mobilized for action. These gangs, composed of white teenagers and young men in their twenties, many of the roughest of whom were of Irish descent, had terrorized black people for years. For weeks, in the spring and summer of 1919, they had been anticipating, even eagerly awaiting, a race riot. On several occasions, they themselves had endeavored to precipitate one, and now that racial violence threatened to become generalized and unrestrained throughout Chicago, they were set to exploit the chaos.[1] "Remember it's the Ragen Colts you're dealing with," one of that gang's spokesmen warned a frightened black man on Sunday, July 27, the first night of the riot. The territory west

[1] For more information on the "athletic clubs," see Chapters VI and VII.

of Wentworth Avenue and extending south from 43rd to 63rd Street, he added, was the Colts'. "We intend to run this district. Lookout." [2] That first evening of bloodshed, 27 blacks fell injured and beaten. Most of these people were the victims of the Ragen Colts and such other west-of-Wentworth gangs as the "Hamburgers," the "Aylwards," the "Dirty Dozen," "Our Flag," the "Sparklers," and the "Standard." Seven more blacks were stabbed, and four wounded by gunfire. Had it not been for the activities of these gangs, the Chicago Commission on Race Relations later observed, "it is doubtful if the riot would have gone beyond the first clash." Lawlessness, violence, and antisocial acts were their forte, however; and undeterred by police, who evidently arrested none of these mobsters during the riot, the athletic clubs made ready to escalate the racial warfare.[3]

Although angered and grieved by the refusal of Officer Callahan to arrest the white stone-thrower at the beach, Chicago's black men and women were not dismayed. They had expected little else of a police force which they had come to view as the armed representative of white hostility. The events of that first evening were no revelation, either. Black people in Chicago had ample reason to fear the athletic clubs, and they had also come to anticipate law enforcement that was biased in favor of white hoodlums. At the same time, blacks were not disposed to sacrifice their lives cheaply. They were armed and stood ready to defend themselves—not, however, by engaging in armed forays into white neighbor-

[2] Chicago Crime Commission, *Illinois Crime Survey,* part three (Chicago: Illinois Association for Criminal Justice, 1929), 1003–4; *Chicago Daily News,* August 2, 1919. See Map 4, the western portion of the black belt being Wentworth Avenue.

[3] Chicago Commission on Race Relations, *The Negro in Chicago* (Chicago: University of Chicago Press, 1922), 5, 11–17, 598, 601, 667. The Cook County Grand Jury investigating the riot stated: "These gangs have apparently taken an active part in the race riots and no arrests of their members have been made as far as this Jury is aware"; report in papers of the Chicago Commission on Race Relations (CCRR), Illinois State Archives, Springfield.

hoods, as marauding bands of whites would do to them, but by attempting to repulse the gangs that either invaded the territory of the black belt or threatened its peripheries. Blacks usually employed such individual tactics as sniping, while whites resorted to mob warfare. Their primary weapons were thus firearms and knives, while those of whites were bricks, stones, fists, baseball bats, iron bars, and hammers.[4]

Calm had returned to the city late in the evening of July 27, and the streets were empty when dawn appeared on Monday. But the ominous problem was how to prevent future outbreaks. It was already becoming sultry at eight o'clock that morning, with prospects of still one more day of temperatures in the nineties, when Mayor William H. Thompson's train steamed into Chicago. The mayor, being an enthusiastic cowboy, had traveled with most of his cabinet and numerous political boosters to Cheyenne, Wyoming, for the Frontier Days festivities; now he was back to solve the city's problems. Almost immediately an experienced South Side police officer offered Thompson his unsolicited opinion that the only way of averting further racial slaughter was to request the aid of the state militia. "Unless the militia is called and the entire south side put under martial law," said Captain Michael Gallery, "the race riots of Chicago will make those of East St. Louis look like a pygmy." Thompson rejected the captain's advice, however, preferring to rely exclusively on the city police. Violence was indeed scattered and meager that morning, and Adjutant General Frank S. Dickson, whom Governor

---

[4] Chicago Commission, *Negro in Chicago*, 5, 16, 18, 21, 33–40, 599, 601; Allen D. Grimshaw, "Actions of Police and the Military in American Race Riots," *Phylon*, XXIV (Fall 1963), 271–89; Grimshaw, "A Study in Social Violence: Urban Race Riots in the United States" (unpublished Ph.D. dissertation, University of Pennsylvania, 1959), 229. The Chicago Commission on Race Relations reported that in "only two cases were Negroes aggressively rioting found outside of the 'Black Belt' [page 18]." Also (page 21), among white men, 69 per cent were shot or stabbed, and 31 per cent were beaten; almost the opposite was true for black men, the figures being 35 and 65 per cent, respectively.

Frank O. Lowden had dispatched to the troubled city, predicted that the police force was sufficient to ward off renewed outbreaks of racial warfare. After conferring with his chief of police for an hour, the mayor ordered every policeman placed on reserve for duty in the South Side black belt. "The rioting must cease," declared Chief John J. Garrity; but should the violence flare up again, he would surround the boundaries of the black belt with a cordon of bluejackets. No one could leave or enter without official permission. "Every resource of the police force will be used." Garrity warned, "to put an end to violence if it becomes necessary to fill every jail in Chicago." [5]

Although such uncompromising rhetoric was commendable, it was no substitute for a comprehensive and racially neutral plan of action. What would be the net effect of stationing the bulk of the city's 3,500-man force along the confines of the black belt—say, on the "dead-line," Wentworth Avenue? Should the city administration pursue this strategy, then black people in virtually every other section of the city— for example, in the Loop, the downtown business district, or in the hostile Irish and Polish territory west of Wentworth and between the black belt and the stockyards—would be unprotected and, on occasion, absolutely vulnerable to the depredations of roaming white mobs. But this was the city's policy, evidently the only one it had, except for the establishment of curfews and the barring of sales of all alcoholic beverages.[6]

The restoration of calm on Monday was illusory, for late that afternoon violence erupted again. Waiting on streetcorners near the gateways to the stockyards were white gangs

[5] Diary of Mrs. Frank O. Lowden, July 28, 1919, in the possession of her daughter, Mrs. C. Phillip Miller, Chicago; *Chicago Daily Journal,* July 25, 28, 1919; *Milwaukee Journal,* July 28, 1919.

[6] Grimshaw, "Actions of Police and the Military in Race Riots," 271–89; Grimshaw, "A Study in Social Violence," 264–65; Chicago Commission, *Negro in Chicago,* 33–40. Chicago was not unique; few if any cities in 1919 had devised effective plans for combating racial violence.

Leaving the stockyards, black and white workers board a streetcar

and workmen, many of them brandishing wooden clubs, iron pipes, and hammers. Pouncing upon black workers as they passed through the gates, the mobs viciously assaulted their prey. Some blacks escaped, managing to elude their pursuers by outrunning them or by boarding passing streetcars just in time. Others, however, were not so fortunate. Oscar Dozier had quit his late afternoon shift and was walking toward home when he encountered a howling, cursing band of whites. For four blocks Dozier ran, but eventually some of the whites overtook the exhausted black man, knocked him to the pavement, and stabbed him repeatedly in the chest. He bled to death in the street. Streetcars were not always safe havens; in fact, they were often easy targets. Returning at six o'clock from the stockyards to the black belt, John Mills had boarded an eastbound streetcar on 47th Street. Just a few blocks later, the car suddenly slammed to a halt as a mob of fifty white youths rushed into the street to surround it. One of the leaders had already climbed atop and disengaged the trolley pole; and as so often happened with the city's mobs during those days of race rioting, about 400 whites, including boys and girls four and five years old, lined the sides of the street cheering on the active nucleus of teenagers. Mills and five other black men, knowing beyond all doubt that they were the hated objects of this assault, leaped from the car and began to run. The hard core of the mob, trailed now by nearly 2,000 enthusiastic onlookers, gave chase. Mills was tackled by his assailants and pummeled to death, his skull fractured.[7]

[7] *Chicago Herald-Examiner,* July 29, 1919; *Chicago Daily Tribune,* July 29, 1919; Peter M. Hoffman (comp.), *The Race Riots: Biennial* [Cook County Coroner's] *Report, 1918–1919* (Chicago: n.pub., n.d.), 23, 28–29, 35–36, 45, 48–49, 50–52; Grimshaw, "Urban Racial Violence in the United States: Changing Ecological Considerations," *American Journal of Sociology,* LXVI (September 1960), 116–17; Grimshaw, "A Study in Social Violence," 213–14, 223; William A. Westley, "The Escalation of Violence through Legitimation," *Annals,* CCCLXIV (March 1966), 121; Chicago Commission, *Negro in Chicago,* 6–9, 10–11, 17–18, 22–23, 37–38, 656, 659; Frederic Thrasher, *The Gang: A Study of 1,313 Gangs in Chicago* (Chicago: University of Chicago Press, 1927), 47.

Whites stoning the black to death

Crowds armed with bricks searching for a black

The arrival of the police

Yet whites had no monopoly on the commission of atrocities. By the late afternoon of July 28, the nucleus of black belligerency had massed at 35th and State Streets, with no fewer than 4,000 people milling around that intersection. At about 4:30, as black people told each other in excited voices that an army of whites was assembling preparatory to an invasion of the black belt, Casmero Lazeroni, a sixty-year-old peddler, innocently steered his horse-drawn wagon into 36th Street from State. Within seconds he was in the midst of the angry mob, which hurled stones at the elderly man before dragging him from his cart and stabbing him to death. Mobs that night also murdered a white laundryman and a white shoemaker.[8]

Throughout the evening carloads of whites sped through the streets of the black belt discharging their weapons as they passed, and blacks retaliated with sniper fire. Posted as guards around the Wabash Avenue YMCA between 37th and 38th Streets were the numerous black students and war veterans who resided there; crouched on fire escapes and peering out windows, they waited. Then, the YMCA's director, A. L. Jackson, recalled, the "cars came through, and they came directly east and turned north on Wabash . . . shooting as they came. My boys, of course, returned the fire. . . ." Snipers fired at practically every vehicle speeding through the black belt, not only at potentially-hostile automobiles but even at the ambulances and hearses carting away the injured and dead. Snipers also mistook the backfiring of police motorcycles for the gunfire of marauders, and they unloaded their firearms in the direction of the noisy reports. When they had no rifles or pistols, snipers used bricks and missiles.[9]

[8] *Chicago Daily Tribune,* July 29, 1919; *Chicago Herald-Examiner,* July 29, 30, 1919; Hoffman, *Coroner's Report,* 42–44, 49–50; Chicago Commission, *Negro in Chicago,* 29, 31, 658, 663–64; copy of telegram from Crockett, Chicago, July 28, 1919, to Military Intelligence Branch, War Department, in Glasser Files, Justice Department Papers (RG 60), National Archives.

[9] *Chicago Herald-Examiner,* July 29, 1919; interviews in Chicago with Mr. Chester Wilkins, June 25, 1969, and Mr. A. L. Jackson,

On Monday, no single site was the focus of more violence than the intersection of 35th and Wabash. For it was here, at the Angelus, an apartment house occupied by whites, that an afternoon of rumors exploded into an evening of bloodshed. In growing hysteria, blacks repeated the story that thousands of whites had mobilized only a few blocks away, at 35th and Wentworth, for the purpose of "cleaning up the black belt." A black woman, others said, had been murdered while returning from work at the stockyards. Finally, there was the rumor that a white tenant had fired a shot from the Angelus, wounding a black boy. The fact that no one had actually seen or heard the shot did not deter a mob of blacks from storming the building. Pointing to one of the apartments, people in the crowd shouted: "He shot from that window. . . . That is the window over there." A police search uncovered no weapons, but this did not assuage the mob, and both its anger and size mounted. A confrontation with the police appeared inevitable. Massed near one corner of 35th and Wabash were 1,500 blacks. Stationed at the intersection of the two streets were nearly 100 officers, twelve mounted, the rest on foot. Then somebody hurled a brick at the policemen; they responded with a volley of gunfire into the heart of the mob. Other shots rang out, from both sides, and numerous black men slumped to the pavement, four of them dead.[10]

White mobs snowballed in size throughout the city that evening. On a South Side streetcorner at about 8:30, for example, five white boys were debating the city's selection of movie shows when a taxicab driver shouted at them that a riot was in progress at 47th Street. Hurriedly, the boys

---

June 27, 1969; Hoffman, *Coroner's Report,* 45–46, 54–55; Chicago Commission, *Negro in Chicago,* 18–19.

[10] *Provident Hospital in the Race Riot of July, 1919* (no imprint), pamphlet in NAACP Papers, in the possession of Middle Atlantic Youth Division of the NAACP, Washington, D.C. (NAACP-2); Chicago Commission, *Negro in Chicago,* 29, 31–32, 661; *Chicago Defender,* August 2, 1919; Hoffman, *Coroner's Report,* 55–56; *Chicago Daily News,* July 29, 1919.

boarded an elevated train, rode it to 47th Street, and became
a part of the mob. For several hours, the white men and boys
roamed the South Side, attacking any black on sight, and although police dispersed the rioters several times, each inter-
ruption was only temporary; the mob always regrouped. At
11:30, it came upon Lieutenant Louis C. Washington, a
black war veteran, his wife, and two other couples. As the
black men and women walked along 43rd Street on their way
home from the theater, Washington recalled, "I heard a yell,
'One, two, three, four, five, six,' and then they gave a loud
cheer, 'Everybody, let's get the niggers! Let's get the niggers,'
and we noticed some of them crossed the street and walked
on up even with us." Then, a half-dozen white men stood
directly in front of Washington's party, and seconds later,
"they swarmed in on us," some of them with pistols, others
wielding knives. One of the black men lurched over, a bullet
in his leg. Washington was stabbed, but before he fell, he
plunged his knife into the breast of one of his assailants.
After several minutes of battle, the mob fled, abandoning the
wounded white youth, who died before an ambulance could
transport him to the hospital.[11]

As the sanguinary character of the rioting finally became
evident to Mayor Thompson, he urged Governor Lowden to
mobilize the state militia and "hold them in readiness in one
of our armories, to make them quickly available for the enforcement of the law when the necessity demands." That evening 3,500 troops filtered into Chicago's armories, several of
which were in or near the black belt. Yet the soldiers would
remain billeted in the armories until Thompson requested
their forceful presence in the violence-ridden streets. It was
obvious that they were needed right away. Undermanned in
the first place, the city's police force now had over 80 per
cent of its men stationed in or around the black belt, leaving
violence to rage unrestrained in almost every other district of

[11] Hoffman, *Coroner's Report,* 40; *Chicago Daily Tribune,* July 29,
1919; Chicago Commission, *Negro in Chicago,* 24–25.

the city. Virtually every minute of that day the overworked police stations, especially on the South Side, received telephone and radio calls for police reserves to break up riots, for ambulances to haul away the injured and hearses to cart off the dead, and for information to corroborate or dispel rumors. Dead-tired, numerous police officers could not perform their duties properly; yet so many others did not even try that police behavior over-all was far less than impartial. A. L. Jackson noted that although the police force had stationed thousands of its men on the South Side, many simply sat on the curb near 35th Street. There were other forms of dereliction of duty, however, that were much more harmful to black people.

Horace Jennings, lying wounded in the street, sighed when he saw a patrolman walking toward him, but his feeling of relief quickly turned to fright with the realization that the man in uniform was also his enemy. "Where's your gun, you black son of a bitch? You damn niggers are raising hell. . . ." Then the officer smashed him over the head with his nightstick, knocking Jennings unconscious. After being left near death at the hands of a mob, Joseph Scott was commanded to "come out of there, you big rusty brute, you. I ought to shoot you." The policeman arrested Scott, struck him repeatedly, and pushed him roughly into a patrol wagon. Earlier twenty-five whites had assaulted Scott on a streetcar, but the police had arrested none of them, partly out of fear of the mob. Instances of brutality and actual police collusion with white lawlessness were not rare; indeed, it was often the black victim of the assault rather than the mob itself who was arrested, and policemen frequently vanished into the shadows of alleys and side streets rather than confront the lawless bands of whites who boldly paraded the main arteries. Chicago's white officers, the Illinois state criminologist said after the riot, tended to apprehend blacks rather than whites because they felt they were "taking fewer chances if they 'soaked' a colored man." The state's attorney, coroner's jury, and the grand jury investigating the riot all concurred in the opinion that white officers were "grossly unfair in making arrests." [12]

One possible resolution of this inequity would have been the infusion of the 3,500 mobilized militiamen into the black belt. The soldiers would have freed a like number of policemen to patrol unprotected sections of the city; and a well-disciplined military troop might have proved to be less biased in its enforcement of the law than a police force with a long history of hostility toward blacks. Certainly, the chances were that blacks would have more confidence in the soldiers than they had in the police. Whites, too, probably would have been more obedient to the commands of an unknown quantity such as the troops. Even so, neither the mayor nor the governor ordered the militia out of the armories and into the streets.

Monday's death toll was seventeen. An additional 172 blacks and seventy-one whites had sustained injuries. Yet midnight marked no end to the warfare, and as Tuesday morning arrived with scarcely a pause in bloodshed, a new source of unrest menaced the city. In a mass meeting on Monday Chicago's traction workers had hooted down a compromise wage settlement and had voted to strike the next morning. Surface and elevated trains would cease to run at 4 A.M. Tuesday, thus opening fresh possibilities for the terrorization of black people who had to walk to work through hostile neighborhoods.[13] Few black workers reported to the stockyards on Tuesday morning. Only nineteen blacks of the 1,500 employed at Armour punched in for work, and only twenty-three of the 2,500 at Swift; and Morris, Wilson, and the other

[12] Report of Grand Jury in CCRR Papers; Hoffman, *Coroner's Report,* 25; *Chicago Herald-Examiner,* July 29, 1919; Chicago Commission, *Negro in Chicago,* 6, 9–11, 33–40, 599, 601–2. Even though twice as many blacks as whites were injured during the riot, twice as many blacks were also arrested by the police and indicted.
[13] *Chicago Daily Tribune,* July 28, 29, 1919; *Chicago Herald-Examiner,* July 29, 1919; "Chicago Afoot," *Survey,* XLII (August 9, 1919), 703–4; Chicago Commission, *Negro in Chicago,* 7, 10–11, 667.

Blacks being escorted by police from the neighborhood of 48th Street and Wentworth Avenue to a safety zone

Blacks being searched in a police station

packers reported similarly low turnouts.[14]

Another development of Tuesday morning was the spreading of violence to the Loop. Still insatiate despite a full evening of bloodshed, a mob of 100 whites, many of whom were soldiers and sailors seventeen to twenty-two years old, began to hunt for blacks in the downtown district. Wherever they were spotted—in railroad stations, restaurants, hotels—black men and boys were dragged into the streets and beaten insensible or shot. Often the motive was not only inflamed racial hatred but also robbery and vandalism. Black men lay dead and wounded in gutters, their pockets turned inside out, while at streetcorners stood the white gangsters, boldly dividing up their profits of watches, cash, and rings.[15]

Still, there was no decision to enlist the aid of the militia. Governor Lowden had been on a train bound for Lincoln, Nebraska, when the news of Monday's renewed bloodshed reached him. He had boarded a special train at Burlington, Iowa, and hastened back to Chicago, arriving at 5:30 A.M. Later that morning he issued a press statement. Pleading for cooperation among public officials at all levels, he added pointedly that although the troops were in the armories ready for action, he could not order them out until Thompson had asked for their services. "We will act on the advices of the mayor," explained Adjutant General Dickson. "We will preserve order at any place he thinks the troops should be sent." So far, however, we "have not received any request. . . ." Such a stipulation was in noticeable contrast to Lowden's actions of September 1917, when not only without a request from Thompson, but in strict opposition to the mayor's wishes, he had dispatched state troops to Chicago to prevent

[14] Hoffman, *Coroner's Report*, 38–39, 54; *Chicago Herald-Examiner*, July 30, 1919; *Chicago Daily Journal*, July 29, 1919; *Chicago Daily News*, July 29, 1919.
[15] *Chicago Daily Journal*, July 29, 1919; *Chicago Defender*, August 2, 1919; *Chicago Herald-Examiner*, July 30, 1919; *Chicago Daily Drovers Journal*, July 29, 1919; Hoffman, *Coroner's Report*, 39, 50; Chicago Commission, *Negro in Chicago*, 7, 19-20, 36.

an antiwar delegation from convening there.[16]

In the absence of streetcars and elevated trains, an incredible array of makeshift vehicles flooded the Loop on Tuesday to carry passengers. Crawling the streets were pickle trucks, laundry coupes, produce wagons, motorcycles with sidecars, and countless private automobiles with their routes chalked on their sides. Montgomery Ward hired six steamboats to transport employees up the Chicago River, and passenger ships also operated along the lake front.[17]

Also on Tuesday rumors began to proliferate throughout the city.[18] Many of them were extreme distortions of the number of deaths, insidious exaggerations that fostered a desire to even the score on the basis of "an eye for an eye," a white victim for a black victim, and vice versa.[19] During the first three days of rioting, for example, two leading newspapers listed 155 whites and 151 blacks as having been injured; the true tallies were 136 whites and 263 blacks.[20] Another prevalent rumor was "the Morgue Myth." Excited visitors to the morgue reported that all the bodies lying there were riot

[16] *Chicago Daily News,* July 29, 1919; *Chicago Daily Journal,* July 29, 1919. In a letter to the author, dated November 30, 1963, Lowden's biographer, William T. Hutchinson, suggested that the governor probably saw no inconsistency between these two actions. According to Professor Hutchinson, Lowden in 1917 was caught up in the nationwide fear of sedition. The Chicago race riot was not, on the other hand, suggestive of a treasonable plot. In 1917, moreover, Lowden waited for a request from officials in East St. Louis before dispatching troops to that city's race riot. Several of Lowden's remarks during the Chicago riot strongly indicate, however, that politics was a prime motivation for not sending the troops in under his own authority and for placing the full burden for such an action on Thompson. For further discussion of this point, see Chapter VI.

[17] *Chicago Daily News,* July 29, 1919; *Chicago Herald-Examiner,* July 30, 1919.

[18] Regarding the interplay of generalized beliefs, incidents precipitating violence, and collective hostility, see G. W. Allport and L. Postman, *The Psychology of Rumor* (N.Y.: Henry Holt, 1947), 193–98.

[19] Graham R. Taylor, "Race Relations and Public Opinion," *Opportunity,* I (July 1923), 199.

[20] See Chicago Commission, *Negro in Chicago,* 22–23, 25–26; Lt. Donald G. Van Buren to Military Intelligence, July 28, 29, 1919, Glasser Files.

victims. The *Whip* blew up the toll of rioting fivefold when it proclaimed in bold headlines: "One Hundred Dead and 1,000 Injured." The police likewise abetted the exaggerations, one officer complaining, for example, that he had had to pay "death dues" on seventy-five policemen.[21] A persistent fabrication was that from four to 100 corpses had been seined out of Bubbly Creek, a stagnant branch of the Chicago River into which the refuse of the stockyards was dumped.[22] Another frequent distortion was that blacks had looted a national guard armory of ammunition and thousands of Springfield rifles and were preparing to invade. Partly as a result of these rumors of blacks' arming, the press quoted Alderman Joseph McDonough of the Fifth Ward as saying that the black people possessed "enough ammunition . . . to last for years of guerrilla warfare," and that he had witnessed several police captains frantically warning white South Side residents: "For God's sake, arm. They are coming; we cannot hold them." [23]

Although only ten women sustained wounds during the riot, eight accidentally, the white newspapers asserted that there had been frequent attacks by black men on white women, with the *Chicago Daily News* even reporting one murder of a white female.[24] To these fabrications the black press added gruesome descriptions of murders which stimulated the craving for vengeance. The *Defender,* for example,

[21] Minutes of the CCRR, March 12, 1920, in CCRR Papers, and in Julius Rosenwald Papers, University of Chicago Library; the *Whip* quoted in *Topeka Plaindealer,* August 8, 1919; *Chicago Daily Journal,* August 1, 1919; *Chicago Daily News,* August 1, 1919. Because of the allegedly inflammatory language in this edition of the *Whip,* the militia bought up all available copies and destroyed them; there is a copy, however, in NAACP-2 Papers.

[22] *Chicago Daily News,* July 29, 1919; Chicago Commission, *Negro in Chicago,* 32–33, 570–71; *Chicago Broad Ax,* August 16, 1919.

[23] *Chicago Daily Tribune,* July 29, 1919; *Chicago Daily News,* July 30, 1919; *Chicago Herald-Examiner,* July 29, 30, 1919; Chicago Commission, *Negro in Chicago,* 21, 28–29, 517, 598.

[24] *Chicago Daily News,* July 29, 1919; *Chicago Daily Tribune,* July 29, 1919; *Chicago Herald-Examiner,* July 29, 1919; Chicago Commission, *Negro in Chicago,* 17, 30–31.

erroneously informed its inflamed readers: "The homes of blacks isolated in white neighborhoods were burned to the ground and the owners and occupants beaten and thrown unconscious into the smoldering embers." The *Defender* also fostered a hideous and totally fabricated account of the murder of a black woman and her baby: "An unidentified young woman and a three months old baby were found dead on the street. . . . She had attempted to board a car there when the mob seized her, beat her, slashed her body into ribbons and beat the baby's brains out against a telephone pole. Not satisfied with this," the *Defender* added, "one rioter severed her breasts and a white youngster bore [them] aloft on a pole, triumphantly." All the while, policemen watched, not making "any attempt to make rescue until too late." [25] This horrifying story spread throughout the country by way of the wire services, and was repeated even by such knowledgeable people as T. Arnold Hill of the Chicago Urban League and Walter White of the NAACP.[26]

Tuesday evening, as the rumors gained momentum, the rioting which had abated during the afternoon both revived and again spilled over the confines of the black belt and stockyards district. Italian residents on the West Side, for example, aroused by tales about a black man having murdered a neighbor girl, set upon a black youth who happened to ride by on his bicycle. His body riddled with bullets and stab wounds, the boy died an awful death, but according to rumors, the mob, in addition, had saturated the corpse with gasoline and ignited it.[27] Race rioting also erupted on the

[25] *Chicago Defender*, August 2, 1919; *The Messenger*, II (September 1919), 12–13; Chicago Commission, *Negro in Chicago*, 30, 572, 576.

[26] Walter White, "Chicago and Its Eight Reasons," *Crisis*, XVIII (October 1919), 296; telegram from T. A. Hill, Chicago, to L. Hollingsworth Wood, New York, July 29, 1919, Rosenwald Papers; *Milwaukee Journal*, July 29, 1919; *New York Times*, July 31, 1919; *Chicago Herald-Examiner*, July 29, 1919.

[27] Hoffman, *Coroner's Report*, 19, 21; *Chicago Daily Journal*, July 30, 1919; *Chicago Herald-Examiner*, July 30, 1919; *Chicago Daily*

North Side, where nearly 5,000 whites hunted down black people in the streets. On the South Side, however, few men and women ventured outside their homes. Parts of the district were closeted in darkness, the result of rioters having shot out most of the street lamps. Trucks and ambulances sped through the black streets, and there was comparative silence except for the pinging of snipers' pistol and rifle shots.[28]

By early Wednesday morning the violent disorders of the past two and a half days had cut short thirty-one lives. Even though the outbursts of late Tuesday had been sporadic, the threat of renewed and perhaps even more virulent racial bloodshed hung over the city, and although it was not at all certain that the police force could subdue further rioting, the governor and the mayor had as yet evinced no willingness to cooperate. They maintained separate command posts, and seldom conferred, if at all. Governor Lowden, in fact, without giving recognition to the efforts of police, attributed the tapering off of violence almost solely to the untested presence of the militia. "I shudder to think," he said, "what might have happened Tuesday if the lawless element responsible for this rioting had not known that 4,000 men, armed and equipped to deal with them, stood ready to act in the zone of violence." You know, Lowden added, that "the second day of an unsuppressed riot is invariably worse than the first, but the fact that the troops were in readiness undoubtedly prevented more serious outbreaks." Yet the militia was not so efficacious a deterrent as

---

Tribune, July 30, 1919; *Chicago Daily News,* July 31, 1919; *St. Louis Globe-Democrat,* July 30, 1919; *New York Times,* July 30, 1919; and *Washington Post,* July 30, 1919. This rumor even reached the halls of the U.S. Senate: see the speech of Tennessee's Senator Kenneth McKellar in *Congressional Record,* LVIII, 3392–93.

[28] *Chicago Herald-Examiner,* July 30, 1919; *Chicago Daily Tribune,* July 30, 1919; *Chicago Daily Journal,* July 30, 1919; R. H. Aishton to W. T. Tyler, and Aishton to M. Clagget, both July 30, 1919, in papers of U. S. Railroad Administration (RG 14), National Archives, Suitland, Maryland (L 19–19); in NAACP-2, affidavits of riot victims and witnesses Count J. Teffner, Dr. E. Haskell Hardeman, W. W. Gibbs, Gordon H. Jackson, and John Taylor.

the governor assumed, for while the troops had been billeted in the armories, unchecked mobs had murdered seventeen Chicagoans and wounded hundreds of others.[29]

After touring the riot area, Thompson declared that he foresaw no exigency that would necessitate the calling out of the militia. Other Chicagoans, however, including all the city's major newspapers, were equally certain that only the infusion of a few thousand troops could restore order, and all day demands for the militia inundated the mayor's office.[30] Citizens also sought out the governor to persuade him to declare martial law. But again Lowden refused, asserting that the mayor was responsible for the maintenance of law and order. He added later: "The troops are to be had for the asking." Thompson responded that the governor could order the militia into service without the mayor's consent. A Democratic alderman spoke for a large portion of Chicago when he complained that "nothing except rotten politics is preventing the calling out of troops." [31]

At a special meeting of the city council all but five of the twenty-five aldermen present favored petitioning for the militia. Alderman McDonough of the Irish ward bordering the black belt warned Chief of Police Garrity, who was before the council to plead for 2,000 special patrolmen, that "unless something is done at once I am going to advise my people to arm themselves for protection." A North Side alderman likewise decried the inadequacies of the police force: "We have a small negro colony, and I wish to give warning that if you take our policemen away [to reinforce the black belt] you are likely to have riots in our ward. You ought to use troops to patrol the peaceful districts and replace the policemen." Yet Garrity was obdurate, and at noon Wednesday the coun-

[29] *Chicago Daily Journal,* July 31, 1919; Hoffman, *Coroner's Report,* 25–27.

[30] *Chicago Daily Journal,* July 30, 31, 1919; *Chicago Daily Tribune,* July 31, 1919; *Chicago Daily News,* July 31, 1919.

[31] *Chicago Daily Journal,* July 30, 1919; *Chicago Daily Tribune,* July 30, 1919.

The wrecked house of a black family in a riot-torn area

cil voted funds for 1,000 special patrolmen, of whom 200 were to be pensioners and the rest untrained applicants from the civil service list who would patrol outlying districts.[32]

Painful memories of the conduct of the state militia at East St. Louis undoubtedly deterred the leaders of the black community from soliciting Thompson and Lowden's assistance. On Wednesday, however, after a two-day conference, black ministers, social workers, and professional and business leaders issued a statement:

> We solemnly call on the mayor of our city and the governor of our state . . . to stop the wholesale murder of defenseless people, even if it is necessary to use the whole militia to do so. We feel that these two officials of our government are responsible, because the state militia and the police force are under them and will obey whatever orders are given by their chiefs.

Thompson's immediate response was that the troops would be summoned "if and when they are needed." The press did not report Lowden's comments, if indeed there were any, while General Dickson was quoted as stating that he still had received no request for the militia from Chief Garrity. "The soldiers are at the disposal of the chief if he sees need of them." [33]

[32] *Chicago Daily Journal,* July 30, 1919; *Milwaukee Journal,* July 30, 1919; *Chicago Herald-Examiner,* July 31, 1919; *Chicago Daily News,* July 30, 1919. The views of outside experts also confirmed the need for the militia. For example, Major General William G. Haan, commander of troops in Washington during its riot, wrote: "In Chicago the troops should have been put in earlier. They seem to have had them there, but they didn't use them. I think a number of lives were lost there that might have been prevented": Haan to Brigadier General C. R. Boardman, August 5, 1919, Haan Papers, State Historical Society of Wisconsin.

[33] *Chicago Daily News,* July 30, 1919; *Chicago Broad Ax,* August 2, 1919; *Chicago Defender,* August 2, 1919; *Chicago Daily Tribune,* July 31, 1919; *Chicago Daily Journal,* July 30, 1919; *Chicago Whip,* February 19, 1927, as quoted in Harold F. Gosnell, *Negro Politicians: The Rise of Negro Politics in Chicago* (Chicago: Phoenix Books of University of Chicago Press, 1967), 58; NAACP *Branch Bulletin,*

For the people of the black belt the restoration of order was imperative. "My people have no food," complained black realtor and banker Jesse Binga. "Retailers in the district have run out of stocks and outside grocery and butcher men will not send their wagons into the district." The black belt's residents had mobbed other drivers so frequently that few dared return, and the icemen's and milk drivers' unions forbade deliveries by their members. Accumulating in alleys and on sidewalks were piles of garbage, which not only reeked but were sources of disease and even epidemic. Funds, in addition, were depleted, since black men and woman generally had not worked that week.[34]

A variety of considerations coalesced during the evening of July 30 to persuade Thompson finally to ask for the militia. The employers of large numbers of black workers had exerted pressure on the mayor, and the blacks' supplication of that afternoon apparently had had its effect, too. Moreover, the fatigue of the police was evident to even the most casual observer. "Why don't they use the soldiers?" groaned patrolmen in the black belt.[35] Perhaps above all, however, was the fear of a widespread plot to burn the black belt; the fire department reported thirty-seven conflagrations in five hours that evening, many of them set within a few minutes on the same blocks. At 51st Street and Shields Avenue, for example, three blocks west of Wentworth, there had been for years a black

III (August 1919), supplement thereto, in CCRR Papers; unpublished autobiography of Ida B. Wells-Barnett, 375–85, in possession of Mrs. Barnett's daughter, Mrs. Alfreda Duster, Chicago; Joseph A. Logsdon, "The Rev. Archibald J. Carey and the Negro in Chicago Politics" (unpublished M.A. thesis, University of Chicago, 1961), 72–73.

34 *Chicago Daily Tribune,* July 31, 1919.

35 *Ibid.; Chicago Daily Journal,* July 31, 1919; *Chicago Daily News,* July 31, 1919; *Chicago Herald-Examiner,* July 31, August 1, 1919; *Chicago Whip,* August 9, 1919; Chicago Commission, *Negro in Chicago,* 40; Van Buren to Military Intelligence, July 30, 1919, in Glasser Files; in CCRR Papers, Hqs., Mobilized State Forces, Field Orders Nos. 1, 2, July 30, 1919; John G. Oglesby, Acting Governor, to Adjutant General of the State of Illinois, [July 30], 1919.

enclave of nine families, but that night the Ragen Colts tried to burn it to the ground. Throughout the afternoon, reported Harriett White, one of the black residents, there had been rumors of a mob that intended to "run all of the niggers out of this section tonight." Repeated telephone calls to the police had brought only a brief visit by about ten mounted policemen at 6:30. Two hours later the Colts arrived, 200 strong, and they "started throwing rocks, bricks, and other missiles and shooting into . . . houses. . . ." Then they began storming through the front doors, smashing furniture and throwing it through windows, and putting the torch to everything. "Bricks, stones and shots entered my home, forcing me to leave," recalled Mrs. White. Having done their work, the Colts left a warning: "If you open your mouth against 'Ragen's' we will not only burn your house down, we will 'do' you."[36]

Shortly before 10 P.M., the 6,200 troops then in the city moved out of the armories and into the region bounded by Wentworth and Indiana, and 18th and 55th Streets. Although some of the soldiers, as one of them later admitted, "went down . . . thinking that Negroes were the most to blame" and with "the intention . . . to clean them up," the behavior of the militia was exemplary. "Use butts and bayonets—fire as a last resort," were the instructions. "Draw no color line—a white rioter is as dangerous as a Negro rioter and must be handled with the same brand of firmness." Disciplined and impartial, the militia cracked down especially hard on the athletic clubs. Still later that night a second force materialized to frustrate the rioters; rain began to fall, and rioters and curiosity seekers scurried into their homes. After that, the violence was sporadic and sparse.[37]

[36] Affidavit of Harriett White, in NAACP-2; Hoffman, *Coroner's Report,* 30–32, 34–35, 37–38, 53; *Chicago Daily Tribune,* July 31, 1919; *Chicago Daily Journal,* July 30, 1919; Chicago Commission, *Negro in Chicago,* 14, which erroneously lists the date of the attack as July 29, 1919.

[37] Minutes of the meeting at City Club of Chicago, February 25,

Blacks under the protection of militia buy badly needed provisions in the black belt

Black men and white soldiers meet and talk

On Thursday, as black workers again ventured west of Wentworth Avenue to journey to the stockyards, it became evident that the hostility of numerous white employees had not waned. One worker, for example, savagely struck a black man with a hammer. A mob then pursued the dazed man through the sheep pens and finally fatally toppled him with shovels and brooms. When police and soldiers rescued a second black man after a severe beating, the white workers retaliated and a vicious battle ensued. The stockyards were not yet safe for any but white workers.[38] Aside from the bloodshed at the stockyards, however, the riot areas were conspicuous for their lack of violence. Truckloads of fresh food, milk, and ice entered the black belt, and on Friday the meat packers established emergency pay stations at the Urban League, Wabash YMCA, and Jesse Binga's bank. Also that day, the traction workers voted to end the strike; resumption of streetcar and elevated service would begin at five the next morning. But most important, black men and women could again step outside their barricaded residences.[39]

On Saturday morning, the meat packers conferred with General Dickson and the deputy chief of police to conclude arrangements for the return to work, under a cover of machine guns, of twelve to fifteen thousand black men and women. Nailed on trees and telephone poles, a host of signs and flyers authorized by the packers had begun to appear in the black belt as early as Friday evening. "FELLOW

1920, copies in CCRR and Rosenwald Papers; *Chicago Daily News,* July 31, 1919; *Chicago Daily Tribune,* July 31, 1919; Chicago Commission, *Negro in Chicago,* 7, 11, 40–43; Sterling Morton, "The Illinois Reserve Militia during World War I and After," oral history, December 4, 1959, in Chicago Historical Society.

[38] Hoffman, *Coroner's Report,* 42–43; *Chicago Daily Journal,* July 31, 1919; *Chicago Herald-Examiner,* August 1, 1919; *Chicago Daily Tribune,* August 1, 1919.

[39] *Chicago Herald-Examiner,* August 1, 2, 1919; *Chicago Daily Tribune,* August 1, 2, 1919; *Chicago Daily News,* August 1, 1919; *Chicago Daily Journal,* August 1, 1919; interview with Mr. A. L. Jackson, June 27, 1969; National Urban League *Bulletin,* IX (January 1920), 17–18; Chicago Commission, *Negro in Chicago,* 44.

Black stockyard workers being paid at the YMCA

Black men buy ice from a freight car switched into the black belt

Milk for babies was distributed

WORKERS," began the poster signed by the "efficiency clubs" of Armour, Morris, and Wilson. "We go back to work Monday 7:00 A.M. Sharp. Use the Elevated Road," on which the police would station guards. "Keep Cool and use your heads. . . . The riot is over. LET'S FORGET IT. We need food and work for our families, so do you. STEADY AND COOL IS THE WATCHWORD." There were other signs, too, from Alderman R. R. Jackson, the Urban League, and the "Committee of Colored Citizens," all giving their assurances that there would be "proper police protection" in the stockyards and on the elevated. At the same time, however, the white workers of the stockyards showed their anger by circulating petitions demanding that the companies draw the color line in employment. But the unions, having issued a plea to their members to abstain from violence and to black workers to have confidence in the labor movement, protested bitterly against the packers' plan for Monday. "These men," the representatives of the Stockyards Labor Council told the packers, "will be on the killing floor of the packing plants. They will have cleavers and knives," and they "know how to use them. The machine guns will not be able to stop what will happen unless they mow down the workers, white and black. You must be insane to attempt such a thing." But the unions' remonstrance was to no avail; further evidence of the racial enmity in the stockyards was essential to dissuade the packers from adopting their shortsighted plan.[40]

That evidence was quick in arriving, for early Saturday morning incendiaries fired the ramshackle dwellings of Polish and Lithuanian laborers who resided in the neighborhood behind the stockyards. The dry frame huts flared up like kin-

[40] Report from Director, Division of Negro Economics, to Secretary of Labor, September 12, 1919, in Labor Department Papers (RG 174), National Archives, 8/102-E; posters and flyers in NAACP-2; *Chicago Herald-Examiner,* August 4, 1919; Chicago Commission, *Negro in Chicago,* 45; *Chicago Daily Tribune,* August 2, 1919; *New Majority,* August 2, 1919; Illinois State Federation of Labor *Weekly News Letter,* August 23, 1919.

dling; 948 immigrants were rendered homeless and the damage approached $250,000. The authorities never affixed the responsibility for the conflagration. Governor Lowden ascribed it to IWW plotters who had blackened their faces in order to cast blame on black people. If so, they were guilty of ineptitude, for the fire destroyed all the possessions of several "Wobblies." The immigrants and the fire department accused black men who, they claimed, had fired the buildings in order to retaliate against the threats of certain white stockyards' employees to murder all blacks who sought reemployment. To this accusation, however, the rejoinder of black Alderman L. B. Anderson was indeed plausible. "It is preposterous," he said, "to think that any colored man would go west of Halsted Street without a guard of police or militia in these times. . . . Do you think," he asked, "that a colored man would go into this district back of the yards to set fires when . . . colored men have refused to go to the stockyards to get paid even though their families were starving? Impossible!" The grand jury charged the fires to the athletic clubs, saying that white gangsters had ignited them "for the purpose of inciting race feeling by blaming same on blacks." Regardless of the identity of the culprits, it was clear to the packers that the black workers could not safely return Monday, a decision that Lowden, J. Ogden Armour, and Louis F. Swift announced several hours later.[41]

Sunday and Monday were uneventful, despite a bomb scare, a menacing mob bearing placards on which were inscribed the words "Kill the Coons," and a series of threatening letters to blacks in contested neighborhoods warning them to evacuate their residences lest the "13," a mysterious organ-

[41] *Chicago Herald-Examiner,* August 3, 1919; *Chicago Whip,* August 9, 1919; *Chicago Daily Tribune,* August 3, 4, 1919; ". . . critical analysis of . . . testimony taken by coroner's jury," undated, in NAACP-2; *Narod Polski,* XXIII (August 13, 1919), in Foreign Language Press Survey, University of Chicago; Hqs., Mobilized State Forces, Field Orders No. 4, August 2, 1919, CCRR Papers; Van Buren to Military Intelligence, August 2, 1919, in Glasser Files; Chicago Commission, *Negro in Chicago,* 16, 20–21, 539–40.

Scenes from a fire in the immigrant neighborhood "back of the yards"

ization, "burn and bomb out and hunt them down through the streets and alleys." On Tuesday an Irish alderman sought to capitalize on the rampant racial antipathy by introducing a motion that the city council establish segregated zones, but his resolution was ruled out of order. Further outbursts of violence that day were meager.[42]

Throughout Wednesday, August 6, representatives of the packers notified their black employees to report the next day. "Practically all of them," the militia headquarters informed commanders in Chicago, "will come in on special trains on the elevated railroad which will discharge at the various stations in the Yards. . . ." The next morning, under the protection of 1,500 policemen, a militia regiment, 350 special deputies and fifty regular deputics, and scores of detectives, 12,000 black workers reported, including 9,000 nonunion men. As they entered the gates, nearly 10,000 white unionists walked out. The NAACP's Walter White, who, after putting on "some old clothes," spent the morning at the stockyards with the black workers, reported that "the only thing that prevented serious clashes was the presence of thousands of police and state troops. There was considerable hooting and muttering and the tension was very great." Later that day handbills in three languages circulated in the vicinity of the stockyards announcing a mass meeting for August 9, to approve either a Chicago general strike or a stockyards strike for the closed shop, the express purpose of which was to exclude nonunion blacks.[43]

[42] *Journal of the City Council of Chicago, 1919–1920,* 1115; this portion of the *Journal* was mailed to the author by the Reference Librarian, Chicago Municipal Reference Library, September 19, 1963; also *Chicago Herald-Examiner,* August 4, 5, 1919; *Chicago Daily Tribune,* August 4, 5, 1919; Hqs., Mobilized State Forces, Field Orders No. 5, August 4, 1919, CCRR Papers.

[43] *New Majority,* August 9, 16, 1919; Alschuler Hearings, August 13, 1919, 30–38, in Papers of Federal Mediation and Conciliation Service (RG 280), Suitland, Maryland, 33/864; Walter White to Mary White Ovington, August 7, 11, 1919, in NAACP Papers, Library of Congress (C-76); Hqs., Mobilized State Forces, Field Orders No. 6, August 6, 1919, CCRR Papers; *Chicago Daily Journal,* August 6–9,

In the early afternoon of August 8, the adjutant general ordered the militia commanders to withdraw from Chicago. The next day, as the last of the troops marched triumphantly through the Loop, the governor and the adjutant general were chauffeured to the city hall. Having informed Lowden that the mayor had departed for the weekend, a curious city official inquired whether or not the governor's business with Thompson was urgent. Lowden replied ironically: "There is no significance in our visit. We just came to see the men with whom we have been cooperating." [44]

The withdrawal of the state militia officially terminated the rioting of the past fourteen days. Dead were thirty-eight, including twenty-three black men and boys. At least 537 were injured, of whom 342 were black. Yet even though black people had suffered the brunt of the bloodshed, they had also been arrested by police at twice the rate of whites, prompting one skeptical white judge to declare: "I want to explain to you [police] officers that these colored people could not have been rioting among themselves. Bring me some white prisoners." [45] The police, in addition, had shot to death seven blacks but no whites.

This was the awesome toll of the Chicago race riot. But what were the causes? Aside from the nation's history of racial violence and the general unrest evident in the Red Summer and the Red Scare, what had brought the city of Chicago to the point where a racial altercation at a beach could spark such a thunderous explosion of violence and bloodshed? Was it the oppressiveness of the ninety-five-degree heat? It was, in part. Was it an accident? Far from it. It was obvious, after two days of violence, that the ecology of the Chicago riot was

11–13, 1919; *Chicago Herald-Examiner,* August 7–9, 1919; *New York Times,* August 8–10, 12, 1919; *Chicago Daily Tribune,* August 7–9, 1919. The state troops were withdrawn on August 8, and the striking workers returned to the stockyards on Monday, August 11, 1919.

[44] *Chicago Daily Journal,* August 8, 9, 1919; *Chicago Daily News,* August 8, 1919.

[45] *Chicago Defender,* August 9, 1919; *Chicago Daily Tribune,* August 7, 1919.

quite unlike that of other race riots; and what the ecology of violence revealed probably more than anything else was that the origins of the riot were imbedded deep in the social, economic, and political structure of the city.

Some sociologists have called the Chicago race riot a "communal" riot or even the "ideal-type" riot. For the Chicago bloodshed was primarily "ecological warfare," involving "a direct struggle between the residents of white and Negro areas." "In no other major urban race riot," a foremost investigator of urban race riots has written, "has a white neighborhood characterized by such high prejudice and such an intensity of anti-Negro social tensions immediately abutted on the central concentration of Negro population." The stockyards and the black belt—these were the two neighborhoods, precisely demarcated by Wentworth Avenue. The Chicago riot, unlike the massacre in East St. Louis, where a black enclave in the downtown section had been invaded, homes burned, and defenseless people mutilated, was no "pogrom." Blacks and whites in Chicago waged pitched battles. Indeed, of all the riots in 1919, a historian has observed, it was Chicago "in which Negroes most fully demonstrated their intention to fight back. . . ." To be sure, whites invaded the black belt; but they usually did so hurriedly, in automobiles, and they often encountered retaliation by sniper fire. In other riots, the bulk of the racial clashes erupted in black neighborhoods and their peripheries. Yet, in Chicago, 41 per cent occurred in the predominantly white district of the stockyards, and 34 per cent in the black belt. Moreover, although many of America's race riots had erupted only after whites had charged blacks with such "sacred" violations of white womanhood as rape, the Chicago bloodshed was purely secular in its causes. There were accusations of sexual violations, but they came later, in the form of rumors, to legitimize, rationalize, and justify the brutality that was happening.[46]

[46] Chicago Commission, *Negro in Chicago,* 598; Allen D. Grimshaw, "Lawlessness and Violence in America and Their Special Manifestations in Changing Negro-White Relationships," *Journal of Negro*

Fundamental to an explanation of the Chicago race riot, and thus an essential beginning point, is the World War I migration—that influx of Southern black people which doubled the city's black population in less than three years, thereby bringing to a climax racial tensions and animosities in labor, housing, and politics that had threatened to erupt for years.

History, XLIV (January 1959), 52–72; Grimshaw, "Urban Racial Violence in the United States," 109–19; Grimshaw, "A Study in Social Violence," 36–37, 47–56, 95, 209–11; Morris Janowitz, "Patterns of Collective Racial Violence," in National Commission on the Causes and Prevention of Violence, *Violence in America,* prepared under the direction of Hugh Davis Graham and Ted Robert Gurr (N.Y.: Signet edition, 1969), 396; Arthur I. Waskow, *From Race Riot to Sit-In* (Garden City, N.Y.: Doubleday & Company, 1966), 10, 58–59.

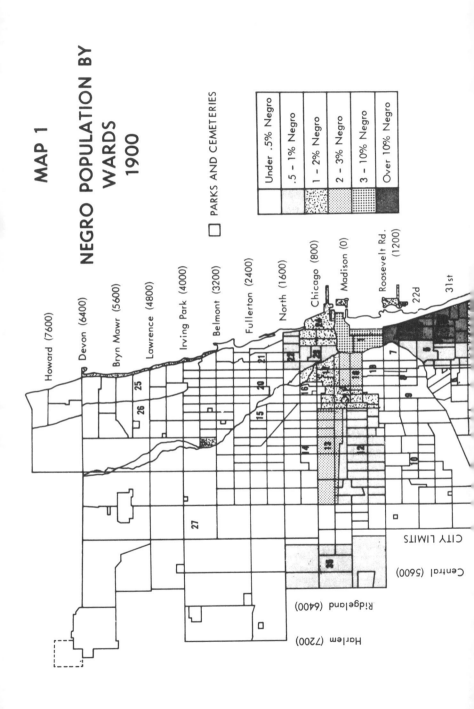

MAP 1

NEGRO POPULATION BY WARDS
1900

☐ PARKS AND CEMETERIES

	Under .5% Negro
	.5 – 1% Negro
	1 – 2% Negro
	2 – 3% Negro
	3 – 10% Negro
	Over 10% Negro

Howard (7600)
Devon (6400)
Bryn Mawr (5600)
Lawrence (4800)
Irving Park (4000)
Belmont (3200)
Fullerton (2400)
North (1600)
Chicago (800)
Madison (0)
Roosevelt Rd. (1200)
22d
31st

CITY LIMITS
Central (5600)
Ridgeland (6400)
Harlem (7200)

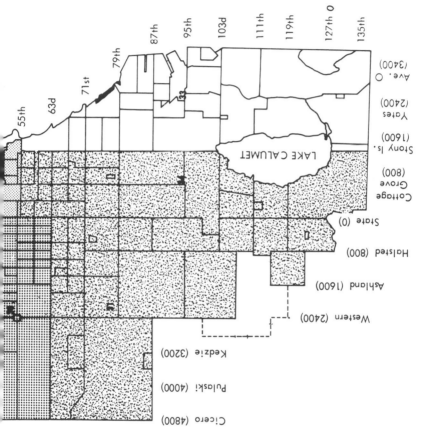

WARD BOUNDARIES OF CHICAGO AS USED IN UNITED STATES CENSUS OF 1900

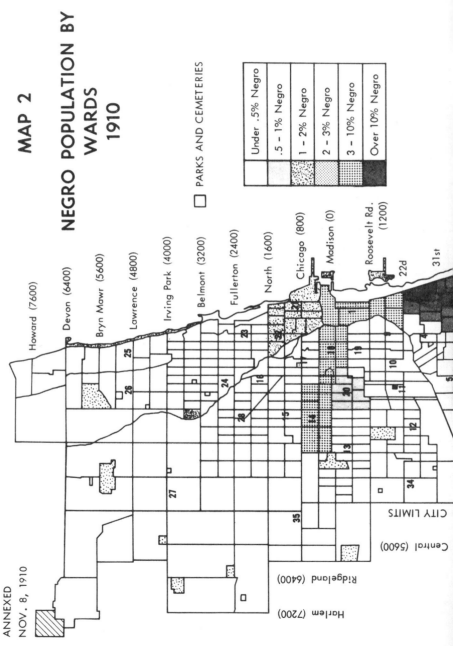

MAP 2

NEGRO POPULATION BY
WARDS
1910

ANNEXED
NOV. 8, 1910

	Under .5% Negro
	.5 – 1% Negro
	1 – 2% Negro
	2 – 3% Negro
	3 – 10% Negro
	Over 10% Negro

☐ PARKS AND CEMETERIES

Howard (7600)
Devon (6400)
Bryn Mawr (5600)
Lawrence (4800)
Irving Park (4000)
Belmont (3200)
Fullerton (2400)
North (1600)
Chicago (800)
Madison (0)
Roosevelt Rd. (1200)
22d
31st

CITY LIMITS

Central (5600)
Ridgeland (6400)
Harlem (7200)

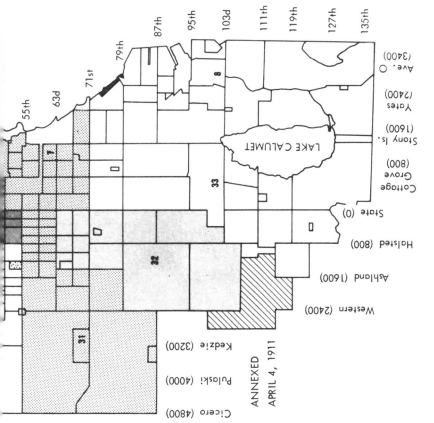

WARD BOUNDARIES OF CHICAGO AS USED IN UNITED STATES CENSUS OF 1910

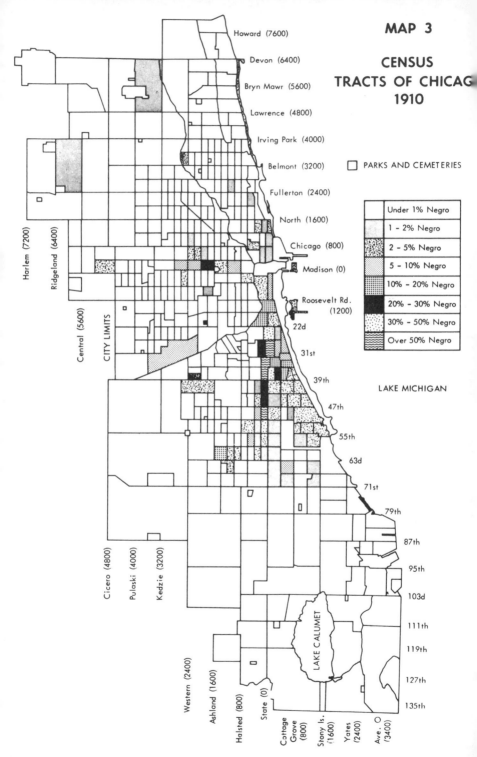

MAP 3

CENSUS
TRACTS OF CHICAGO
1910

Howard (7600)
Devon (6400)
Bryn Mawr (5600)
Lawrence (4800)
Irving Park (4000)
Belmont (3200)
Fullerton (2400)
North (1600)
Chicago (800)
Madison (0)
Roosevelt Rd. (1200)
22d
31st
39th
47th
55th
63d
71st
79th
87th
95th
103d
111th
119th
127th
135th

Harlem (7200)
Ridgeland (6400)
Central (5600)
CITY LIMITS

Cicero (4800)
Pulaski (4000)
Kedzie (3200)
Western (2400)
Ashland (1600)
Halsted (800)
State (0)
Cottage Grove (800)
Stony Is. (1600)
Yates (2400)
Ave. O (3400)

☐ PARKS AND CEMETERIES

	Under 1% Negro
	1 - 2% Negro
	2 - 5% Negro
	5 - 10% Negro
	10% - 20% Negro
	20% - 30% Negro
	30% - 50% Negro
	Over 50% Negro

LAKE MICHIGAN

LAKE CALUMET

Based on unpublished census data for 1910, compiled
by Otis and Beverly Duncan, Population Studies Center, University of Michigan.

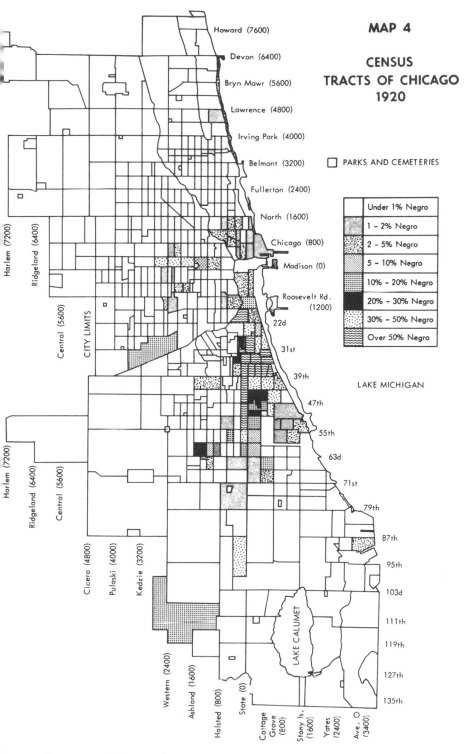

MAP 4

CENSUS
TRACTS OF CHICAGO
1920

Howard (7600)

Devon (6400)

Bryn Mawr (5600)

Lawrence (4800)

Irving Park (4000)

Belmont (3200)

☐ PARKS AND CEMETERIES

Fullerton (2400)

North (1600)

Chicago (800)

Madison (0)

Roosevelt Rd. (1200)

22d

31st

39th

47th

55th

63d

71st

79th

87th

95th

103d

111th

119th

127th

135th

LAKE MICHIGAN

LAKE CALUMET

	Under 1% Negro
	1 – 2% Negro
	2 – 5% Negro
	5 – 10% Negro
	10% – 20% Negro
	20% – 30% Negro
	30% – 50% Negro
	Over 50% Negro

Harlem (7200)

Ridgeland (6400)

Central (5600)

CITY LIMITS

Harlem (7200)

Ridgeland (6400)

Central (5600)

Cicero (4800)

Pulaski (4000)

Kedzie (3200)

Western (2400)

Ashland (1600)

Halsted (800)

State (0)

Cottage Grove (800)

Stony Is. (1600)

Yates (2400)

Ave. O (3400)

d on Ernest W. Burgess and Charles Newcomb, editors,
nus Data of the City of Chicago (Chicago: University of Chicago Press, 1931)

Going into Canaan

WHAT THE PAST YEAR has held for us we know," editorialized Chicago's militant black newspaper, the *Defender,* on New Year's Day. But "what the year of 1916 will bring no man knows. . . ." [1] A black man in the South, receiving a copy of this *Defender* in the mail from a friend, would find little hint of the mass migration which would begin that year.

The news in Chicago on New Year's Day was not of the future but of the immediate holiday season. It told of lodge parties, family reunions, and church socials, and despite the frigid and gusty weather, there was much to celebrate. The Pullman car conductors and porters, for example, boasted of the ten per cent wage increases which the company had just announced. Local personages from the black community were in the news. There was a photograph in the *Defender* of

[1] *Chicago Defender,* January 1, 1916.

74

Binga Dismond, track star at the University of Chicago, who was studying for admission to medical school; and reporters noted from Boston that the fiery Ida B. Wells-Barnett had been elected to the executive committee of the National Equal Rights League at its annual convention. Yet there was sufficient discouraging news to offset the good. Jack Johnson, the "Greatest Boxer of Them All," according to the local press, had suffered an unexpected defeat at the hands of the "Great White Hope," Jess Willard, the previous spring, and blacks that winter were increasingly suspicious that federal agents had arranged the outcome; Mound Bayou, an all-black town in Mississippi, was in financial collapse because of crop failures; and racial violence had erupted in Muskogee, Oklahoma. The determined black men in that unhappy Oklahoma community, however, claimed that they had "got their spirit from the *DEFENDER,*" and that they had decided to die if necessary to rid their neighborhood of the "filth" of prostitution and the white men it attracted.[2]

This news of the outside world, coming to a man born and raised on a piece of land he had never left, might have been an opening shaft of light to one in darkness as to the realities of the larger world. The *Defender* in those days, however, was not encouraging men to move to Chicago, as it was later to do; in fact, on New Year's Day 1916 it even questioned the wisdom of a black's trying to live in that city, where "conditions make it practically impossible . . . to secure a flat or a house in a desirable neighborhood at anything like a moderate rental, if, in fact, they can be had at all." [3]

But 1916 was the year that heralded the advent of a migration of hundreds of thousands of blacks to the urban industrial North. Chicago's black population practically doubled in the next four years. The school census of May 1914 counted 54,557 black people, and some blacks estimated that at least that many more arrived between 1916 and 1918. Per-

[2] *Ibid.*
[3] *Ibid.*

haps this latter estimate is inflated, and certainly it does not accord with the federal census; but it is also apparent that a sizable portion of the black minority has, even in recent and more sophisticated censuses, proved itself to be invisible to the enumerators. At any rate, by 1920, according to the federal census, the number of blacks in Chicago had soared to 110,000, and the vast preponderance of this increase was made up of migrants who had been Southern and to a large extent rural up to World War I.[4]

Other Northern urban industrial complexes were almost as magnetic in their appeal as Chicago; altogether over 450,000 blacks flocked to the North between 1916 and 1918. But it was Chicago more than any other northern city that represented "the top of the world" and "freedom" to Southern blacks. It was Chicago, renowned for its World's Columbian Exposition of 1893 and famous for its mail order houses, mass-production industries, and vast railroad network, that was "a synonym for the 'North.'" To Southern blacks, Chicago was not only a city; it was a state of mind.[5]

[4] Department of Commerce, Bureau of the Census, *14th Census of the United States, 1920* (Washington: Government Printing Office, 1922), III, 274–76; Otis D. and Beverly Duncan, *The Negro Population of Chicago* (Chicago: University of Chicago Press, 1957), 34, 90; Chicago Commission on Race Relations, *The Negro in Chicago* (Chicago: University of Chicago Press, 1922), 79; Allan H. Spear, *Black Chicago: The Making of a Negro Ghetto, 1890–1920* (Chicago: University of Chicago Press, 1967), 139–46; Bureau of the Census, *13th Census of the United States, 1910* (Washington: Government Printing Office, 1913), III, 512–14. Frank D. Loomis (ed.), *Americanization in Chicago* (Chicago: Chicago Community Trust, n.d.), 7; Junius B. Wood, *The Negro in Chicago* (Chicago: Chicago Daily News, ca. 1916), 6–7; estimate of migration by James W. Poe, president, Colored Citizens' Patriotic League, May 10, 1917, in Files on East St. Louis, in U.S. Department of Labor Papers (RG 174), Box 205, National Archives (Poe estimated that within the past eighteen months between 400,000 and 700,000 blacks had migrated to the North, with 54,000 coming to Illinois, the highest total for any state); Robert E. Park in Chicago Urban League, *Annual Report*, I (no imprint), 4; Philip Hauser's figure for the decade 1910–1920 is 454,300: T. Parsons and K. B. Clark (eds.), *The Negro American* (Boston: Beacon, 1967), 75.

[5] See Emmett J. Scott, *Negro Migration during the War* (N.Y.: Oxford University Press, 1920), 102.

One 1916 migrant to Chicago was Shot Pinckney.[6] A sharecropper, Pinckney farmed with his own family and 300 others on a 2,000-acre Mississippi plantation. "We were never paid money," he later recalled, "only credit at the Commissary." Naturally he had thought about leaving the plantation and Mississippi, but because of the size of his family (a wife and six children) and because of the surveillance of the overseers and guards (". . . they wouldn't let us go anywhere except to work. . . ."), he had become resigned to living out the rest of his years there. But in the autumn of 1916 "a new comer" working in one of the cotton gins approached him and asked: "How would you like to leave this plantation and go up north and make some money?" Fearful that they might be overheard, Pinckney quickly replied: "You are either drunk or just a plain, simple, damn fool." That evening, however, the stranger visited his shack, and Pinckney and his wife agreed to leave for the North if the stranger could suggest a way to escape. But, Pinckney asked, "How are we to get by the guard at the 'Big Gate'?" The next morning Pinckney followed the stranger's instructions and asked the overseer for permission for his family to leave the plantation "so we could see a circus which we heard would be in town" on Saturday. The overseer looked at Pinckney with "a squinting, suspicious expression in his eyes," but he finally consented. The stranger had persuaded other families to request permission, and they, too, were issued passes to show the guards at the "Big Gate." "We all left walking Friday night about midnight," each family having with it only a meager amount of personal belongings "lest we arouse suspicion and jeopardize our chances of escape." Waiting a mile away at "the little station on the branch track" was something that Pinckney and

[6] The author has fabricated the name, for the source from which this information was taken contained none: interview in Ardis Harris, "Bronzeville, A City within a City," June 7, 1939, in WPA Project, "The Negro in Illinois," the files of which are in the George Cleveland Hall Branch, Chicago Public Library.

his family had never seen before—a train. They boarded it, and at about 5:30 felt it lurch and then creep forward, "as if to make less noise as possible; gradually picking up more and more speed after it had reached the main line." Occasionally the train would jerk to a stop, but Pinckney and his family did "not know what station it was, as we were not allowed to look outside the train, or even raise the window-blinds until the train had crossed the Mason and Dixon line." But even before it had left Mississippi, each car in the train was "packed to every available foot of . . . space," and thus jammed together the migrants traveled to Chicago. Employment was awaiting Pinckney at the stockyards. The stranger probably profited as well as the workers, for he was doubtless a labor agent for Northern industries.

Pinckney's departure from the South was rather unique, but historically there was nothing unusual about the interstate migration of Southern blacks. A series of migrations had followed the withdrawal of federal troops from the South after Reconstruction. In 1879, under the leadership of "Pap" Singleton of Tennessee and Henry Adams of Louisiana, thousands migrated to Kansas, idealized as the home of John Brown and free-soil victories. Blacks in 1889 moved from southern Alabama to Arkansas and Texas; and during the 1890's they flowed into the mineral regions around Birmingham, Alabama. The spread of the boll weevil produced a migration from Southern cotton fields to the canebrakes of Louisiana, and when sugar planters reduced their acreage in 1914 because of the prospect of free sugar another movement commenced.

In a sense, the World War I migration was merely an acceleration of this longstanding process. Between 1916 and 1918, however, not only did far more blacks migrate than ever before, but the direction of the migration shifted as well. The decennial movement of black people from 1880 to 1910 had been 20.5 miles southwest, 9.5 miles southwest, and 5.8 miles southwest; but, in 1920, the movement was 21.5 miles northeast.[7] It was the forces that reversed the direction of the migration which, above all, distinguished the "Great Northern Drive" from the earlier migrations.

Of these forces, one set compelled countless blacks to flee the South, while the other lured them to the North. "I am in the darkness of the south," lamented a dweller of Alabama in pleading for a train ticket to Chicago, ". . . o please help me to get out of this low down country [where] i am counted no more thin a dog."[8] Disfranchisement, segregated facilities, inequality before the courts, mistreatment by police, lynchings and other kinds of physical violence, abuse and verbal insults to women, and governmental neglect of sanitation, lighting, and streets—these were among the social and political forces driving blacks out of the South. "Anywhere north will do us," wrote a Louisianian who epitomized the zeal to escape the caste system of the South; and, he added, "I suppose the worst place there is better than the best place here."[9] A Texas black voiced a similar sentiment when he indicated that although he preferred to migrate to Chicago, he primarily wanted "to leave the South and go and [any] Place where a man will be any thing Except a Ker. . . ."[10]

Education, or rather the inaccessibility of it, was a potent driving force. Black parents longed to provide better opportunities for their children, and basic to this desire was school-

[7] W. O. Scroggs, "Interstate Migration of Negro Population," *Journal of Political Economy*, XXV (December 1917), 1034–43; Joseph A. Hill, "Recent Northward Migration of the Negro," *Monthly Labor Review*, XVIII (March 1924), 475; Charles S. Johnson, "How the Negro Fits in Northern Industries," *Industrial Psychology*, I (June 1926), 401–2; R. R. Wright, Jr., "The Migration of Negroes to the North," *Annals*, XXVII (May 1906), 97; Louise V. Kennedy, *The Negro Peasant Turns Cityward* (N.Y.: Columbia University Press, 1930), 28.

[8] Emmett J. Scott (comp.), "Additional Letters of Negro Migrants of 1916–1918," *Journal of Negro History*, IV (October 1919), 440.

[9] *Ibid.*, 442.

[10] Scott (comp.), "Letters of Negro Migrants of 1916–1918," *Journal of Negro History*, IV (July 1919), 298. See also S. Fincher to Robert S. Abbott, from Chamblee, Georgia, n.d., in the Carter G. Woodson Papers, Library of Congress.

ing. "I want a good paying job," wrote a Mississippian, "that I may be able to educate my children." In Southern districts, however, and especially in areas with high percentages of cotton tenancy, the school terms for blacks were as much as two months shorter than those for whites. It was not sufficient simply to pay taxes, for as one Louisianian complained: "Our poll tax paid, state and parish taxes yet . . . we cannot get schools." Investment in public school property and equipment in the South was five to ten times more per white child than per black child, and the disparity between salaries for teachers of whites and teachers of blacks was equally great. An extreme example of this was a portion of Louisiana in which the annual salaries averaged $28.89 per white pupil and $.87 per black pupil.[11] It was thus effective advertising for Chicago when the *Defender* displayed in its pages two photographs, one of a frame, single-room "Jim Crow School" in Abbeville, Louisiana, the other of an expansive, stone-columned building housing Chicago's Robert Lindblom High School, "where no color line is drawn" and "one of the many reasons why members of the Race are leaving the south." [12]

The incomes of most Southern blacks, especially agricultural wage hands, sharecroppers, and tenant farmers, had never been more than paltry. Immediately before America's entry into World War I, natural disasters exacerbated this economic driving force, and hunger, malnutrition, and pellagra burgeoned as indices of these misfortunes. The boll weevil in 1915 and 1916 ravaged the cotton crops of Louisiana, Mississippi, Alabama, Georgia, and Florida; and of these five

[11] Scott, "Letters of Negro Migrants," 304, 305, 337; Scott, "Additional Letters," 432–38, 444; Department of the Interior, Bureau of Education, *Bulletins* No. 38 and No. 39 (Washington: Government Printing Office, 1917), 7–8, 28, 34; 9, 11, 283; Henry Allen Bullock, *A History of Negro Education in the South; from 1619 to the Present* (Cambridge: Harvard University Press, 1967), 87, 176–85; Department of Labor, Division of Negro Economics, *Negro Migration in 1916–17* (Washington: Government Printing Office, 1919), 35, 38–40, 94, 106–7.
[12] *Chicago Defender,* April 7, 1917.

states all but Louisiana also experienced disastrous rains and floods. The resultant destitution prompted blacks to moan: "De white man he got ha'f de crap [crop]. Boll-weevill took de res'. Ain't got no home. Ain't got no home." [13] In southwestern Perry County, Alabama, for example, cotton was the sole crop. "We see starvation ahead of us," wrote a black Alabamian, and at least 6,000 of the 24,000 blacks laboring in the immediate region left after the destructive arrival of the boll weevil. The infestation also visited southwestern Georgia, inflicting immense damage to crops in 1916. This along with flooding rains convinced planters that they must turn to such food products as peanuts, corn, velvet beans, oats, sorghum, and sweet potatoes—all crops that required substantially less labor than cotton; the excess in the labor supply was then either turned out penniless or left without any provision being made for its subsistence. Other planters, moreover, would not and sometimes could not advance funds to sharecroppers and tenants with which to plant the next year's crops. "Heavy rains and Boll weavel," a black farmer from southwestern Georgia observed sadly, had caused the loss of thousands of bales of cotton, and now the local planter was "going to see that his personal losses are minimized as far as possible and this has left the average farm laborer with nothing to start out with to make a crop for next year. . . ." And since "nobody wants to carry him till next fall . . . he wants to migrate to where he can see a chance to get work." [14]

Despite the labor depression in the South in 1915 and

[13] George E. Haynes, "Negroes Move North," *Survey,* XL (May 4, 1918), 118; Department of Labor, *Report of the Secretary and Report of the Bureaus, 1917* (Washington: Government Printing Office, 1918), 81; Scott, "Additional Letters," 422.

[14] *Negro Migration in 1916–17,* 17-19, 21, 44, 51, 56, 58–63, 77–80, 82, 86–87, 93, 103; W. E. B. Du Bois, "The Economics of the Negro Problem," in Alexander Trachtenberg (ed.), *The American Labor Year Book, 1917–18* (N.Y.: Rand School of Social Science, 1918), 180–81; George E. Haynes, "Migration of Negroes into Northern Cities," in National Conference of Social Work, *Proceedings, 1917,* 495; Scott, "Additional Letters," 442, 452, 453.

1916, there was a contemporaneous increase in the cost of living. "Everything is gone up but the poor colerd peple wages," concluded a black in New Orleans, and it was clear that, whether afflicted by no wages or low wages, the blacks' standard of living was wretched. "Wages is so low and grocery is so high," complained a Mississippian, "untill all I can do is to live." [15] Similar reports from all over the South flowed into the offices of the *Defender,* the Chicago Urban League, and employment offices.

Obviously, these driving forces were not unique to the World War I years. Inequality in its multitudinous forms had been the perennial scourge of Southern blacks, and debt peonage, dispossession, and the increasing unproductivity of the land through natural disaster, poor cultivation, and the planting of a single crop were virtually as old as the cotton culture itself. During the war, however, the abundance of Northern jobs provided escape. As A. L. Jackson, executive secretary of Chicago's all-black Wabash Avenue YMCA, explained to members of the City Club of Chicago: "The negro had wanted to come north all the time and he came when at last he had a chance to earn a living." [16] Jobs were abundant in Chicago, for at the very time that its industries cried out for workers to satisfy the insatiable demands for war products, two factors depleted the labor force. On the one hand,

[15] Scott, "Additional Letters," 414, 416–19, 420, 423, 426, 453; Scott, *Negro Migration,* 14.

[16] "Chicago's Negro Problem," City Club of Chicago *Bulletin,* XII (March 17, 1919), 75. See also "Reasons Why Negroes Go North," *Survey,* XXXVIII (June 2, 1917), 227; Scott, *Negro Migration,* 16–17.

The primacy of the economic motive in migrating has been convincingly demonstrated; see *Negro Migration in 1916–17,* 76, 86–87; Charles S. Johnson, "How Much Is the Migration a Flight from Persecution?" *Opportunity,* I (September 1923), 272–74; Johnson, "The American Migrant: The Negro," National Conference of Social Work, *Proceedings, 1927,* 554–58; Wright, "Migration of Negroes to the North," 104; "More Testimony on Negro Migration," *Survey,* XXXVIII (July 14, 1917), 340; August Meier, *Negro Thought in America, 1880–1915* (Ann Arbor: Ann Arbor Paperbacks of University of Michigan Press, 1966), 61–62.

A black family arrives in Chicago from the South

A plantation home in the rural South from which blacks migrated

the war caused immigration to the United States to dwindle from 1,218,480 in fiscal year 1914 to 366,748 in 1916, and to 110,618 in 1918. To restrict further the availability of immigrant labor, foreign belligerents conscripted their eligible nationals residing in the United States. In 1918 the net immigration had ebbed to only 6,023. The result in Chicago was a decline in the foreign-born percentage of the population from 33.5 per cent in 1910 to 28.4 per cent in 1920. On the other hand, 4,791,172 Americans served in the armed forces during World War I, creating additional voids in the labor force. The sources from which industries obtained replacements for immigrants and servicemen were women, machines, Southern whites, and, above all, blacks.[17]

Chicago was the logical destination of many of the migrants. Jobs were plentiful there and wages were high, especially in industries like slaughtering and meat packing, iron and steel forging, electrical machinery, and machine-shop products.[18] Moreover, Chicago's employment opportunities, particularly in the stockyards, were well publicized in the South. A frequent rumor was that the stockyards needed 50,000 men and women immediately, and that the packers would provide temporary quarters. "The packing houses in Chicago for a while seemed to be everything," a black in Hattiesburg, Mississippi, recalled; ". . . you could not rest in your bed at night for Chicago." Throughout the war Southern blacks discussed the migration, and more often than not the discussions centered on Chicago. A common evening pastime

[17] Department of Labor, Bureau of Immigration, *Annual Report of Commissioner General of Immigration, 1914* (Washington: Government Printing Office, 1915), 3; *Ibid., 1916*, 3; *Ibid., 1918*, 9; Helen Jeter, *Trends of Population in the Region of Chicago* (Chicago: University of Chicago Press, 1927), 34–35.

Blacks felt that a prime ingredient in the Chicago race riot was the influx of "20,000" Southern whites to the city. For example, see Walter White, "Chicago and Its Eight Reasons," *Crisis*, XVIII (October 1919), 294. White believed that they "spread the virus of race hatred." Even if they did, they were not indispensable to the forces that culminated in rioting.

[18] See Jeter, *Trends of Population in Chicago*, 13.

in Hattiesburg was sauntering to the depot to ask the Chicago porters on the Gulf and Ship Island Railroad numberless questions about the city. Hastily formed conclaves then spread news about such topics as Chicago's climate, the public schools, voting, and jobs throughout the black community. Out of these discussions, representatives were often appointed whose function it was to notify Chicago industries, newspapers, and placement agencies that a certain number of black people were available for employment and to request train tickets. These groups ranged in size from two or three families to more than 1,000 persons.[19]

The massive railroad network emanating from Chicago made it the most accessible destination for numerous blacks, especially those from Mississippi, Arkansas, Alabama, Louisiana, and Texas. Although the majority of the migrants paid their own fares, others traveled to the city on train passes, and club rates often eased the financial burden of the trip for still others.[20] Regardless of the travel arrangements, the incontrovertible fact was that thousands of black migrants had boarded trains for Chicago. ". . . I have seen it on Saturdays and Sundays when there wasn't standing room in the negro car," wrote a white railroad man from Hattiesburg in the spring of 1917, "and some days we would pull a special car for them." Every weekend for the past six months, he noted, "There would be a bunch collect here, sometimes as many as 150 at a time, and leave in parties. Most have gone to Chicago. . . ."[21]

In addition, Chicago's railroad lines connected it with practically every Southern town where lynchings occurred; and there was, as T. Arnold Hill of the Chicago Urban League

[19] Chicago Commission, *Negro in Chicago,* 577; Scott, *Negro Migration,* 26–27, 29, 102; Scott, "Letters of Negro Migrants," 305, 308–9, 313, 319, 322–23, 331, 338, 340; Scott, "Additional Letters," 417, 418, 422, 427, 441, 444, 446, 447, 451, 452.

[20] Scott, "Additional Letters," 414, 417–19, 422, 430, 433, 443.

[21] Quoted in Files on East St. Louis in RG 174, Box 205, 13/65; and see "Northern Invasion Starts," *Chicago Defender,* January 20, 1917.

observed, a correlation between Southern mob violence and the influx of migrants to Chicago. "Every time a lynching takes place in a community down south," he told a reporter, "you can depend on it that colored people will arrive in Chicago within two weeks. We have seen it happen so often that whenever we read newspaper dispatches of a public hanging or burning . . . we get ready to extend greetings to the people from the immediate vicinity of the lynchings." [22]

Letters from migrants to relatives and friends generated "the moving fever," especially when they contained money, which was concrete proof of prosperity and could easily be converted into a train ticket.[23] A carpenter supplied glowing reports about Chicago to his brother in Hattiesburg, telling him that he had just been promoted and received a raise. "I should have been here 20 years ago. I just begun to feel like a man." His children were enrolled in "the same school with the whites and I don't have to umble to no one." Moreover, he had registered to vote, and he proudly announced that "there isnt any 'yes sir' and 'no sir'—its all yes and no and Sam and Bill." [24] Similarly, a laborer from Chicago's Calumet region informed a friend in Alabama that the city fulfilled all the hopes with which he had undertaken his migration. The people were patriotic, the schools integrated, and he wondered sometimes how the industries could afford to be so generous with salaries "the way they work labors, they do not hurry or drive you." Work was plentiful, and money was abundant "and it is not hard to get." [25] Mrs. Rosena Shephard

[22] Carl Sandburg, *The Chicago Race Riots* (N.Y.: Harcourt, Brace & Howe, 1919), 26, 51–54; Scott, *Negro Migration,* 47; *Negro Migration in 1916–17,* 79, 88, 91, 107.

[23] Some observers claimed that nine out of ten migrants came at the insistence of friends or relatives, usually as a result of letters: Shelby M. Harrison and associates, *Public Employment Offices* (N.Y.: Russell Sage Foundation, 1924), 609.

[24] Scott, "Additional Letters," 459. This letter is also in the Woodson Papers, which was the source of many of Scott's letters and perhaps the most significant source of manuscript information regarding the World War I migration.

[25] *Ibid.,* 464.

heard her neighbor boasting about her daughter who had gone to Chicago. Six weeks had gone by with no news at all; then came word that she was earning $2.00 a day as a sausage-packer. "If that lazy, good-for-nothing gal kin make $2 a day," Mrs. Shephard exclaimed when she heard this news, "I kin make four," and she left for Chicago.[26] Dr. Alexander H. Booth watched his patients set out from his Southern community, and he wondered whether he would ever be paid the fees that the departing migrants had long owed him. To his surprise, the payments started to arrive in letters from the North which told him that "home ain't nothing like this." The doctor packed his bags to join them.[27] Because of letters, visits home by migrants, and rumors, the South was, as a Floridian remarked, "ringing with news from Chicago," news that could transform indecision into an affirmation to try it for oneself.[28]

In addition to spontaneous responses to the driving forces and to the lure of Chicago, the process of migration was also stimulated by a government agency, private labor agents, certain industries, and the press. Until Southern planters protested, for example, the United States Employment Service sought to fill the requisitions of Northern employers with Southern blacks.[29] Independent labor agents also scoured the South, inducing blacks to pull up stakes. To stem this flow, Southern states, counties, and city councils began to exact prohibitive license fees to discourage the recruiters. Birmingham required a $2,500 tax of labor agents, as did the State of Alabama, thus making it a $5,000 proposition before an agent could begin recruiting in that city; and when Alabama's

[26] *Ibid.*, 457–58; and Charles S. Johnson, "The New Frontage on American Life," in Alain Locke (ed.), *The New Negro* (N.Y.: Atheneum edition, 1968), 281.

[27] Johnson, "The New Frontage," 282.

[28] Scott, "Additional Letters," 418.

[29] Department of Labor, *Report of the Secretary and Reports of Bureaus, 1918* (Washington: Government Printing Office, 1919), 114; and correspondence regarding government "Recruiting of Labor," in War Labor Policies Board Papers (RG 1), National Archives.

courts of county commissioners or county boards of revenues began to exact their fees, the cost would spiral still higher. Other areas were equally apprehensive, but, as practically every strange face in Southern towns was identified as a labor agent, much of this legislation was directed at phantoms.[30] Other recruiters were actually bunco artists who would vanish after collecting $2.00 per head in exchange for promises of train tickets and jobs in Chicago.[31]

Labor agents affiliated with certain Northern industries, however, did pose a real threat to the maintenance of the Southern labor force. Between July 1916 and January 1917, for example, the Pennsylvania Railroad imported 12,000 blacks to do unskilled labor; but it ceased to do this when it became a much less expensive operation simply to hire blacks after they had arrived on their own tickets.[32] The Illinois Central Railroad also issued passes on which hundreds of blacks traveled to Chicago, and steel mills and tanneries in the Chicago area did likewise. But passes and prepaid tickets were essential only during the initial stage of the migration, for after that it became a self-generating movement.[33]

[30] John G. Van Deusen, *The Black Man in White America* (Washington: Associated Publishers, 1938), 38; St. Clair Drake and Horace Cayton, *Black Metropolis* (N.Y.: Harcourt, Brace, and Co., 1945), 58–59; Scott, *Negro Migration,* 72–85; *Negro Migration in 1916–17,* 12, 27–28, 62–63, 65, 74, 86, 100, 110; Harrison, *Public Employment Offices,* 605–6; Wood, *Negro in Chicago,* 9–10.

[31] Scott, "Letters of Negro Migrants," 329–31; *Chicago Defender,* April 21, 1917. In De Ridder, Louisiana, alone, 1,800 blacks paid $2.00 apiece for promises. See *Negro Migration in 1916–17,* 16; Scott, "Additional Letters," 415; *Chicago Defender,* April 21, May 12, 1917; Johnson, "The New Frontage," 281.

[32] See statement by John T. Emlen of the Armstrong Association, in National Conference of Social Work, *Proceedings, 1917,* 500; J. S. Cullinan to W. B. Wilson, June 26, 1917; and J. T. Watkins to W. B. Wilson, July 14, 1917, in RG 174, 8/102.

[33] Scott, *Negro Migration,* 102, 107, 114; James Weldon Johnson, "The Changing Status of Negro Labor," National Conference of Social Work, *Proceedings, 1918,* 384; see also U.S. Railroad Administration Papers (RG 14), Suitland, Maryland, P 19–3, "Protest against Discrimination against Colored Passengers," regarding prepaid tickets being sent to blacks in the South for travel to the North; *Negro Mi-*

It is possible that the largest employers of black labor in Chicago, the meat packers, also enticed numerous blacks away from the South. This, at any rate, was the contention of many observers familiar with the Chicago labor market. The packers vehemently denied the charge of importation, asserting that, aside from bringing North from Southern branches a few blacks for "specific temporary work," they had "not found importation necessary." [34] For the purpose of affixing responsibility for the Chicago race riot, it is unfortunate that this issue was blurred by charges and countercharges supported by little factual evidence.

Perhaps the most effective institution in stimulating the migration was the *Defender,* which prompted thousands to venture North. It was the *Defender*'s emphatic denunciation of

---

gration in 1916–17, 28; Walter E. Meyer to Walter Lippmann, July 31, 1917; Lippmann to Hugh L. Kerwin, August 6, 1917, in RG 174, 8/102.

[34] Graham Taylor, Chicago, to Julius Rosenwald, Chicago, April 24, 1920, Rosenwald Papers, University of Chicago. This assertion seems to lack credence on two counts. First, in the past the packers had imported black workers, as well as Greek and Polish immigrants and other aliens to break strikes. For example, see "The Great Strike," an unpublished and undated manuscript by Mary McDowell of the University of Chicago Settlement House "back of the yards," McDowell Papers, Chicago Historical Society; R. R. Wright, Jr., "The Negro in Times of Industrial Unrest," *Charities,* XV (October 7, 1905), 71–74; Ernest Poole, "The Meat Strike," *The Independent,* LVII (July 28, 1904), 179–84. Second, a committee of the Illinois State Council of Defense to investigate the East St. Louis race riot maintained that a primary cause of that riot was the importation of blacks by the packers; and, after all, the East St. Louis packers were subject to the dictates of their headquarters in Chicago. See State of Illinois, Council of Defense, Committee on Labor, *The Race Riots at East St. Louis* (Chicago: n.pub., 1917). In congressional hearings on the race riot, two Illinois congressmen, Martin D. Foster and William A. Rodenberg, expressed conflicting opinions about whether migration was induced by the packers. Foster was emphatic that the packers imported blacks. See 65th Cong., 1st Sess., United States House of Representatives, Committee on Rules, *Riot at East St. Louis* (Washington: Government Printing Office, 1917), 4, 7–8, 20; and John H. Walker to V. Olander, July 5, 1917, and to William B. Wilson, July 5, 1917; and Wilson to Walker, July 10, 1917, RG 174, Box 205, 13/65. Still, the subject of labor importation is very debatable; a thorough and conclusive study is badly needed.

the Southern treatment of blacks and its emphasis on pride in the race that increased its circulation tenfold between 1916 and 1918. "Turn a deaf ear to everybody," a typical editorial advised in 1916. "You see they are not lifting their laws to help you. Are they? Have they stopped their Jim Crow cars? Can you buy a Pullman sleeper where you wish? Will they give you a square deal in court yet?" Blacks were slaves in the South, and they have remained slaves, so to the South "we have said, as the song goes, 'I hear you calling me,' and have boarded the train singing, 'Good-bye, Dixie Land.' " [35]

"MILLIONS TO LEAVE SOUTH," was the *Defender's* banner headline on January 6, 1917. "Northern Invasion Will Start in Spring—Bound for the Promised Land." That coming May 15 was to be the date of "The Great Northern Drive," and its announcement precipitated a massive outpouring of letters to the *Defender,* the Urban League, and various churches requesting and indeed pleading for jobs, information, transportation, and housing.[36] And when the *Defender* declared later that there were no special trains designated to leave Southern stations on May 15, and that this date had been set simply because it was "a good time to leave for the north, so as to become acclimated," it was already too late.[37] The exodus, the hegira, "The Flight Out of Egypt," the "Black Diaspora," had begun.

Reinforcing the desire to migrate were the success stories, the photographs of Chicago's public facilities to which all had equal access, and the advertisements of job openings and of rooms to rent and houses to buy which the *Defender* prominently displayed in its pages. As a rebuttal to "southern prop-

[35] October 7, 1916; and see Sandburg, *Chicago Race Riots,* 52.

[36] Kennedy, *Negro Peasant Turns Cityward,* 53; *Negro Migration in 1916–17,* 29–30; Scott, *Negro Migration,* 29–30; Arna Bontemps and Jack Conroy, *Anyplace But Here* (N.Y.: Hill and Wang, 1966), 161–74; Roi Ottley, *The Lonely Warrior: The Life and Times of Robert S. Abbott* (Chicago: Henry Regnery, 1955), 159–72; and see Woodson Papers and Scott letters, most of which were written in response to these announcements.

[37] *Chicago Defender,* May 12, 1917.

agandists who . . . painted harrowing pictures of dire conditions suffered here," the *Defender* told its readers of Robert A. Wilson, formerly of Atlanta, who arrived in Chicago with a nickel and a penny. He spent the nickel for streetcar fare to the *Defender*'s offices and the penny for a bag of peanuts "to satisfy that pang of hunger." The newspaper directed him to the Urban League, which found him work at a foundry. Since that happy day, the *Defender* added, Wilson had acquired an automobile, house, and bank account, and had brought his family from the South; and "thus ends the romance of the lone nickel, the Lincoln penny, and the man who made opportunity a realization." [38] That blacks could and did make good in Chicago was a constant theme of the *Defender;* it was the South, not the North, that was unfit for human habitation.

To blacks the *Defender* symbolized the freedom attainable in the North; its exhortations to depart "the land of suffering" impelled countless people to peddle household goods and personal belongings accumulated over a lifetime in order to purchase tickets for the North. Its validity rested with the knowledge that it was not controlled by the white community as was much of the local black press, and with the violent reactions it provoked among white Southerners. To the persistent rumor that blacks would freeze to death in the North, the *Defender* countered that this was "all 'bosh.' IF YOU CAN FREEZE TO DEATH in the north and be free, why FREEZE to death in the south and be a slave, where your mother, sister and daughter are raped. . . . where your father, brother and son are . . . hung to a pole, [and] riddled with bullets. . . ." [39] For whites and blacks who praised the South or held the North in contempt, the *Defender* had nothing but disdain. It used to be preachers, the *Defender* asserted, but now there was a teacher, in Tallulah, Louisiana, who was "licking the white man's hand," and getting "his name in the white papers as 'good nigger'" for "asking that our people

[38] *Ibid.,* March 10, 1917, February 2, 1918.
[39] *Ibid.,* February 17, 1917.

remain here and be treated like dogs. . . ." [40]

Such utterances, of course, outraged whites. Letters arrived at the *Defender*'s offices threatening to kill "some of your good Bur heads" unless the newspaper started advising blacks "to be real niggers instead of fools," and Southern towns outlawed its circulation. The whites of Madison County, Mississippi, adopted a resolution claiming that the *Defender* was German propaganda designed to "revive sectional issues and create race antagonism," and thus "condemned its circulation in this county." [41] Other whites confiscated issues of it, and at least one rural community permitted no correspondence between its black residents and the newspaper.[42] All of this served to elevate the *Defender*'s value and to heighten its persuasiveness. A black leader in Louisiana confided to an official of the Labor Department that each issue of the *Defender* was so eagerly awaited that "my people grab it like a mule grabs a mouthful of fine fodder." [43] And failure to receive a copy could cause real anguish. "I feel so sad in hart," a girl in Macon, Georgia, disconsolately wrote a friend in Chicago, "my definder diden come yesterday." [44]

Blacks who heeded the *Defender* brought with them to Chicago a vision of opportunity, of "a better chance," and of "feeling like a man." Yet for many, perhaps most, the *Defender* had held out false promises. Their aspirations for economic, political, and social rebirth were soon shattered by their reception in the city.

The World War I migration of blacks was, according to a black minister in Atlanta, "the most unique movement in history." For "the colored race, known as the race which is led,

[40] *Ibid.,* January 20, 1917.
[41] *Chicago Broad Ax,* June 15, 1918; and Frederick G. Detweiler, *The Negro Press in the United States* (Chicago: University of Chicago Press, 1922), 21.
[42] Scott, "Letters of Negro Migrants," 330.
[43] *Negro Migration in 1916–17,* 30.
[44] Scott, "Additional Letters," 455.

has broken away from its leaders." [45] Other observers agreed that a striking characteristic of the migration was its individualism. It was "a leaderless mass-movement," wrote black sociologist Charles S. Johnson, and it burst forth "only after a long period of gestation." [46] Aggravated by decades of debasing social and political inequality and economic deprivation, the migrants of 1916 to 1919 were, Johnson added, "ready for the spark of suggestion which touched them off and sped them blindly northward." They were so ready, in fact, that they deserted their established leaders.

Numerous black business and professional men, who had derived social status and relative prosperity from Southern segregation, had remained silent in the past and had not remonstrated against the inhumane treatment and subsistence wages which the race had had to endure. Other blacks forfeited their credibility and positions of influence by heaping inflated and transparent praise upon the South as "our home" and upon the Southern white man as "our friend," and by damning the North as a place where blacks could do little but freeze or starve to death.[47] But younger blacks were restless and dissatisfied, and would not accept the plantation and caste system under which their parents had suffered. Blacks naturally felt that they were powerless to object to mistreat-

[45] "Negro Migration as the South Sees It," *Survey,* XXXVIII (August 11, 1917), 428.

[46] Johnson, "How the Negro Fits in Northern Industries," 403; Scott, *Negro Migration,* 6, 13, 44–45; T. Arnold Hill, *The Negro and Economic Reconstruction* (Washington Associates in Negro Folk Education, 1937), 26; "Negro Migration as the South Sees It," 428; Miles Mark Fisher, "The Negro Church and the World War," *Journal of Religion,* V (September 1925), 486; W. E. B. Du Bois, "The Migration of Negroes," *Crisis,* XIV (June 1917), 66; "A Letter from Dixieland," *Chicago Defender,* November 4, 1916.

[47] In Woodson Papers, letter from unsigned, Pensacola, Florida, to editor of *Chicago Defender,* October 24, 1916; and memoranda quoting *Fort Worth Record,* July 22, 1917; *New Orleans Times-Picayune,* December 9, 1916; *Birmingham* (Alabama) *Age-Herald,* September 25, 1916; *Atlanta Independent,* December 16, 1917; *Southwestern Christian Advocate,* December 7, 1916; *Dallas Express,* October 4, 1917.

ment by whites. "We dare not resent . . . or show even the slightest disapproval," lamented a minister in rural Alabama.[48] Being powerless, however, did not mean that blacks had to continue to endure indignity; and whether black leaders could have protested against the system or not, the migrants disregarded their advice when opportunity beckoned from the North.[49]

The migrants, Ray Stannard Baker noted, were "acting for themselves, self consciously. . . ." And in doing so they had to combat much more than resistance from members of their own race; they had to overcome the efforts of whites to check the migration. Blacks "are being snatched off the trains . . . and a rested [sic]," a Mississippian reported to the Chicago *Defender*, "but in spite of all this, they are leaving every day and every night. . . ." Despite threats even of death, the flow of migrants continued undeterred.[50]

The migration was a positive movement in other ways. Although jobs and better wages were usually the initial stimulant, the migrants were searching for a share in the freedom that had been denied them for so long. Many blacks viewed the migration as a divinely inspired deliverance from the land of suffering. During the era of the Civil War, the Biblical story of the exodus of the Israelites from Egypt had fueled the hopes of the slaves for freedom, and plantation songs abounded with predictions of a new Moses to free them from their oppressors. But there was no exodus to the Promised Land after the war. There was emancipation, but for millions of blacks this was a cruel hoax which turned out to be but

[48] Scott, "Additional Letters," 420.

[49] Scott, *Negro Migration*, 45; *Negro Migration in 1916–17*, 95; and in Woodson Papers, *Dallas Express*, August 11, 1917; Robert E. Jones, editor, *Southwestern Christian Advocate*, to Robert E. Park, March 2, 1917.

[50] Baker, "The Negro Goes North," *World's Work*, XXXIV (July 1917), 319, as quoted in Spear, *Black Chicago*, 138; *Chicago Defender*, March 24, April 7, 1917; March 24, 31, 1919; *Negro Migration in 1916–17*, 110; newspaper clippings in NAACP Papers, Library of Congress (C-373); Scott, *Negro Migration*, 72–85; Scott, "Additional Letters," 412, 420, 427, 435, 451–52; Wood, *Negro in Chicago*, 9–10.

another form of bondage. Then came World War I and the migration to "Beulah Land"; countless blacks again saw God's hand at work pointing the way to freedom. A group of 147 blacks from Hattiesburg, for example, knelt down, kissed the ground, and held a prayer service after "Crossing over Jordan," the Ohio River. The men stopped their watches, the women sobbed, and then all sang the songs of deliverance, beginning with, "I done come out o' de land of Egypt; ain't that good news." [51]

Many, perhaps most, of the migrants to Chicago were "totally unprepared" for the adjustments they would have to make to the city. This at least was the opinion of an observer like Chester Wilkins, chief Red Cap at the Illinois Central Station. Wearing overalls and housedresses, they arrived, Wilkins recalled, with little more than coca sacks filled with their belongings, and some stepped off the trains carrying chickens, goats, pigs, and stocks of sugar cane. "Many of them didn't know where they were going . . . [except that] they knew somebody in Chicago," and they had only the vaguest notions of where to find their friends. [52]

The adjustment that the migrants would have to make was threefold: from rural to urban, from servitude to citizenship, and to a new set of mores regulating race relations. Culturally isolated from the rest of the world, the migrants had moved to a metropolis and black neighborhood with a dynamic group life. They had found recreation and amusement in a Saturday trip to town when they lived in the South; now they lived in a city. The South could be hostile, but the North could be impersonal, unsympathetic, and lonely; to a great extent, group relations supplanted the intimate and personal

[51] Johnson, "How the Negro Fits in Northern Industries," 405; Ottley, *Lonely Warrior*, 161–67; E. Franklin Frazier, *The Negro Family in Chicago* (Chicago: University of Chicago Press, 1932), 80–82; Herbert Horwill, "A Negro Exodus," *Contemporary Review*, CXIV (September 1918), 299; *Negro Migration in 1916–17*, 101; Scott, *Negro Migration*, 45–46.
[52] Interview with Mr. Wilkins, Chicago, June 25, 1969.

relations the migrants had known. Attuned to an agricultural work routine which was dependent upon the seasons and the weather and which had given permanence to personal relations, the migrants now sought daily employment at hourly wages in mass-production industries. The time clock and factory discipline, not the sun, would determine their schedules. Functioning to a far lesser degree in Chicago were the various social controls exercised in the South, among them neighborhood gossip, the respect of friends, family unity, and, perhaps above all, the fear of being chastened or criticized by the church for misbehaving. And absent in the city, of course, was "the plantation tradition," as Charles S. Johnson defined it, "with its almost complete dependence upon the immediate landowner for guidance and control in virtually all those phases of life which are related to the moving world outside." [53]

The migration had done more than transplant blacks from one location to another; it had transplanted them from one culture to another, from peasantry to proletariat. To make the adjustment, the newcomers would need the counsel of patient friends. But to whom could they turn? Often they could not turn to their former leaders, for even though numerous black business and professional men eventually left the South, many were not able to reassert their leadership in Northern cities. Some were discredited, and others, because of the disparity between the educational standards of the North and the South, could not continue to practice their professions in Chicago. Although some ministers reestablished their churches in the North, others could not penetrate or compete on a paying basis with the better established of Chicago's

[53] George E. Haynes, "Conditions Among Negroes in the Cities," *Annals,* XLIX (September 1913), 110–11; Charles S. Johnson, *Shadow of the Plantation* (Chicago: Phoenix Books of University of Chicago Press, 1966), 2–6, 9, 202, 210; Johnson, "How the Negro Fits in Northern Industries," 400–1; E. Franklin Frazier, *The Negro Family in the United States* (Chicago: Phoenix Books of University of Chicago Press, 1966), 75–76, 227–31; Johnson, "The New Frontage," 279, 285–88.

black churches. Businessmen generally lacked the capital and experience to reestablish themselves in Chicago. When they migrated, many of these former leaders had to seek employment in the stockyards, foundries, and other factories, just as their former followers had. Many of the migrants thus tended to look to the established black residents for leadership.

Many of Chicago's "Old Settlers," however, rejected the new arrivals, and they did so largely because of the very personality traits, attitudes, mannerisms, and habits that demanded adjustment. A "retrospective myth" among the old settlers was that the migrants had "brought discrimination with them." The migrants, they complained, "made it hard for all of us." There was a time, they claimed, when blacks could work downtown in the Loop, eat in any restaurant, and be attended by white doctors; but this was before the migration. "The whites were not always prejudiced like they are now," said one embittered lady. Her children used to attend "the white kids' parties," and "the white children and colored children got along fine." But now the whites just shouted expletives at the blacks. Adverse reactions to the Southern blacks increased the insecurity of the older city dwellers, who had never been positive of their status in Chicago. Fearing that the conduct of the migrants might prove an obstacle to their advancement, they disassociated themselves from their Southern brothers. To the migrant, on the other hand, conditioned by racial separation, the distance between the Northern blacks and himself made it seem to him that they were "acting like white." The rejection of the new arrivals augmented their already critical scarcity of leadership; they thus sometimes relied on irresponsible leaders for direction, or else they suffered from lack of direction.[54]

[54] Robert C. Weaver, *The Negro Ghetto* (N.Y.: Harcourt, Brace, 1948), 23–24, 28; W. Lloyd Warner, *Color and Human Nature* (Washington: American Council on Education, 1941), 149; Drake and Cayton, *Black Metropolis*, 73–76; "Colored Chicago," *Crisis*, X (September 1915), 234–36; Frazier, *Negro Family in Chicago*, 90; George E. Haynes, "Race Riots in Relation to Democracy," *Survey*, XLII

Fortunately, there were churches and social service agencies that were eager to aid the newcomers. Few of these churches were white, however; these institutions generally fled in panic before the influx of migrants. Apparently rather than attempt to integrate except in a token manner, for example, the First Baptist Church in 1918 sold its building on the South Side to the black Olivet Baptist congregation. With the blacks "steadily pushing down the alleys southward with their carts of furniture," wrote the First Church's historian, that body decided to relocate farther south. Forty-seventh Street still stood as "a breakwater" against the "tide," but if it crumbled, he predicted, "there will be some new history for the First Church." [55]

Olivet Baptist was a familiar name to thousands of migrants. Olivet's membership increased from 4,271 in 1916 to 8,430 in 1919, and its annual number of baptisms almost quintupled, until it was the largest Protestant church in the United States. Olivet sponsored clubs for boys and girls and community organizations for women; it conducted a day nursery and free kindergarten for the children of working mothers; and it purchased a building for use as a kitchen and dining room and had the rooms upstairs refurbished for a Working Men's Home. Also headquartered at Olivet was the Bethlehem Baptist Association, which operated an employment bureau and attempted to secure homes for the newcomers. Other churches, among them Quinn Chapel and Bethel

---

(August 9, 1919), 697–99; Carter G. Woodson, *A Century of Negro Migration* (Washington: Associated Publishers, 1918), 186–87.

[55] Perry J. Stackhouse, *Chicago and the Baptists: A Century of Progress* (Chicago: University of Chicago Press, 1933), 202; Bontemps and Conroy, *Anyplace But Here,* 178; Miles Mark Fisher, "History of the Olivet Baptist Church" (unpublished A.M. thesis, University of Chicago Divinity School, 1922), 85–87; *Chicago Defender,* May 18, September 21, October 5, 1918; Miles Mark Fisher, *The Master's Slave: Elijah John Fisher, a Biography* (Philadelphia: Judson Press, 1922), 180–82; Frank Dorey, "The Church and Segregation in Washington, D.C., and Chicago, Illinois" (unpublished Ph.D. thesis, University of Chicago, 1950), 63–76.

African Methodist Episcopal Church, likewise assisted the migrants.[56]

The most heavily endowed secular agency aiding the migrants, and the most active one, was the Chicago Urban League.[57] Founded in 1915 as an affiliate of the National League on Urban Conditions among Negroes, it made its objective to facilitate, through interracial cooperation, the adjustment of blacks to city life and to promote equal industrial opportunity. From the spring of 1917 to the outbreak of the riot, the League secured employment for over 20,000 black men and women; as many as 55,000 in all sought jobs and dwellings from the organization during this period. The placement service was, in fact, so important both to the black community and to Chicago's industries that in March 1919 it took over the operations of Chicago's black belt office of the United States Employment Service when this branch folded because of a cut in federal appropriations.[58]

Proper deportment in public, cleanliness, healthy children, the prevention of juvenile delinquency, and economy in pur-

---

[56] S. Mattie Fisher, "Olivet as a Christian Center," *Missions*, X (March 1919), 199–202; Olivet Baptist Church, *Facts and Figures* (no imprint), pamphlet in Papers of the Chicago Commission on Race Relations (CCRR), Illinois State Archives, Springfield; Fisher, "Olivet Baptist Church," 81, 83–89, 91, 95, 97; Fisher, *Master's Slave*, 178–79; Carter G. Woodson, *The History of the Negro Church* (Washington: Associated Publishers, 1921), 278; *Crisis*, XIV (May 1917), 36; Quinn Chapel AME Church, *120th Anniversary Record, 1847–1967* (Chicago: n. pub., 1967); *Chicago Defender*, March 17, 24, 31, June 2, October 27, 1917.

[57] Regarding the heavy financial backing by industrialists of the Urban League and the Wabash Avenue YMCA, see Chapter IV. The history of the League is Arvarh E. Strickland, *History of the Chicago Urban League* (Urbana: University of Illinois Press, 1966).

[58] Chicago Urban League, *Annual Report*, I (no imprint), 10; *ibid.*, II, 6; and *ibid.*, III, 2; State of Illinois, Department of Labor, *Third Annual Report* (Springfield: Illinois State Journal Co., 1921), 16; *Negro Migration in 1916–17*, 23–24; Scott, *Negro Migration*, 104; *Chicago Broad Ax*, June 29, 1918; Chicago Commission, *Negro in Chicago*, 365–66; *Chicago Defender*, April 28, December 8, 1917, March 16, 1918; A. L. Foster, "Twenty Years of Interracial Goodwill through Social Service," in Chicago Urban League, *Two Decades of Service, 1916–1936* (no imprint), *passim*.

chasing food—these were among the League's other goals. Blacks "cannot afford to be careless and indifferent," the League's secretary, T. Arnold Hill, explained in a letter to black leaders. The race was on trial, he added, and white employers would judge their workers on the basis of *"general behavior, good manners, good conduct, and attention to dress and cleanliness,* as well as *efficient service. . . ."* Also, to help the migrants adjust, the League divided the city into several districts and sent club women to instruct new citizens "about the things they should do and know in order to become better citizens and more efficient workmen." Regarding health, the "block visitors" instructed the newcomers that necessities for avoiding tuberculosis and infant mortality were fresh air and sunshine, and eating regularly. Children should be scrubbed, their hair combed, and they should be kept "in school as long as you are able." To save money, "eat vegetables and less meats." And, above all, refrain from "loud conversations," boisterousness, and vulgarity on streetcars and in public places. For "bad action and conduct are embarrassing . . . and reflect not only upon the individual, but react upon the masses" of the race.[59]

Deportment of the migrants was also a major concern of the *Defender.* "A Few Do's and Don't's" of the *Defender* were: Do not loaf on the corner of 35th and State Streets and "make insulting remarks about women"; avoid raucous laughing and talking; send peddlers to the rear; do not stick your head out of the window, for this is a custom observed only in "backwoods towns" of the South; honor "streetcar etiquette" and if at all possible bathe and change clothes after quitting work and before boarding the streetcar; and do not

[59] T. Arnold Hill to Arthur T. Aldis, July 5, 1917, with enclosures regarding "Public Meetings," "Block Work," "Suggestions for Block Visitors," and minutes of meeting of Chicago Urban League, January 9, [1918?], in Arthur T. Aldis Papers, University of Illinois, Chicago Circle Campus; National Urban League, "A Contribution to Democracy: The Record of Some Results of Cooperation by Two Races," *Bulletin* of National Urban League, VIII (January 1919), 13–15; *Chicago Defender,* November 23, 1918.

"appear on the street with old dust caps, dirty aprons and ragged clothes." The *Defender*'s apprehension and that of the Urban League were practically identical: the fear that whites would choose to judge misbehavior not in terms of individual acts but in terms of undesirable racial traits. And it was for this reason that most of the *Defender*'s "don't's" related to behavior which might be observed by whites.[60]

Like the Urban League, Chicago's all-black Wabash Avenue YMCA was heavily financed by industrialists and especially by the packers, and it, too, instructed the migrants as to proper conduct in public. Armour, Morris, Swift, and the other packers sponsored "efficiency clubs" at the YMCA. Organized by foremen at the stockyards, these clubs, according to the YMCA's secretary, "promoted everything else that happened" for numerous black workers—picnics, glee clubs, concerts and recitals, Liberty Loan drives, "Thrift," "Health," "Go-To-Night-School," and "Clean Up" campaigns, lectures on the packing industry, and athletic leagues. The YMCA Industrial Baseball League fielded eight teams from the stockyards, including the Swift Premiums, Libby-McNeill Giants, and Morris Cadets, and in 1918 these teams played before almost 12,000 spectators.[61]

The aid and counsel of the Urban League, the *Defender*, the Wabash Avenue YMCA, and other social service agencies were invaluable. But too often they were inadequate, especially when the migrants encountered unrestrained white hatred.

The reception given the migrants by certain nationality

[60] *Chicago Defender*, March 24, June 2, July 14, 28, August 4, 11, October 20, November 17, 1917; February 2, March 23, April 6, May 25, July 13, September 14, 1918; June 7, 1919; Peter M. Hoffman (comp.), *The Race Riots: Biennial* [Cook County Coroner's] *Report, 1918–1919* (Chicago: n. pub., n.d.), 22; *Chicago Broad Ax*, October 19, 1918.

[61] Interview with Mr. Jackson, Chicago, June 27, 1969; G. R. Arthur, "The Y.M.C.A. Movement among Negroes," *Opportunity*, I (March 1923), 17–18; *Chicago Defender*, June 1, 15, August 10, 24, September 21, October 5, 12, 1918.

groups, among which the Polish and particularly the Irish were conspicuous, was, at times, violently hostile. Mutual antagonism between the Irish and the blacks was legendary, and its origins were firmly rooted in the country's past. Arising from opposing political affiliations and competition in the labor market, this enmity evinced itself early in Chicago. There as elsewhere during the Civil War, for example, black and Irish laborers fought bloody battles. In July 1864, a dozen blacks underbid Irish longshoremen for the job of unloading a lumber boat. Five hundred Irish workers retaliated by attacking and forcing them to flee the docks for their lives. "It was degrading," the Irish said in their defense, "to see blacks working upon an equality with themselves, and more so, while their brothers were out of employment." This mutual antagonism did not abate in succeeding decades. As the city's black neighborhood filled to overflowing between 1914 and 1919, the quest for housing during the acute wartime and postwar shortage, the urge for political dominance and patronage, and conflicting attitudes toward unionization further exacerbated Irish-black relations.[62]

Wentworth Avenue demarcated the two neighborhoods, being the eastern boundary of the Irish and the western boundary of the blacks. The avenue was the "gang line," moreover, and to trespass spelled "trouble." The poet Langston Hughes discovered this disagreeable fact for himself on the first Sunday he spent in Chicago. It was 1918, and Hughes was a high school student. He "went out walking alone to see what the city looked like," but "wandered too far

[62] *Chicago Tribune*, July 15, 17–18, August 11, 1862; August 5, 1863, July 15, 1864, November 13, 1866; Carl Wittke, *The Irish in America* (Baton Rouge: Louisiana State University Press, 1956), 125–32, 268; Ralph Davis, "The Negro Newspaper in Chicago" (unpublished M.A. thesis, University of Chicago, 1939), 13–14; St. Clair Drake, *Churches and Associations in the Chicago Negro Community* (Chicago: [WPA], 1940), 136; Drake and Cayton, *Black Metropolis*, 180; Jacque Voegeli, *Free but Not Equal: The Midwest and the Negro during the Civil War* (Chicago: University of Chicago Press, 1967), 34–35.

outside the Negro district, over beyond Wentworth, and was set upon and beaten by a group of white boys, who said they didn't allow niggers in that neighborhood." The black eyes and swollen jaw that he suffered were reminders not to cross Wentworth again. Thousands of blacks, however, had to cross Wentworth. They labored in the Union Stock Yards, which were situated across Wentworth Avenue and at the western border of Canaryville, the Irish territory. Going to and from work, the blacks often encountered violence from the Irish "athletic clubs," which were organizations of adolescents sponsored by ward bosses and operating with little police interference. Numerous black children resided in school districts which encompassed areas east and west of Wentworth. Rather than permit their children to attend schools in the Irish district, parents requested either that their children be transferred to the more overcrowded and rundown schools in the black belt or that the principals and teachers escort the black students. Violence nevertheless persisted. Blacks and Irish discovered in enemy territory were frequently greeted with cries of "He is from the east side," or "Hit him, he is from the west side." [63]

A final form of reception, and perhaps the most important, involved an almost total absence of understanding by the preponderance of whites who experienced only occasional and meager contacts with any blacks. In Chicago, because of extreme residential segregation, there was a paucity of social interchange between the races. Consequently, there was a decided lack of interracial understanding, and even then observers warned of the creation of two separate worlds in the cities, one black, one white. Whites had long before stereotyped blacks, and Chicago's newspapers perpetuated these stereo-

[63] Proceedings of meeting of Committee on Racial Contacts, March 11, 1920, in CCRR Papers; Hughes, *The Big Sea* (N.Y.: Hill and Wang, 1963), 33; Chicago Commission, *Negro in Chicago*, 12, 16, 43, 115, 251–52, 479–80, 482, 484; Frederic M. Thrasher, *The Gang: A Study of 1,313 Gangs in Chicago* (Chicago: University of Chicago Press, 1927), 15–19, 202–3, 212, 452–86.

types in their portrayals of blacks. Also, the few contacts between the races were ordinarily in surroundings—such as on rush-hour streetcars and elevated trains—not conducive to an accurate appreciation of anyone, black or white. Finally, in order not to offend the whites, blacks often affected mannerisms which conformed to the docile, convivial, happy-go-lucky stereotypes. The employment of these safety devices further retarded interracial understanding.[64]

The primary stereotypes of blacks were that they were mentally inferior, immoral, emotional, and criminal. Some secondary beliefs were that they were innately lazy, shiftless, boisterous, bumptious, and lacking in civic consciousness. Still other stereotypes held that they consistently sold their votes, carried razors, habitually shot craps, and had one front tooth filled with gold with their first earnings.

Men generally believe only what they want to believe, and Chicago's newspapers assisted them in this pursuit. By far the most numerous of the news items pertaining to blacks were those devoted to crime and vice, and riots and clashes. The labeling of "negroes" in articles aggravated the disproportionate coverage allotted criminality, immorality, emotionality, and mental inferiority. The press also reinforced the secondary stereotypes. One example among hundreds appeared in the *Chicago Tribune* of March 11, 1918: "MISTAH JACKSON'S AIM BAD: WOUNDS TWO NOT INTENDED. Charles Jackson, colored, may be handy with a razor, but he's erratic with a gun." The *Tribune,* which referred frequently to the city's "darkies," was the most derisive of the city's white newspapers in its treatment of racial news. But even the newspaper which was the most tolerant and fair-minded, the *Daily News,* printed racist slurs. One of its cartoons was entitled: "Meditations of Hambone." Hambone, with his long, floppy shoes, sad eyes, and enormous, minstrel lips, would mutter such words of wisdom as: "Some folks c'n see dey duty so plain dey alluz able t' git erway f'um it fo' it

<hr>

[64] Chicago Commission, *Negro in Chicago,* 523–63; Jane Addams, *Social Control* (N.Y.: NAACP, n.d.), 2.

gits to 'em!!" [65] Apart from perpetuating and reinforcing stereotypes, Chicago's press also generated fears that the migrants were "infesting" the city. The *Tribune* proclaimed: "HALF A MILLION DARKIES FROM DIXIE SWARM TO THE NORTH TO BETTER THEMSELVES." [66]

In March 1919, A. L. Jackson of the Wabash Avenue YMCA informed a gathering of prominent white Chicagoans: "If we are to avoid the dynamite that there is in this interracial problem, white people must get a better understanding of the negroes." "The difficulty in the situation," he explained, "is in part due to the fact that the white man ordinarily obtains his idea of the negro from his colored laundress, from a porter, or from some ill-clad workman who brushed against him unceremoniously in the streetcar." These "classes do not represent the average negro," for "it takes all kinds of negroes to make a race. . . ." [67]

With preconceptions compounded by so few points of real contact, whites generalized grievously about the race as a whole on the basis of extremely limited and artificial associations. For many whites the only point of contact was in public transportation; and what whites did not know or refused to believe was that a sizable portion of the "dirty and ill-smelling" blacks about whom they complained were the victims of inadequate washroom facilities for cleaning up after work. Many engaged in work—such as at the stockyards—which left an indelible odor on both blacks and whites. But most white passengers preferred to believe the stereotype, and refused to acknowledge that innumerable blacks were exceptions to it. [68]

[65] *Chicago Daily News,* August 28, September 2, 1918; *Chicago Defender,* August 31, 1918; Charles S. Johnson, "Public Opinion and the Negro," *Opportunity,* I (July 1923), 202–4; Chicago Commission, *Negro in Chicago,* 436–594; Graham R. Taylor, "Race Relations and Public Opinion," *Opportunity,* I (July 1923), 198.

[66] Quoted in Chicago Commission, *Negro in Chicago,* 530.

[67] "Chicago's Negro Problem," 76.

[68] Chicago Commission, *Negro in Chicago,* 238, 303–4; Taylor, "Race Relations and Public Opinion," 197; T. Arnold Hill, "Race Antagonism—Its Cost and Its Cure," *Life and Labor,* IX (September 1919), 238; *Chicago Defender,* March 23, May 25, 1918.

Another major point of interracial association was between the black as a menial and the white as his customer. Living in a white man's world, the black generally knew more about the white man than the white man knew about him. The black menial investigated white behavior patterns because his livelihood depended upon his ability to please his customer. By becoming "an expert cajoler of the white man and a veritable artist at appearing to be that which he is not," Stanley B. Norvell, a Chicago black, explained, he reaped larger tips. And it was not just "George, the porter," who "conned" the white man with a "yas sah." To avoid arousing the suspicion and distrust of whites, blacks other than menials assumed the pose of flunkey; as an avoidance and accommodative mechanism, it raised fewer problems. But, as Norvell noted, the end result of the lack of intercourse between the races and the currency of stereotypes was that the "white man of America knows just about as much about the mental and moral calibre, the home life and social activities of . . . colored citizens as he does about the same things concerning the habits of the thus far unexplored planet of Mars. . . ." "He is just a 'nigger,'" Norvell concluded, and the white man "takes him for granted. . . ." [69]

Whites thus conceived of the black person as either an unruly, unclean, contemptible creature, possibly deserving punishment, or as a meek, docile, nonresistant menial, or even combinations of the two. They were therefore unprepared for the emergence of the "New Negro" whose self-respect and aspirations had been kindled by the war and who was determined to defend himself militantly against aggression.

The influx of over 50,000 blacks in a brief period greatly complicated existing problems in Chicago. These problems were primarily those of housing, politics, and labor. Before

[69] William M. Tuttle, Jr. (ed.), "Views of a Negro during 'the Red Summer' of 1919," *Journal of Negro History*, LI (July 1966), 209–18; J. O. Houze, "Negro Labor and the Industries," *Opportunity*, I (January 1923), 20; Taylor, "Race Relations and Public Opinion," 197.

the migration of 1916 to 1918, there was a modicum of inter-change between the races. It was not much, but it was more than existed in 1919, when whites attempted to drive blacks away from their residential districts with bombs, when politi-cians raised the racial issue in an extraordinarily partisan manner, and when labor unions, struggling for their very ex-istence, counted the blacks either all for them or all against them. In 1919, the heightened problems of housing, politics, and labor created such inflexible racial attitudes that the door to mutual racial understanding in Chicago was closed, and violence was bound to result.

Labor Conflict and Racial Violence

WELL, are you going to join or not?" the smokehouse floor steward impatiently asked the black worker in June 1919. "No, I would rather quit than join the union," was the angry reply. "If you don't join tomorrow, these men won't work with you." "Fuck you!" "God damn you!" Then the black man drew a knife from the pocket of his overalls. "He was big enough to eat me . . . ," the floor steward recalled, so "I called for help." The union men, "practically all of them are in the union except . . . these three colored fellows," came to his assistance. It was after this encounter that the white men in the smokehouse at the stockyards walked out, declaring that they could no longer work with nonunion blacks. Similar confrontations were occurring simultaneously in various shops at the yards. Leaving dead hogs hanging on hooks on the conveyor belts or after only partially dressing the beef, hundreds of workers informed their foremen that black men on the floor were nonunion, and that they would not return until these men were discharged or made to join the union. Black resistance to unionization—and, with it, interracial abuse and violence—mounted in the weeks before the riot. "Fuck the union, fuck you in the [union] button," raged a black worker. Knives and revolvers proliferated on both sides. "If I catch you outside I will shoot you," a black man warned an insulting committeeman. And the unions became even more aggressive. "Where is your button?" demanded a white organizer. "I ain't got none on," was the reply, "but [if I did] I would put it on the end of my prick." [1]

The factors precipitating the Chicago race riot of 1919 included housing and politics. But the riot was also a violent outcrop of the long-standing discord between white and black job competitors in the Chicago labor market. In fact, several contemporaries claimed that labor was perhaps the most significant cause of the riot. [2]

Later students of the riot, while admitting that interracial labor friction might have precipitated some violence, have listed it as but a minor cause. For example, the most exhaustive study, *The Negro in Chicago* by the Chicago Commission

[1] Hearings of Judge Samuel Alschuler, U.S. arbitrator in the Chicago stockyards, June 20, 1919, 1–83, 110–11; June 21, 220, 249–58, 303–45, 382–86; June 23, 392–93, 493–505, 511–13, 534–36, 546–47, 550, all in Records of the Federal Mediation and Conciliation Service, Suitland, Maryland (RG 280), 33/864.

[2] Certain contemporary observers of the racial violence in 1919, among them Mary White Ovington, A. Philip Randolph and Chandler Owen of *The Messenger,* Graham Taylor, Walter F. White, Dr. Roscoe C. Giles, Dr. George E. Haynes, and James Weldon Johnson, felt that labor conflict was perhaps the major cause of the Chicago riot: see Miss Ovington to J. R. Shilladay, August 11, 1919, and to Bolton Smith, August 15, 1919, in NAACP Papers, in the possession of Middle Atlantic Youth Division of the NAACP (NAACP-2), Washington, D.C.; in *ibid.,* White's "Notes on Chicago . . . ," September 17, 1919; *Brooklyn Daily Eagle,* August 25, 1919; *Brooklyn Standard Union,* August 25, 1919; *Boston Herald,* November 10, 1919; *Buffalo Express,* August 25, 1919; Report from Director, Division of Negro Economics, to Secretary of Labor, September 12, 1919, in Labor Department Papers, National Archives (RG 174), 8/102-E; *The Messenger,* II (September 1919), 11–21.

on Race Relations, concluded that it was relatively unimportant since "race friction" was "not pronounced in Chicago industries." [3] Allan H. Spear in *Black Chicago* has similarly asserted the the riot "had little to do with labor conditions. . . ." [4] Both the Chicago Commission and Spear support this contention by pointing out that during the riot there was an almost total absence of violence in the stockyards, which was by far the largest single area of employment for black Chicagoans. And, indeed, there was far less bloodshed there than knowledgeable observers had feared. But this is a simple matter to explain; fearing bodily harm, black workers stayed home.[5] And what happened when blacks returned to work? White workers murdered one black man and severely injured another, and when police and soldiers intervened, a vicious battle ensued between them and the angry whites. Several days later the packers notified nonunion black workers that order had been restored to the yards, and that additional police and soldiers armed with rifles and machine guns would be there to insure their safe return to work. Labor disagreed, arguing that the situation was still volatile. The packers "thought that if they would be able to jamb [*sic*] the colored laborers," charged President John Fitzpatrick of the Chicago Federation of Labor, "that is, the great body of colored laborers, and the white union men in the stock yards . . . that there would be murder there, and that they would destroy our organization. There was no other purpose in it,

[3] Chicago Commission on Race Relations, *The Negro in Chicago* (Chicago: University of Chicago Press, 1922), 2–3, 395, 399, 412.

[4] Allan H. Spear, *Black Chicago: The Making of a Negro Ghetto, 1890–1920* (Chicago: University of Chicago Press, 1967), 163. The other recent study of events leading up to the riot is Arthur I. Waskow, *From Race Riot to Sit-In, 1919 and the 1960s* (Garden City, N.Y.: Doubleday & Company, 1966), 39, 53, 56–57. Waskow contends that friction in the labor market was significant and he quotes numerous contemporaries to that effect, but he makes no attempt himself to establish that relationship, and he apparently feels that other causes were more important.

[5] *Chicago Daily Tribune,* August 3, 1919.

absolutely no other purpose in it. . . ." [6]

In addition, the Chicago Commission noted that Chicago's black union membership totaled about 12,000, or "almost exactly the same as the proportion of white [union] members to the white population in Chicago." The Commission's arithmetic was not only fallacious but grossly misleading, however, for it was obvious that prior to the riot black workers were more resistant to organization by white-dominated unions than any other race or nationality. Of the 12,000 black union members, for example, 1,200 belonged to seventeen locals of the Railway Men's International Benevolent Industrial Association, an all-black union which was formed in protest against the exclusionist membership policies of the railway brotherhoods and those of most of the railway unions of the American Federation of Labor. Even more important, the Commission's arithmetic did not reveal that proportionately more blacks than whites were blue-collar workers. Although black people comprised 4.1 per cent of the city's total population, they accounted not only for over 6 per cent of the adult population but for an even higher percentage of the productive portion of the population between the ages of twenty and forty-four. On the other hand, a smaller percentage of the black population were children and old people; and proportionately more blacks than whites worked at jobs with union representation. Contrary to the Commission report, upwards of 20,000 black workers, or from 50 to 75 per cent more than the 12,000 black members in 1919, would have had to be unionized in order to have been on a par with the proportion of white union members.[7]

Labor historian Herbert Gutman has made a plea to histo-

[6] Alschuler Hearings, August 13, 1919, 38, RG 280, 33/864; Cook County, Illinois, Office of the Coroner, *Transcript of Evidence Concerning the Race Riot,* July and August, 1919 (mimeographed), in Graham Taylor Papers, Newberry Library.

[7] Chicago Commission, *Negro in Chicago,* 406–12; Bureau of the Census, *14th Census, 1920* (Washington: Government Printing Office, 1922, 1923), III, 274; IV, 1076–80.

rians "to explore in detail the confrontation of the black worker and industrial America in particular settings." [8] The history of the black worker in Chicago from the Pullman strike of 1894 to the race riot of 1919 provides such an opportunity, in part because the race riot was in many ways the tragic culmination of those twenty-five years of conflict between blacks and whites in the labor market.

Although friction and sometimes bloodshed had marked the job competition between Chicago's whites and blacks for decades, a new seed of racial discord in the city's labor market was planted at the stockyards in 1894. In that year, masses of packing and slaughterhouse workers conducted a sympathetic strike with Eugene V. Debs' American Railway Union, and, in the midst of it, black strikebreakers were hired for the first time in the history of the meat packing industry. Although the packers initially disclaimed any intention of adopting this practice, less than a week later black strikebreakers were working, eating, and sleeping in the stockyards. Their presence fired racial animosities. "Cases of attacks on colored men were numerous yesterday," the *Chicago Record* reported on July 19. "Swinging from the cross-tree of a telegraph pole . . . near the entrance to the yards, the effigy of a negro roustabout was suspended. A black false face of hideous expression had been fixed upon the head of straw, and a placard pinned upon the breast of the figure bore the skull and cross-bones with the word 'nigger scab' above and below in bold letters. . . ." [9]

The strike ended in August, and the black strikebreakers were intimately associated with the defeat. The workers had

[8] Introduction to Sterling D. Spero and Abram L. Harris, *The Black Worker* (N.Y.: Atheneum edition, 1968), xi.

[9] *Chicago Record,* July 17, 19, 27, August 3, 1894; *Chicago Daily Tribune,* July 13, 15, 1894; *Chicago Times,* July 19, 1894; and other references cited in Alma Herbst, *The Negro in the Slaughtering and Meat-Packing Industry in Chicago* (Boston: Houghton Mifflin, 1932), 17–20; Spero and Harris, *Black Worker,* 265.

been thoroughly vanquished. They seemed "unmanly and without self-respect," recalled Mary McDowell of the settlement house "back-of-the-yards." "A community cowed is a sad sight to one who has been used to freemen." [10]

Labor conflict and racial violence rocked other parts of the state of Illinois in the 1890's, and repercussions were felt in Chicago. The names Spring Valley, Carterville, Virden, and Pana became synonymous with black strikebreakers and bloody industrial warfare at southern Illinois coal mines. In 1895, after striking Italian immigrant miners in Spring Valley had murdered an uncounted number of black strikebreakers, 500 of the decedents' black brothers in Chicago held "enthusiastic" meetings "preparatory to assisting their brethren . . . to wipe a colony of five thousand Italians off the map." [11]

Latrobe Steel in Chicago imported 317 black workers from Birmingham in 1901, but the intended strikebreakers refused to work as "scabs" and asked to be returned to Alabama. Stating that he had a decent-paying job in Birmingham, one of the steelworkers said that he had no idea that he "would be asked to take the place of any man on strike" or he "never would have left the South. . . ." Other Alabamians in Chicago at this time did not fare so well. In 1902, the University of Chicago imported eighty nonunion black laborers from Tuskegee Institute to break a strike at a campus construction site. But when union workers in the building trades refused to work alongside the Tuskegeans, the University discharged

[10] *Chicago Daily News*, July 29, 1904.

[11] *The Albion Journal*, August 8, 1895; *Inter-Ocean* (Chicago), August 14, 1895; and unidentified clipping, all quoted in "The Negro in Illinois," a WPA Project, the files of which are in the George Cleveland Hall Branch of the Chicago Public Library; Earl R. Beckner, *A History of Labor Legislation in Illinois* (Chicago: University of Chicago Press, 1929), 68–70, 386; Paul M. Angle, *Bloody Williamson* (N.Y.: Knopf, 1952), 96–104; Philip Taft, "Violence in American Labor Disputes," *Annals*, CCCLXIV (March 1966), 130; Arna Bontemps and Jack Conroy, *Anyplace But Here* (N.Y.: Hill and Wang, 1966), 142–44.

the blacks. "No matter how expert a colored man may be," remarked the *Inter-Ocean* of Chicago, "it is said that it is next to impossible for him to secure membership in a union in Chicago." Paul Laurence Dunbar, the black poet, noted in 1903 that Chicago's troubled race relations "arise out of an industrial situation. . . ." But what Dunbar saw of exclusionist white unions and black strikebreakers was only a mild precursor of the violent racial crises that would explode in the immediate months ahead.[12]

For, meanwhile, the workers at the stockyards were building a new union—the Amalgamated Meat Cutters and Butcher Workmen (AMCBW). Chicago was its target, for "if a start could be made in Chicago," the center of the industry, the AMCBW's president Michael Donnelly wrote Samuel Gompers, "our success nationally would be virtually established." Success was slow in coming, but by 1902 Donnelly could proudly announce that twenty-one locals had been chartered in Chicago and that the union rolls had burgeoned to 4,000. Accompanying organizing successes, moreover, were concrete gains in wages and hours.[13]

Yet these benefits went only to skilled workers, and at the turn of the century less and less skill was required in the industry because of the minute subdivision of labor. The "facts are these," Homer D. Call, the AMCBW's secretary-treasurer, explained to Frank Morrison of the AFL. "Twenty

[12] *Inter-Ocean,* July 28, 1901, August 19, 1902, July 5, 1903, quoted in L. Townsley's memoranda in "Negro in Illinois."

[13] Herbst, *Negro in Meat-Packing,* 20–21; Donnelly, Kansas City, to Gompers, Washington, D.C., December 29, 1896, AFL Papers, State Historical Society of Wisconsin; AMCBW *Proceedings, 1899,* 14–18; *1900,* 5–6; *1902,* 12, 15–16, 23; *1904,* 14; *1906,* 10; AFL *Proceedings, 1896,* 93; Mollie Daley to Mary McDowell, August 1, 1902; M. Donnelly to To Whom It May Concern, September 19, 1902, both in Mary McDowell Papers, Chicago Historical Society; AMCBW *Official Journal,* II (December 1901, February, August 1902, October 1903), 13; 18; 71, 72; 23; H. D. Call in *Chicago Record-Herald,* August 1, 1904; Mary McDowell, "The Story of a Women's Labor Union," *Commons,* VII (January 1903), 1–3; AMCBW *Official Journal,* II (March 1903), 1–12.

years ago the trade of the butchers was one of the best in the country." Then, after the consolidation of smaller packing houses into a handful of "large packing houses . . . they began a system to crowd out the expert butchers and replace them by cheaper men in every way. . . ." The owners "divided the business up into gangs consisting of enough to dress the bullock, one man doing only one thing . . . which makes it possible for the proprietor to take a man in off from the street . . . and today the expert workers are in many cases crowded out and cheap Polackers and Hungarians put in their places. . . ." The skilled worker realized that this specialization enabled unskilled workers with muscle to replace him; it appeared inevitable that unless a minimum wage were obtained for the unskilled, cutthroat job competition would drive all wages down. The unskilled were "the club held above our heads at all times," complained a skilled butcher. "If the packers refuse to agree to any minimum wage for the unskilled," asked Call, "how long will it be before they attempt to reduce the wages of the skilled men?" [14] The skilled workers thus championed the demand for a minimum wage of 20 cents an hour.

This was the union's objective, but it still faced an obstacle that had perpetually plagued unionization of the stockyards —the vast heterogeneity of races and nationalities that com-

[14] U. S. Commission on Industrial Relations, *Final Report and Testimony* (Washington: Government Printing Office, 1916), IV, 3328–30; Call, Syracuse, to Morrison, Washington, D.C., February 20, 1899, AFL Papers. See also *Report of the Commissioner of Corporations on the Beef Industry* (Washington: Government Printing Office, 1905), 17–19; W. Joseph Grand, *History of the Union Stockyards* (Chicago: Thomas Knapp Co., 1896), 49–51; John R. Commons, *Trade Unionism and Labor Problems* (Boston: Ginn & Co., 1905), 225; J. C. Kennedy, *Wages and Family Budgets in the Stock Yards District* (Chicago: University of Chicago Press, 1914), 7; William Hard, "The Stock Yards Strike," *Outlook,* LXXVII (August 13, 1904), 887; *Chicago Record-Herald,* August 1, 1904; Mary McDowell, "A Lost Strike, but Not a Dead Cause," *Union Labor Advocate,* V (October 1904), 12; "The Butcher Workman's Strike," *Railroad Trainmen's Journal,* XXI (October 1904), 768–69.

peted for jobs; no other potentially divisive force more ominously threatened the union's goal of solidarity.[15] For how could there be dialogue and unity if people could not even speak the same language or understand each other's customs? Racial jealousies and antagonisms crumbled, however, as the unskilled enthusiastically joined the union because of dissatisfaction with the prevailing wage of 15 to 18½ cents an hour, and blacks joined as well as whites. Many of the 500 black workers in the Chicago yards had become members, U. S. Labor Commissioner Carroll D. Wright reported to President Theodore Roosevelt. The women's local reportedly greeted its black applicants with "a hearty welcome," and Mary McDowell noted that "black men sat with their white comrades" at union meetings. This fellowship extended beyond the confines of the meeting room. The AMCBW held a funeral for "Bro. Wm. Sims (colored) tail sawyer at Swift's east house," with sixty-eight whites and seven blacks attending.[16]

Negotiations with the packers over the minimum wage were fruitless, breaking down in late June 1904, and when the packers announced a wage reduction, 23,000 packing house workers struck. Seven thousand mechanical tradesmen later joined the strike, which dragged on for ten weeks before the workers sporadically drifted back to work. The AMCBW had launched its strike in the face of a depression. Outside the stockyards each morning as many as 5,000 men stood lined up to replace the strikers. The strike was further

[15] Call, Syracuse, to McDowell, Chicago, November 22, 1902, McDowell Papers.

[16] "The Great Strike," unpublished and undated manuscript in *ibid.*; Wright to Roosevelt, September 8, 1904, in *Bulletin* of Bureau of Labor, X (January 1905), 2; Commission on Industrial Relations, *Final Report and Testimony*, IV, 3471, 3330; Mary McDowell, "The First Women's Union," *Official Journal*, II (October 1902), 28–29; Graham Taylor's remarks in *Chicago Daily News*, July 30, 1904; *Official Journal*, II (May 1903), 23–27; *Chicago Daily News*, July 29, 1904; A. Kaztauskis, "From Lithuania to the Chicago Stockyards," *Independent*, LVII (August 1904), 241–48; David Brody, *The Butcher Workmen: A Study of Unionization* (Cambridge: Harvard University Press, 1964), 41; Herbst, *Negro in Meat-Packing*, 22–24.

doomed because the strikers' resources were so paltry compared to the combined assets of the packers. Moreover, the heterogeneous nationalities and races, which had united confidently in 1903 and 1904, were in the final analysis divided and weak.[17]

Despite the hopelessness of the strike, the arch villains to emerge from the defeat were the packers and their strikebreakers, especially the black ones. One observer estimated that upwards of 18,000 blacks served as strikebreakers, with almost 1,400 arriving in one trainload. Although these figures probably were exaggerated, to white workers the disturbing presence of the blacks seemed to be everywhere. For example, five white women strikebreakers, who had been hired by a black man representing Armour, reported seeing numerous black strikebreakers, including boys thirteen and fourteen years old. They worked in the canning room, ate their meals in a massive improvised dining room one floor below, and at night slept in the canning room which "had forty cots arranged as close together as possible." One night during the strike, Ernest Poole, a journalist, and John R. Commons, a labor economist, sneaked into the stockyards. They climbed a fence, then dropped inside. After walking several minutes, "at last at the end of one dark hall we could see a glow of light and, as we drew nearer, we heard a roar of voices." They had

[17] AMCBW *Proceedings, 1904,* 33, 92–93, 193; *ibid., 1906,* 7–10, 12; *Chicago Daily Tribune,* July 13, 1904; *Chicago Record-Herald,* July 13–16, 24–26, 1904; *Official Journal,* V (July 1904), 33; Edna Louise Clark, "History of the Controversy between Labor and Capital in the Slaughtering and Meat Packing Industries in Chicago" (unpublished M.A. thesis, University of Chicago, 1922), 116 ff.; Ernest Poole, "The Meat Strike," *Independent,* LVII (July 28, 1904), 80; *Report of the Commissioner of Corporations on the Beef Industry,* 39–51; Samuel Gompers to Thomas I. Kidd, July 26, 1904, Gompers Letterbooks (91), Library of Congress; Samuel J. Naylor, "The History of Labor Organization in the Slaughtering and Meat Packing Industry" (unpublished M.A. thesis, University of Illinois, 1935), 21–60; and letters between Frank Morrison and Homer D. Call, in Morrison Letterbooks, CXXVI, CXXVIII, in AFL-CIO Headquarters, Washington, D.C.; brought to the author's attention by Professor Robert Babcock of Wells College.

come upon a boxing ring, around which, "sitting and standing
. . . with whoops and cheers some five thousand negroes
were watching." Apparently craps and other kinds of gambling, deadly assaults with knives and guns, fires, and even
smallpox also existed inside the guarded walls of the stockyards. Extensive preparations were made to house and feed
the strikebreakers. Carpenters constructed bunk beds in four
tiers. Wagonloads of mattresses and provisions were taken
into the plants. But nothing could make living conditions inside the stockyards better than deplorable. Male and female
workers were only superficially segregated, and vice and li-
centiousness flourished. A social worker in the stockyards reported that J. Ogden Armour, upon witnessing the filth,
drunkenness, gambling, and illicit sex relations in these temporary housing facilities, moaned: "My God, I can't stand
it." The packers chartered weekend excursions to the black
belt, but these were not sufficient either to relieve the monot-
ony of the strikebreakers or to assuage the anger and disgust
of local citizens. One group of businessmen at a mass meeting
adopted a resolution deploring the importation of "Greeks
and negroes, most of whom are brought from the vilest slums.
. . . [They] are a menace to the city of Chicago. . . ." [18]
    Since the violence of the 1894 strike had alienated public
opinion, the union in 1904 posted on trees and fences notices

[18] R. R. Wright, Jr., "The Negro in Times of Industrial Unrest,"
Charities, XV (October 7, 1905), 70; *Chicago Daily Tribune,* July 13,
24–26, 1904; *Chicago American,* August 26, 1904; William M. Tuttle,
Jr., "Some Strikebreakers' Observations of Industrial Warfare," *Labor History,* VII (Spring 1966), 193–96; notarized statement of five
women strikebreakers, August 18, 1904; "The Great Strike"; Harry
O. Rosenberg, "The Packing Industry and the Stockyards," manuscript in McDowell Papers; Mary McDowell, "A Quarter of a Century in the Stock Yards District," Illinois State Historical Society,
Transactions (1920), 81; Eric W. Hardy, "The Relation of the Negro
to Trade Unionism" (unpublished M.A. thesis, University of Chicago,
1911), 35–36; Upton Sinclair, *The Jungle* (N.Y.: The Heritage Press,
1965), 262–65; "The Community's Interest in the Stock Yards
Strike . . . ," *The Commons,* IX (September 1904), 404–5; Herbst,
Negro in Meat-Packing, 24–27; Ernest Poole, *The Bridge: My Own
Story* (N.Y.: Macmillan, 1940), 92–98.

which admonished the strikers "to molest no person or property, and abide strictly by the laws of this country." Morning and night, Mike Donnelly paraded up and down the lines of pickets, saying: "Leave the scabs alone! Obey the law! Keep out the militia and we'll win." These exhortations notwithstanding, the strikers' animosities frequently boiled over, and eventually even Donnelly considered drowning black strikebreakers. A mob of 500 mauled a black laborer and his ten-year-old son, and in another skirmish white strikers stabbed both eyes of a black strikebreaker. Other black people were hauled off streetcars. A full-scale riot threatened to erupt when 2,000 angry strikers hurled brickbats and other missiles at 200 black strikebreakers and their police escorts. Harry Rosenberg, a worker at Mary McDowell's settlement house, reported witnessing a mob of women and children chasing a black man down the street, crying: "Kill the fink, kill the fink," and in late August union pickets fatally stabbed a black suspected of strikebreaking.[19]

Their fortunes waning in late August, union leaders desperately wired Booker T. Washington. "Hundreds of negroes are acting as strikebreakers," they informed Washington, as they begged him to come to Chicago to lecture on the subject, "Should negroes become strike-breakers?" He declined the offer.[20]

The words "Negro" and "scab" were now synonymous in the minds of numerous white stockyards workers; and, lest they forget, racist labor officials and politicians were present to remind them. The strike, wrote one such union official, was broken "by such horrid means that a revelation of them

[19] Poole, *The Bridge,* 93–97; Rosenberg, "The Packing Industry"; Poole, "The Meat Strike," 184; "The Stockyards Strike and Immigrant Workers," *Charities,* XIII (February 4, 1905), 413; *Chicago Daily Tribune,* July 16, 1904; *Chicago Record-Herald,* July 22, 24, 27, August 1, 18, 21, 23, 25, 1904.

[20] Herbst, *Negro in Meat-Packing,* 26–27; *Chicago Record-Herald,* August 24, 1904; *Chicago Daily Tribune,* August 24, 26, 1904; *New York Tribune,* August 25, 27, 1904; cited in Spero and Harris, *Black Worker,* 267; Wright, "Negro in Times of Industrial Unrest," 70–73.

makes the soul sicken and the heart beat faint with an awful fear." It was broken by blacks, most of them "huge strapping fellows, ignorant and vicious, whose predominating trait was animalism." [21] South Carolina's Senator Ben Tillman traveled to Chicago a month after the end of the strike. "It was the niggers that whipped you in line," he told a group from the stockyards district. "They were the club with which your brains were beaten out." [22]

It was not mere words, however, but another strike, the bloody teamsters' strike of 1905, that made more indelible the image of blacks as a "scab race." Lasting over 100 days, the strike resulted in close to twenty deaths and over 400 serious injuries. Just days after the teamsters struck in April, trainloads of black men began streaming into Chicago. Shootings, knifings, and stonings soon paralyzed the city's commerce. Showers of bricks and stones greeted the black drivers as they attempted to deliver milk, coal, and other merchandise, and the injuries inflicted were recorded in the box scores of strike victims that Chicago's newspapers printed as front-page news. Pummeled with brass knuckles, "right ear almost torn off"; injured by bricks, severely bruised and cut, "struck on head and left leg with clubs during riot at Rush and Michigan"; struck on the head by a brick "said to have been thrown from the tenth floor"; beaten into unconsciousness, "three shovels broken over his head"—these were but a few of the injuries described.[23]

Fearing that these acts of violence would erupt into full-scale rioting, the city council enacted an order requesting the corporation counsel to file an opinion "as to whether the importation of hundreds of Negro workers is not a menace to the community and should not be restricted." The employers'

[21] John Roach, "Packingtown Conditions," *American Federationist,* XIII (August 1906), 534.

[22] *Chicago Broad Ax,* October 15, 1904; quoted in Spear, *Black Chicago,* 39.

[23] *Chicago Daily Tribune,* May 2–4, 1905; Wright, "Negro in Times of Industrial Unrest," 73.

association responded by consenting not to import any more black strikebreakers, but it refused to discharge any of its black drivers.[24]

Not only was the employers' gesture futile, but its very futility indicated that new elements had entered into the relationship between labor conflict and racial violence in Chicago. In this dispute, unlike the stockyards strike of eight months before, the hostility of striking whites toward strikebreaking blacks had been generalized into hatred for the black race as a whole; any black man was a potential target. In addition, no longer did mob assaults violate just one district; presaging the 1919 riot, racial violence spread throughout the city but it was especially prevalent in the blue-collar neighborhood to the west of the black belt. "You have the negroes in here to fight us," the teamsters' president told the employers' association, "and we answer that we have the right to attack them wherever found." Moreover, as Graham Taylor of the Chicago Commons settlement house observed, the "great intensity of class consciousness" in the teamsters' strike forged a firm bond between strikers and their families, neighbors, other wage-earners, and even the little children who supported them by hurling rocks at the strikebreakers. Finally, the besieged blacks were determined to defend themselves, whereas in 1904 they had generally fled.[25]

Some of the nonstrikebreaking black victims were mistaken for nonunion drivers. One of these was a dishwasher, who was kicked and beaten and had his head smashed through a car window. When policemen came to his aid, the crowd began to yell: "That's what they will all get." Another was a porter who was attacked by a crowd that ran after him screaming that he was a scab; beaten into unconsciousness,

[24] Spear, *Black Chicago,* 39–40; and *Chicago Daily Tribune,* May 2–6, 10, 12, 1905.

[25] *Ibid.;* Graham Taylor, *Chicago Commons through Forty Years* (Chicago: Chicago Commons Association, 1936), 118; *Lietuva* (Chicago), May 12, 1905, in Foreign Language Press Survey (FLPS), University of Chicago Library.

the porter died several days later of a fractured skull. The only offense of other black people, however, was that their color was "black and displeasing." A black medical student was pummeled to the ground. Even a black union member was pelted with rocks; when he called out to his attackers that his employer was not involved in the strike, one of them replied that being a "nigger" he deserved a beating anyhow.[26]

Perhaps there was no better example of white solidarity during these turbulent weeks than the sympathy strike conducted by hundreds of grade school students. Protesting the delivery of coal at school buildings by black strikebreakers employed by the Peabody Coal Company, the students hurled missiles at the drivers and organized a "skilled pupils' " union with a kindergarten local affiliated. "We are on strike. Hurrah for the unions," read the paper badges of the students who threw bricks, stones, and pieces of wood at classmates who refused to join the picket line. Many parents supported the strike, some asserting that they would never permit their children to return to school so long as scabs continued to deliver coal. They also sanctioned violence. One father, for example, told a judge that his son was "amply justified" in flinging coal at black drivers because these men were "black" and "nonunion." Even teachers encouraged the strikers. "I will invite the pupils to strike," one principal allegedly said, "if the dirty niggers deliver coal at this school." [27]

Black people appeared resolved to defend themselves. When a white man made a crude remark about a black strikebreaker who was standing at the rear of a custom house, the black man leaped down from the platform and leveled a revolver at the white. "Why, I was only joking," the white man quickly said. "You're just white trash and I ought to shoot you anyhow," was the reply.[28]

[26] *Chicago Daily Tribune,* May 4, 9, 12, 14, 1905.

[27] *Ibid.,* May 12–24, 1905. See also *The Commons,* X (June 1905), 325–26, 329–30.

[28] *Ibid.,* May 7, 9, 15, 1905.

It was this resolve that helped to precipitate unrestrained violence in mid-May. An eleven-year-old white boy died on May 16, after two black strikebreakers leaving work at the Peabody Coal Company had fired into a group of jeering children. Hysteria swept the neighborhood as enraged mobs hunted for blacks. White anger swelled so that black people feared to appear in the streets. Then, on the evening of May 20, rioting surged out of control. Whites, parading down the streets proclaiming their intention of "driving the blacks off the face of the earth," met armed resistance. Surrounded by attackers, another strikebreaker from Peabody fired and fatally wounded a white man. The next day, as the rioting spread to other districts, police were unable to prevent the outbreaks and disturbances that grew bloodier as night approached. That evening a black man was murdered by a white bartender in a saloon brawl, and other black men were dragged off streetcars. In the black belt, where blacks marched the streets crying "Justice" and "Down with the white trash," white men were chased and beaten. When the violence subsided on May 22, two people were dead and a dozen severely injured; it had been, as Allan Spear has written, "the bloodiest racial conflict in the city before the riot of 1919." [29] Labor conflict, it was readily apparent, could easily escalate into racial violence.

The image of black people as a scab race no doubt continued to fester in the minds of white workers, even though black strikebreakers did not reinforce it often again until 1916. Pullman car porters and other black men and women replaced striking railroad car cleaners in the spring of that year. Fed in dining cars and sleeping in the Pullmans, the blacks, according to the employer, were hired "not as strikebreakers, but with the understanding that their positions would be permanent," and they were "proving themselves much more efficient in every way than the cleaners who left. . . ." Most of these workers stayed on the job after

[29] *Ibid.,* May 17, 19, 21–23, 1905; and Spear, *Black Chicago,* 40.

breaking the strike.[30]

Also in 1916, as a result of increased meat production to feed Europe's armies and a sharp decline in immigration, the lines of men waiting outside the stockyards each morning evaporated. "In the past years," Mary McDowell wrote a friend, "we have seen three to five thousand men and women waiting every morning for work and have been told that while there was such a surplus of labor a raise in wages could not be given to the unskilled workers." [31] Surely, now, this must change.

Union leaders realized that the moment was propitious for organizing all the stockyards workers in this mass-production and minutely specialized industry into some sort of industrial unionism. Under the leadership of John Fitzpatrick, president of the Chicago Federation of Labor (CFL), and William Z. Foster, an organizer for the railway carmen's union, all the trade unions in the yards with the exception of the Amalgamated Meat Cutters and Butcher Workmen (AMCBW) united in July 1917 to form the Stockyards Labor Council (SLC).

Next to persuading the nationals to lay aside jurisdictional jealousies for the benefit of central organization, the SLC's most formidable problem was that of unionizing black workers, of whom there were between 10,000 and 12,000 in the

[30] Mark L. Crawford, Commissioner of Conciliation, to Secretary of Labor, April 17, 1916; Clive Runnels to Crawford, April 14, 1916; John Fitzpatrick to William B. Wilson, March 30, 1916, all in RG 280, 33/192; Chicago Commission, *Negro in Chicago*, 430–32. For the Illinois Central Shopmen's strike of 1911–1912 and the Knab and Henrici restaurants' strikes, in all of which black strikebreakers were used, see Philip Taft and Philip Ross, "American Labor Violence . . . ," in National Commission on the Causes and Prevention of Violence, *Violence in America,* prepared under the direction of Hugh Davis Graham and Ted Robert Gurr (N.Y.: Signet edition, 1969), 306–7; Commission on Industrial Relations, *Final Report and Testimony,* IV, 3244–53, 3280, 3328, 3533–37; *Naujienos* (Chicago), March 13, April 15, 1916, in FLPS.

[31] McDowell, Chicago, to [?] Mechem, Chicago, [?], 1916, McDowell Papers; Commission on Industrial Relations, *Final Report and Testimony,* IV, 3459–3531.

yards, or about one quarter of the total laboring force.[32] The CFL asked Samuel Gompers for a method by which the SLC could grant membership to blacks without violating the constitutions, rituals, and other color bars of the nationals. His solution was that the AFL would award federal charters to all-black locals if no serious objections were raised by the nationals. Despite the established unworkability of federal locals, and the cries of "Jim Crow" that they would arouse, the SLC embarked confidently on its campaign to organize black workers. To assist in the drive, the Illinois coal miners donated two black organizers, and several others later joined the team.[33]

The stockyards, rather than the steel mills or other mass-production industries, became the focus of the unions' efforts to solicit black membership. Not only were the packers by far the major employers of black labor in Chicago, but, nearly as significant, success in organizing black workers in the yards was generally considered a gauge of the ability of the unions to organize blacks in any of Chicago's industries, and indeed even in other industries throughout the country. "As Sam Gompers has said," Foster wrote Fitzpatrick in 1918, "the stockyards movement has blazed the way and shown labor

[32] George E. Haynes, memorandum regarding the proportion of blacks employed in meat packing in Chicago, January 1916–February 1919, to H. L. Kerwin, March 14, 1921, RG 280, 170/1365. See also [Fred L. Feick] to Louis F. Post, *ca.* December 1917, RG 280, 33/864; Monroe Work (ed.), *Negro Year Book, 1918–1919* (Tuskegee Institute: Negro Year Book Co., 1919), 13; Bureau of the Census, *14th Census: Manufactures, 1919* (Washington: Government Printing Office, 1923), IX, 312, 316–17, 322, 326, 346; Brody, *Butcher Workmen*, 85; Clark, "History of the Controversy," 27–28. Less than 500 black workers were retained in the stockyards after the strike: *Reports of the U. S. Immigration Commission*, Part 2 (Washington: Government Printing Office, 1911), XIII, 13, 196, 249, 503.

[33] Herbst, *Negro in Meat-Packing*, 28–34; William Z. Foster, "How Life Has Been Brought into the Stockyards," *Life and Labor*, VIII (April 1918), 64; Brody, *Butcher Workmen*, 85–87; William Z. Foster, *The Great Steel Strike and Its Lessons* (N.Y.: B. W. Huebsch, 1920), 211–12; Gompers to Fitzpatrick, August 22, 1917, Gompers Letterbooks (237); Spero and Harris, *Black Worker*, 270.

how to organize the basic industries. In this big movement"
of industrial unionism, he added, "everybody is looking to us
in Chicago to take the lead." Moreover, the slaughtering and
meat packing industry was Chicago's largest, employing over
one eighth of the city's wage-earners and ranking first in value
added by manufacture and total value of its products.[34]

A mass organization drive began in September 1917, with
parades, smokers, hall and street meetings, and the distribution of 50,000 pieces of literature in various languages.
"Brothers in all the Packing Houses. . . . BE MEN—JOIN
THE UNION," read the handbills summoning black workers
to a union meeting. The strike failures of 1894 and 1904
haunted union members, and it was rumored that the packers
wanted a strike and had imported an enormous labor reserve
of blacks to break it and crush unionization. And indeed it
seemed to workers to be a fact, though a much disputed one,
that employers were importing black laborers from the rural
South.[35]

On March 30, 1918, however, through the intervention of
the federal government, Judge Samuel Alschuler, who had
been appointed U. S. Administrator for Adjustment of Labor
Differences in Certain Packing House Industries, awarded the
eight-hour day and other benefits to workers in the yards.
These awards, the workers felt, were a tremendous union victory. Fitzpatrick jubilantly proclaimed to an excited crowd of
thousands assembled in a Chicago public park: "It's a new

[34] See census figures in footnote 32, this chapter; Foster to Fitzpatrick, June 22, 1918, John Fitzpatrick Papers, Chicago Historical
Society; David Saposs, "How the Steel Strike was Organized," *Survey,*
XLIII (November 8, 1919), 67–69; Spero and Harris, *Black Worker,*
260.

[35] Investigation by R. T. Sims to E. N. Nockels, January 19, 1917,
enclosed in Frank Morrison to W. B. Wilson, February 22, 1917, in
U. S. Department of Labor Records, National Archives (RG 174),
205, 13/65; handbill in RG 280, 33/864; Illinois Federation of Labor
Weekly News Letter, September 28, 1918; *Butcher Workman,* III
(November 1917), 2; the colloquy in U. S. Senate, 65th Cong., 3rd
Sess., Committee on Agriculture and Forestry, *Government Control
of the Meat-Packing Industry* (Washington: Government Printing Office, 1919), 1498–1503.

day, and out in God's sunshine, you men and you women, black and white, have not only an eight hour day but you are on an equality." [36] Union membership soared in the weeks following these awards.

"I suppose you have heard from official sources that the Stockyards will soon be a hundred percent organized," Ida Glatt, an officer of the Women's Trade Union League, happily recounted to Agnes Nestor, former president of the League. "From intimate connection with the white and colored English speaking women workers, I can tell you first hand that the women are just rolling into the organization." The unions' secretaries "do nothing but take in applications from morning to midnight." Black men and women were also participating in the meetings of the SLC.[37]

Not everybody shared Miss Glatt's optimism. Irene Goins, a black organizer who was active in the yards, expressed her disappointment: "My people . . . know so little about organized labor that they have had a great fear of it, and for that reason the work of organizing has proceeded more slowly than I anticipated." Another black organizer, John Riley, echoed Mrs. Goins' disappointment.[38]

[36] File in RG 280, 33/864; 864-A; *Report of the President's Mediation Commission to the President of the United States* (Washington: Government Printing Office, 1918), 16; *Monthly Labor Review*, VI (May 1918), 115–27; *Survey*, XL (April 13, 1918), 35–38, Illinois Federation of Labor *Weekly News Letter*, September 28, 1918; AMCBW *Proceedings, 1920*, 84–85, 109–10, 211–12; *New York Times*, December 26, 1917, January 21, 23, 25, 28, 1918; *Butcher Workman*, III (December 1917), 1; *ibid.*, IV (January 1918), 1, 2; *ibid.*, VII (March 1921), 4; and *ibid.*, VIII (April 1922), 1, 2; Mary McDowell, "Easter Day after the Decision," *Survey*, XL (April 13, 1918), 38; *Radnicka Straza*, February 20, 1918, in FLPS; Herbst, *Negro in Meat-Packing*, 37–41; John H. Keiser, "John Fitzpatrick and Progressive Unionism, 1915–1925" (unpublished Ph.D. dissertation, Northwestern University, 1965), 34–42.
[37] Glatt, Chicago, to Nestor, in England, April 22, 1918, Agnes Nestor Papers, Chicago Historical Society; John B. Lennon to H. L. Kerwin, April 24, 28, 1918, RG 280, 33/1211, 33/1233.
[38] Council of National Defense, Women's Committee, Conference of Departments of Women in Industry of the Middle-West State Divisions, *Report* (no imprint), 8; *Butcher Workman*, IV (October 1918), 5.

Labor's need to organize black workers increased in the fall of 1918. The war was drawing to a close, and accompanying demobilization would be the termination of the government contracts and the federal wartime agencies which had supported union recognition, collective bargaining, and nondiscrimination against union members. Furthermore, employers realized that the Armistice would dump on the labor market 4,000,000 servicemen and a sizable portion of the 9,000,000 war industry workers; and they envisaged the demoralization of the union movement as workers undercut each other for jobs. It was thus imperative for labor to meet with greater solidarity the employers' efforts to reestablish the prewar pattern of industrial relations. But among the obstacles to organization were the black workers, who, union leaders feared, would be pawns of the employers in the future struggle. Southern blacks continued to pour into Chicago; and in recent years, while the black population had more than doubled, the black industrial force had risen even more impressively, from 27,000 to almost 70,000.

The proportion of workers among blacks was much higher than that among whites. For example, whereas 10.5 per cent of all Chicago's males and 11.1 per cent of all its females were between the ages of twenty-five and twenty-nine, 13.7 per cent of the black males and 15.0 per cent of the black females were between these ages. Of the city's black women, 47 per cent fifteen years of age and older were gainfully employed, compared with only 36.6 per cent of native white women and 20.6 per cent of the foreign-born. The meaning of such statistics was evident: that although the wartime increase of Chicago's black population was indeed large, the increase of the black industrial force, especially at the unskilled level, was even more impressive. Moreover, when concentrated in certain industries, this increase was spectacular. In 1910, black men comprised just 6 per cent of the laboring force in the yards; ten years later, they constituted 32 per cent. During the war years, the black laboring force of every packing house, reported Dr. George E. Haynes of the Labor

Department's Division of Negro Economics, had increased rapidly from three to five times over the level of January 1916.[39]

In addition, the image of black strikebreakers had not dimmed during the war. Hotel keepers locked out white waiters in April 1918, hiring blacks in their places. "This is a deliberate attempt to start a race war," Fitzpatrick wrote Secretary of Labor William B. Wilson, and Wilson's conciliator in Chicago agreed that the dispute was "full of danger because of the Race problem." Ten months later black waiters and cooks broke other strikes in four fashionable hotels.[40] Black women broke strikes of egg candlers and garment workers, and on at least two occasions black men replaced striking whites at Armour as checkers and drivers of electric conveyance trucks.[41]

But racial distrust in the labor market was a two-way

[39] Estelle Hill Scott, *Occupational Changes Among Negroes in Chicago* (Chicago: WPA District 3, 1939), 175; *Chicago Daily Journal,* April 3, 1919; Department of Commerce, Bureau of the Census, *Women in Gainful Occupations, 1870 to 1920* (Washington: Government Printing Office, 1929), 11, 31; Haynes' memorandum to Kerwin, March 14, 1921, RG 280, 170/1365; Louise V. Kennedy, *The Negro Peasant Turns Cityward* (N.Y.: Columbia University Press, 1930), 74; E. W. Burgess and C. Newcomb, *Census Data of the City of Chicago, 1920* (Chicago: University of Chicago Press, 1931), 9–10, 50–51, 56 ff.; Bureau of the Census, *13th Census, 1910* (Washington: Government Printing Office, 1913), III, 512–14; *14th Census, 1920* (Washington: Government Printing Office, 1923), IV, 1076–80; L. Houghteling, *The Income and Standard of Living of Unskilled Laborers in Chicago* (Chicago: University of Chicago Press, 1927), 20–21.

[40] Fitzpatrick to Wilson, April 27, 1918, RG 280, 33/1280; John B. Lennon to H. L. Kerwin, April 24, 28, 1918, *ibid.,* 33/1211, 33/1233; Fitzpatrick and Nockels to W. B. Wilson, January 10, 1919, *ibid.,* 170/41; *New Majority,* January 11, 1919; *Forward,* January 3, 1919, in FLPS.

[41] Report on Egg Inspectors' Union, undated; Oscar F. Nelson to H. L. Kerwin, November 3, 1918, both in RG 280, 33/2602; file on garment workers in *ibid.,* 33/369; Commission on Industrial Relations, *Final Report,* IV, 3246–47; Chicago Commission, *Negro in Chicago,* 414–15; Joel Seidman, *The Needle Trades* (N.Y.: Farrar and Rinehart, 1942), 38; Department of Labor, *Report of the Secretary, 1919* (Washington: Government Printing Office, 1920), 50–51; *Chicago Defender,* November 3, December 1, 1917, August 31, 1918.

street, and at numerous times during the war black people suffered the enmity of the labor unions and individual white workers in the shops. One day black workers at Chicago Bearing Metal were shocked to find hanging on the lavatory door a sign reading: "Niggers are not allowed to use this toilet." Apparently the author of the sign was the shop foreman, although he denied it. A sign also appeared at the Acme Packing Company advising workers that thereafter a common room for relaxing would be "For White People Only." Several efforts to segregate dining and lavatory facilities were reported at clothing stores, at one of which the first-floor dining table was "for salesladies only," while in the basement was another table for the firemen tending the furnaces and the black maids.[42] This enmity sometimes burst into violence. Late on a Saturday afternoon in the summer of 1918, six Yellow Cabs were driven beneath the elevated station at 35th Street near State and parked. Having heard that black men had established a substantial business transporting baseball fans to the nearby White Sox games in jitney cars, the taxi drivers had arrived to convince the competition—with force if necessary—that it should relinquish the territory. "Come on, all you black s--s of b-----s!" shouted a white driver as he flourished a revolver, but the police intervened before there was bloodshed.[43]

With the Armistice, the forces of demobilization touched all levels of the economy—especially black Chicagoans, whose employment security was in large measure attributable to the government's demands for war products. They were usually the first to feel the effects of the immediate postwar unemployment that spring. Black women were the first to be discharged; black men and white women soon followed. Sometimes there was even a hierarchy of color; those of black skin were fired first, then those of brown and lighter brown. At the

[42] *Chicago Defender,* October 27, 1917, March 2, July 13, 20, September 7, 14, November 2, 23, 1918.
[43] *Ibid.,* June 8, 22, 1918.

stockyards' National Box Company, where half of the workers and almost all the unskilled workers were black, black women were discharged after a pay raise for women workers. "After they gave that," complained a black woman, "there came a whole lot of white ladies." A woman who wanted to remain at National Box was told she could stay if she were willing to do the grueling work of loading trucks formerly done by men. "If you don't want to do that," her foreman told her, "you will have to go home, because they are going to have all whites." [44]

"For the past few days," a black official of the U. S. Employment Service observed apprehensively in late January 1919, "there has not been a single vacant job in Chicago for a colored man," and "nothing," he added, "would tend more [than unemployment] to cause race friction. . . ." Yet unemployment soared in the next few months. By early May upwards of 10,000 black laborers were out of work, a figure which represented 20 per cent of the city's total unskilled unemployment. Black unemployment prompted the Chicago Association of Commerce in April to wire chambers of commerce in the South: "Are you in need of Negro labor? Large surplus here, both returned soldiers and civilian Negroes, ready to go to work." By May, employment in the stockyards had fallen from over 65,000, the January total, to 50,000. Moreover, returning soldiers added to the figure; and thousands of black troops were mustered out in or near Chicago, many of them Southerners who had little desire to return

[44] Other women verified this report; see hearings on National Box, March 14, 1919, RG 280, 33/864-B, 62–63, 88–105, 108–17, 120, 125–33; Forrester B. Washington, "Reconstruction and Colored Women," *Life and Labor,* VIII (January 1919), 3–5; NAACP, *Report for the Years 1917 and 1918* (N.Y.: NAACP, 1919), 45; Kennedy, *Negro Peasant,* 132–33; T. Arnold Hill, "Recent Developments in the Problem of Negro Labor," National Conference of Social Work, *Proceedings, 1921,* 324; Helen B. Irvin, "Conditions in Industry as They Affect Negro Women," National Conference of Social Work, *Proceedings, 1919,* 522–23; Paul S. Taylor, *Mexican Labor in the United States: Chicago and the Calumet Region* (Berkeley: University of California Press, 1932), 109–15.

home.[45] A. L. Jackson of the Wabash Avenue YMCA pleaded with Chicago industrialists to hire these veterans, and in boosting their qualifications he even invoked the nativism so prevalent in 1919: "These boys are all good Americans. There are no slackers, no hyphens among them." [46] To alleviate the distress, the Chicago Urban League distributed portions of the oversupply of labor to Battle Creek, Flint, and Detroit, and to areas of Wisconsin and Illinois. Even so, it could place only a few hundred workers compared to the many thousands of placements it had made during the war.[47] Later that year, during the prosperous summer months of 1919, black Chicagoans doubtless realized that in the event of a labor depression they were the most expendable, and many did not want to jeopardize their tenuous positions by unionizing.[48]

Another grievance, and one which bothered black and white workers alike, was the high cost of living. Throughout the spring and summer of 1919 newspapers editorialized about "HCL," and "HCL" was in every workingman's vocabulary. Although relative wage earnings in industry were up substantially from 1915, real earnings, because of the high cost of living, were up only 4 to 5 per cent. The cost of living

[45] Dr. Haynes' activity reports for the Division of Negro Economics for the weeks ending March 22–May 31, 1919, in RG 174, 8/102-E, F; Bureau of the Census, *14th Census*, IX, 316; minutes of meetings of the Executive Committee, Bureau for Returning Soldiers and Sailors, February 17, 1919, and undated; Forrester B. Washington to John Fitzpatrick, January 25, 1919, all in Fitzpatrick Papers; *Chicago Defender*, March 1, May 17, 31, 1919; Director General, U. S. Employment Service, *Annual Report . . . Fiscal Year Ended June 30, 1919* (Washington: Government Printing Office, 1919), 81–82; Carl Sandburg, *The Chicago Race Riots* (N.Y.: Harcourt, Brace & Howe, 1919), 31–35.

[46] "Chicago's Negro Problem," City Club of Chicago *Bulletin,* XII (March 17, 1919), 76.

[47] Chicago Urban League, *Annual Report,* III (no imprint), 3; *ibid.,* IV, 10; Sandburg, *Chicago Race Riots,* 17–18, 21–24.

[48] For increased employment that summer, see Dr. Haynes' activity reports for July 1–31, 1919, in RG 174, 8/102-F; and in *ibid.,* Division of Negro Economics, U. S. Employment Service, "Clearance Bulletin," July 29, 1919.

in Chicago had soared almost 75 per cent from December 1914 to June 1919. Food had skyrocketed 73 per cent, clothing 157 per cent, and home furnishings 127 per cent; and the crest of the boom was still not in sight.[49]

To workers in Chicago, "HCL" also denoted profiteering, and profiteering, in turn, meant the "big five" meat packers. The pages of *The New Majority,* the weekly of the Chicago Federation of Labor, and the Illinois Federation of Labor's *Weekly News Letter* persistently assailed the packers for profiteering. Labor was not alone in this assault. The Federal Trade Commission and the Senate Agriculture Committee investigated and prosecuted the "big five" in 1918 and 1919 for violation of the antitrust laws and for profiteering.[50] On the basis of public opinion, the time was ripe for the stockyards' workers to intensify both their organization drive and their demands on the packers.

A particular grievance of the stockyards' workers was the refusal of the packers to bargain collectively. Throughout Judge Alschuler's term as federal arbitrator in the yards, the packers had not once signed an agreement with the workers. Alschuler had had to present two agreements, one for the signatures of the packers, one for the unions. It was obvious to the labor leaders that unless the principle of collective bargaining were established before the expiration of Alschuler's

[49] Paul H. Douglas, *Real Wages in the United States, 1890–1926* (Boston: Houghton Mifflin, 1930), 210, 391. The prices of basic foodstuffs in Chicago were up 100 to 200 per cent from 1915: Bureau of Labor Statistics, *Retail Prices 1913 to December 1919* (Washington: Government Printing Office, 1921), 130–35. See also Mrs. M. A. Gadsby, "The Steel Strike," *Monthly Labor Review,* IX (December 1919), 1751–52; *Monthly Labor Review,* XXI (August 1925), 313; U. S. Children's Bureau, *Children of Wage-Earning Mothers: A Study of a Selected Group in Chicago* (Washington: Government Printing Office, 1922), 13.

[50] United States Senate, 65th Cong., 2nd Sess., *Profiteering,* Sen. Doc. No. 248 (Washington: Government Printing Office, 1918), 7, 14–17; Federal Trade Commission, *Report on the Meat Packing Industry* (Washington, 3 vols.: Government Printing Office, 1919–1920).

term, the temporary gains of the war period were in jeopardy.

In spite of, or possibly because of, the postwar layoffs that affected thousands of workers, and the threat of cutthroat job competition, Judge Alschuler, in mid-February 1919, gave the unions a boost with the announcement of his second awards. He granted wage increases and working hour revisions favorable to labor. Thus it appeared incongruous when the five major packers on April 12 requested that the Secretary of Labor extend Alschuler's administration for one year after the official declaration of peace. The packers evidently did not want to agitate a strike and risk establishing the precedent of collective bargaining until the labor surplus in Chicago was sufficiently formidable to defeat a strike. Objecting to this extension, the unions recommended that the employers at least listen to grievances in the first instance; but the Labor Department could not compel employers to accept collective bargaining, and Alschuler's administration was extended relatively unchanged in May 1919. As in the past, the unions' grievances in the first instance would be submitted to the federal arbitrator.[51]

In early June the stockyards unions kicked off their most spirited organization drive since 1917. Following a parade and the distribution of campaign buttons on June 8, John Kikulski, an organizer of butchers and meat cutters, outlined the goals of "this great campaign," in which "Polish, Irish, Lithuanian, and in fact every race, color, creed, and nationality is to be included. . . ." "While there will be varied differences in our physical makeup and thoughts, there is one thing which we all hold in common, and that is our right to a living wage, and our rights in the pursuit of happiness as American citizens. . . ." In other attempts to organize black workers, and to convince them that labor's cause was theirs,

[51] United States Administrator for Adjustment of Labor Questions Arising in Certain Packing Houses, *Findings and Awards,* February 15, 1919, 11–15; Department of Labor, *Report of the Secretary, 1919,* 52; Herbst, *Negro in Meat-Packing,* 41; pertinent correspondence in RG 280, 33/864.

too, the CFL devoted portions of *The New Majority* to the black race. Prominently displayed in its pages, for example, was a petition of Local 651 of the AMCBW, the best known all-black local in the city, to President Wilson, imploring him to "see that the representatives of Ireland be given a seat at the peace table and be recognized in the formation of the League of Nations." It was not coincidental that Irish union members frequently generated racial friction in the yards, that many union leaders were Irish, or that the black butchers' petition concluded somewhat illogically that Ireland should be assured a seat in the League of Nations "to the end that prejudice and race hatred are entirely eradicated." Another example of the CFL's attempts to identify black workers with the labor movement—in the minds of both blacks and whites—was an article "by John Riley (Negro)" entitled "Tom Mooney Must Be Free." Tom Mooney, a union man, was awaiting execution in San Quentin for murder, and Chicago labor leaders had stoutly protested against his conviction. In fact, Chicago was headquarters of the Mooney Defense Fund. Few crusades were better tailored to establish rapport between the races. The organ of the AMCBW, the *Butcher Workman,* likewise published pointed appeals to black workers. Appearing in the May issue was an article by a black woman. Entitled "The Negro's Greatest Opportunity as I See It," it was both a slashing attack on race prejudice and an announcement that the AMCBW had "broken down the bars and . . . invited us in." "Therefore, the black man should take advantage of this great opportunity [membership in the AMCBW], so that he may be the instrument through which discrimination may be driven out of this country—the home of the free and the home of the brave." [52]

After the June 8 mass meeting, union leaders enthusiasti-

[52] *Sunday Jewish Courier,* June 8, 1919, in FLPS; *New Majority,* April 26, June 14, 21, July 5, 19, 1919; Department of Labor, Division of Negro Economics, *The Negro at Work during the War and during Reconstruction* (Washington: Government Printing Office, 1921), 26–27; *Butcher Workman,* V (May, June, July 1919), 4; 1; 1.

cally promoted the unionization drive, posting organizers at the gates to the stockyards at noon and quitting time. A musicians' local contributed a three-piece band to attract nonunion workers to the speakers' flatbed truck. *The New Majority* even recommended forming a band composed strictly of union men from the yards, adding that it would be "one of the most cosmopolitan groups of musicians in the world"; "everything [would be] represented except an Eskimo and I don't believe they like the smell of stockyards but would make good freezer men." Regarding the response of black workers, *The New Majority* joyfully recalled that A. K. Foote, secretary of Local 651, "was singing the blues a few days ago, but now he has a smile so broad that it is almost impossible to believe that such a change could come over a man." For four weeks, the confidence of the stockyards' unions was unabated. Their slogan was "100 per cent union or bust," and to achieve the goal they stationed seven trucks at the yards' entrances. As enough men and women indicated a desire to become members, the organizers invited them to climb aboard and they were "whizzed over to the union headquarters." [53]

Black and white workers paraded through the black belt on Sunday, July 6, and congregated in a playground near the yards. Brass bands led the way, and the marchers waved miniature American flags and carried placards, on one of which was printed: "The bosses think because we are of different colors and different nationalities that we should fight each other. We're going to fool them and fight for a common cause —a square deal for all." Union leaders delivered speeches at the playground. The seven speakers, of whom three were black, did not betray the advertised purpose of the meeting— to organize black workers. "It does me good . . . to see such a checkerboard crowd," said J. W. Johnstone of the SLC in welcoming the workers. "You are standing shoulder to shoulder as men, regardless of whether your face is black or white." "You notice there ain't no Jim Crow cars here

[53] *The New Majority,* June 21, July 5, 1919.

today," a black AMCBW organizer, C. Ford, told the crowd. "That's what organization does. The truth is there ain't no negro problem any more than there's a Irish problem or a Russian or a Polish or a Jewish or any other problem. There is only the human problem, that's all. All we demand," he concluded, "is the open door. You give us that, and we won't ask nothin' more of you." John Kikulski then addressed the Polish in their native language to explain the need for "cooperation between blacks and whites." [54]

Following the open-air meeting of July 6, the stockyards' organizers initiated a drive to corral the backing of black ministers. They outlined organized labor's goals to the Colored Baptist Ministers' Alliance, and a few days later a union committee attended the African Methodist Episcopal Sunday School Convention, where one member addressed the delegates on the merits of the labor movement. [55]

Yet events just two days after the July 6 parade belied the union leaders' optimism. For it was on July 8, as a hot spell settled on the city, that the most violent strike of the summer occurred. Two thousand employees of the Corn Products Refinery at Argo struck that morning, after the company's president had reneged on an agreement to hold a referendum on the closed shop. Anticipating trouble, the company had requisitioned a shipment of rifles and reinforced its special police force. The next day, during a fracas at the plant's entrance, armed guards shot and killed two strikers and seriously wounded eighteen others, one of whom soon died. A howling, stone-throwing mob of strikers' wives and daughters added to the turbulence by chasing the mayor of Argo, who was also superintendent of the company's machine shops, two miles to Chicago's city limits for threatening local grocers and druggists with discontinuance of the refinery's accounts if

[54] Sandburg, *Chicago Race Riots*, 47; Herbst, *Negro in Meat-Packing*, 42–43; *New Majority*, July 12, 1919; *Chicago Whip*, July 19, 1919; *Butcher Workman*, V (July 1919), 1, 3.

[55] *Chicago Whip*, July 25, 1919.

they extended credit to the strikers.

Ida Glatt, J. W. Johnstone, and other organizers from the Women's Trade Union League and SLC had been busy at Argo for the past year trying to unionize the workers, and there was a deep affinity between this campaign and the sister campaign at the stockyards. The day after the shootings at Argo the strikers and several thousand other Russian, Lithuanian, and Polish workers, mainly from the stockyards district, marched in a guard of honor at the funeral of the murdered men. During the funeral rumor was rife that the company had asked numerous black men to "come back Monday and bring all of your friends." The citizens of Argo feared that their introduction into the plant would ignite another round of bloodshed, but on Monday refinery officials deputized a number of black men whom they strung out in a line in front of the factory. Their presence particularly incensed the strikers, and disorder erupted during which three strikers were wounded. A mother of four was shot in the leg and then beaten down from a trolley wire, but not before she had disengaged it in order to allow strikers to hurl bottles and bricks at a stalled streetcar filled with strikebreakers. Altogether 600 blacks were brought in as strikebreakers in this bloody dispute; doubtless, the immigrant strikers in Argo and around the stockyards did not forget their role in crushing the strike.[56]

A confrontation between labor and management in the yards also was not long in coming. The first week of July witnessed the introduction of 300 mounted policemen to pa-

[56] Oscar F. Nelson to H. L. Kerwin, August 4, 1919; Fitzpatrick to Woodrow Wilson, July 9, 1919; in RG 280, 170/606; *Chicago Daily News,* July 8–10, 14, 1919; *Chicago Herald-Examiner,* July 9, 1919; *Chicago Daily Journal,* July 10–11, 14, 1919; Department of Labor, *Report of the Secretary of Labor, 1920* (Washington: Government Printing Office, 1921), 117; William L. Evans, "The Negro in Chicago Industries," *Opportunity,* I (February 1923), 15; *New Majority,* August 2, 1919; *Annual Report of the Women's Trade Union League [WTUL] of Chicago, June, 1915, to June, 1916* (no imprint), 15; WTUL of Chicago *Bulletin,* VII (August, September, December 1918), 2;2;4.

trol the stockyards district, apparently to reverse the unions' organizing successes. As workers gathered around a union speaker the police would ride into the crowd and disperse it. After protesting to the packers, 10,000 workers walked out on Friday, July 18. Although they returned to the stockyards Monday, it was evident that one of the most serious strikes in Chicago's history was imminent. That evening union members voted to demand wage increases and other benefits, to submit these demands Saturday, July 26—just the day before the outbreak of the race riot—and to allow the packers forty-eight hours either to accept them or prepare for a strike.[57]

Nor was the stockyards the only scene of industrial unrest in Chicago in 1919. Except for New York, no city in the nation had more strikes than Chicago that year.[58] May was the time for renewing numerous labor contracts for the city's industries; beginning in that month, the number of strikes, threatened strikes, and lockouts increased markedly, and, combined with the shooting of a union business agent by a strikebreaker, presaged a turbulent summer. In mid-June, private detectives at the American Car and Foundry Company fired twenty shots into a mob of union men who were intent upon stopping a truckload of strikebreakers from entering the plant; one man died. There were also controversies in steel rolling mills, a shoe company, and a butterine factory. Apparently no area of employment was immune to strikes. At the Patrolmen's Social, Chicago's policemen discussed striking but feared that the city would be placed under martial law if they did; and firemen, municipal clerks, and food inspectors voted to consider walking off the job if the city council

[57] Alschuler Hearings, August 13, 1919, 23–29, in RG 280, 33/864; Fitzpatrick and J. W. Johnstone to W. B. Wilson, August 23, 1919; Wilson to Fitzpatrick and Johnstone, August 28, 1919, *ibid.*, 33/864-C; *Chicago Daily News,* July 17, 21, 1919; *New Majority,* July 26, 1919; *Chicago Herald-Examiner,* July 21, 1919; *Chicago Daily Tribune,* July 21, 1919; and *Chicago Whip,* July 25, 1919.

[58] Edson L. Whitney (comp.), "Strikes and Lockouts in the United States, 1916, 1917, 1918, and 1919," *Monthly Labor Review,* X (June 1920), 1509; *New York Times,* July 20, 1919.

did not approve higher wages. The city's new fiscal year budget did not satisfy other municipal workers, either, and on the first day of July, the city hall's janitors walked out, as did 5,200 street sweepers and garbage handlers.[59]

As evidenced by the bloodshed at Argo, the violent strikes were usually in mass-production industries. And the urge to strike in these industries that summer was infectious. Thousands of workers struck even before formulating demands or affiliating with the locals. The philosophy underlying this tactic was that if a plant's personnel quit *en masse,* organization along industrial rather than craft lines would be facilitated; then the "plant union" could submit demands from the various crafts in a lump—take it all or accept a total shutdown. On July 10, hundreds of women candy workers deserted five factories and then embarked upon compiling their grievances. The contagion spread. The next day, 7,500 nonunion machinists, blacksmiths, and moulders formed a parade inside the Crane Company on the city's South Side, and spontaneously walked out. In mid-July, thousands of nonunion employees also walked out of International Harvester's reaper plant, tractor works, and twine mills.[60]

Lockouts heightened the city's industrial disquiet. Four days after the initial Harvester walkout, over 100,000 carpenters, laborers, structural ironworkers, and other building tradesmen were locked out by the Building Employers' Association, tying up over $100,000,000 in construction operations and cutting off or slashing a half-million incomes. In the days before the riot erupted, there were additional disputes

[59] Department of Labor, *Report of the Secretary, 1919,* 113–17; Illinois Department of Labor, *Second Annual Report* (Springfield: Illinois State Journal Company, 1920), 74–77; *New Majority,* May 10, June 21, July 5, 1919; Illinois Federation of Labor *Weekly News Letter,* May 3, 24, 1919; *Chicago Daily Journal,* June 19, 1919; *Chicago Daily Tribune,* June 29, July 2, 1919.

[60] *Chicago Daily News,* July 10, 18, 1919; *Chicago Daily Tribune,* July 12, 16, 26, 1919; *Chicago Daily Journal,* July 16–17, 1919; *Chicago Herald-Examiner,* July 26, 1919; Department of Labor, *Report of the Secretary, 1920,* 91, 117.

idling thousands of typographers, cigar store clerks, box makers, and other workers. And in the final week, William Z. Foster, John Fitzpatrick, and other union officials in the steel mills of South Chicago escalated their unionizing campaign to its highest pitch; that week they also conducted the strike vote for the massive 1919 steel strike. Other threatened strikes of 36,000 workers, among them all of Chicago's streetcar and elevated railway employees, were scheduled either for the weekend on which the race riot began or for Monday, July 28.[61]

Upwards of 250,000 workers in Chicago were on strike, threatening to strike, or locked out by late July 1919. In other words, one out of every three or four men and women in wage-earning fields in which there was the slightest union activity was a participant in a labor dispute.[62] The unrest was evident to even the most casual observer. The city's polarization between capital and labor was so extreme that summer that it prompted this statement by Ray Stannard Baker: "Labor is more closely organized, more self-conscious, more advanced in its views in Chicago than in any other American city."[63] Labor, with its intense class consciousness, felt it was fighting for its very existence.

[61] Department of Labor, *Report of the Secretary, 1920*, 118, 119, 121; *Chicago Daily News*, July 18–19, 21, 24, 1919; *Chicago Herald-Examiner*, July 23–25, 1919; *Chicago Daily Journal*, July 18, 1919; *Chicago Daily Drovers Journal*, July 19, 1919; Gadsby, "Steel Strike," 1745; Keiser, "John Fitzpatrick," 43–44; *New York Times*, July 27, 1919; Royal E. Montgomery, *Industrial Relations in the Chicago Building Trades* (Chicago: University of Chicago Press, 1927), 100 ff.; Chicago Real Estate Board *Bulletin*, XXVII (August 16, September 25, 1919), 625, 627, 719–20.

[62] Department of Labor, *Report of the Secretary, 1920*, 116–121; Illinois Department of Labor, *Second Annual Report*, 71–77; *Chicago Herald-Examiner*, July 9, 1919; *Chicago Daily Tribune*, July 12, 16, 18, 1919; *Chicago Daily Drovers Journal*, July 19, 1919; *Chicago Daily Journal*, July 17, 1919; Graham Taylor, "An Epidemic of Strikes in Chicago," *Survey*, XLII (August 2, 1919), 645–46; Bureau of the Census, *14th Census*, IV, 1076–81.

[63] Baker, *The New Industrial Unrest* (Garden City, N.Y.: Doubleday, Page and Company, 1920), 112.

The labor unrest affected numberless others—the corner grocer, the shoe repairman, salesmen, newsboys—anyone depending on consumers for his income. The economic basis of discontent was thus present in Chicago. Compounded by Chicago's vast, heterogeneous population, individual discontent was potential mass violence; and the focus of violence was facilitated by the distinguishing physical characteristic of the black people—the skin which to so many white people meant evil, danger, even a threat to their existence.

On that fateful weekend in July, 90 per cent of the whites in the stockyards were unionized, while three fourths of the black workers, or 9,000 people, were still outside the labor movement.[64] What had retarded unionization among black workers in Chicago's stockyards and elsewhere?

Black workers in labor histories too often appear as faceless figures either to be praised, pitied, or damned. But it is evident that black men and women had very real reasons for resisting unionization, if indeed they had the opportunity to join in the first place. Emotional racial antipathy barred them from union membership; many and perhaps even most white union men and women viewed black people as having been foreordained to occupy the lowest rung on the racial ladder. In May 1919 the president of the railway clerks was asked whether Mexicans were to be classified as "white" under an article in the union's constitution. "They are certainly considered white," he replied, "as is the American Indian. . . . This section has always been construed as simply to debar the negro or those who have African blood in their veins." Black workers, whites felt, could not share membership with them; as in housing and politics, the imputation of equality was just too much to bear. A white worker who held that black people were innately inferior, and who at the same time

[64] Sandburg, *Chicago Race Riots,* 8, 44–50, 65; *Chicago Daily Journal,* August 6, 1919; Haynes, memorandum to H. L. Kerwin, March 14, 1921, RG 280, 170/1365.

was proud of his craft, became the double victim of depreca-
tion by association when a black man entered both his trade
and his trade union. As a member of the car workers' union
put it: "I believe that God, in his infinite mercy, made the
negro, but he never made him to be a car worker." Whites
also wanted to control their portions of the labor market, and
they did so by excluding blacks from membership and from
such other union-dominated activities as apprenticeship pro-
grams. And even when unions were enlightened enough to
admit black workers, white members sometimes made conditions so unpleasant that black men and women quit their jobs
before having a chance to seek membership.

Undoubtedly, some white workingmen were willing to admit blacks to their locals, if not as a matter of principle, at
least as a means of self-defense; but too often these locals
were hamstrung by policies at the national union level.[65] Most
unions in Chicago in 1919 probably had no black members at
all. Of the 110 national and international unions of the AFL
represented in the city, nine excluded blacks by constitution
and two by ritual. In addition, five unions restricted membership by tacit agreement and four others accomplished the
same end by making the conditions for membership onerous
for black workers, though not for whites. The plumbers'
union restricted membership by license law; union members
sitting on city and state examination boards refused to license
black plumbers. A survey in 1912 estimated that an additional sixteen unions put all black workers in coordinate or
subordinate locals. Upwards of thirty-seven of Chicago's 110

[65] Abram L. Harris, "Negro Labor's Quarrel with White Workingmen," *Current History*, XXIV (September 1926), 903–7; Herman
Feldman, *Racial Factors in American Industry* (N.Y.: Harper &
Brothers, 1931), 27–28; Charles S. Johnson, "Negro Workers and the
Unions," *Survey*, LX (April 15, 1928), 113–15; "Negroes and Organized Labor," *Survey*, XXXIX (February 9, 1918), 527–28; Brotherhood of Railway Clerks, *Proceedings, 1919* (Cincinnati: n.pub.,
n.d.), 169; Joint Convention of the Brotherhood of Railway Carmen
of America and International Association of Car Workers, *Proceedings, 1905* (Kansas City: n.pub., n.d.), 21.

AFL unions, then, either excluded black men and women or refused to integrate them into the locals. The Chicago Commission on Race Relations, in response to a questionnaire, was informed by twenty-eight other locals that either no black workers were in the trade or "no applications were received." Black people were also alienated from the labor movement by thirteen of the fifteen major unions outside of the AFL. Only the Amalgamated Clothing Workers and the Industrial Workers of the World welcomed black workers, while the remaining thirteen, all transportation unions, raised the color bar in their constitutions.[66]

Where exclusion was not the rule in the labor movement, segregation was frequently the practice. Even though racial separation in trade unions could lead to double standards in wages and hours, union leaders seemed to be blind to these inequities. Writing to Booker T. Washington, for example, the general secretary of the carpenters' union boasted "that we do not draw the color line in our organization, as is evidenced by the fact that . . . we have in the United Brotherhood . . . unions composed exclusively of colored men." After 1900, segregation in the labor movement became widespread, for in that year the AFL placed in its constitution an amendment authorizing federal locals. Thereafter, whenever a national refused to enroll blacks as members, the executive council of the AFL would issue a federal charter to the black workers. The executive council was then supposed to act as the "national" for the federal local. Because of its workload, however, it was rarely in a position to assist the locals in organizing, settling grievances, or negotiating contracts. Realizing its limitations, the AFL usually referred the local's problems to the national having jurisdiction in the field. But this,

[66] F. E. Wolfe, *Admission to American Trade Unions* (Baltimore: Johns Hopkins Press, 1912), 123–25; Spero and Harris, *Black Worker,* 57, 58–62; Lorenzo J. Greene and Carter G. Woodson, *The Negro Wage Earner* (Washington: Association for the Study of Negro Life and History, 1930), 47–53; Chicago Commission, *Negro in Chicago,* 406 ff.

of course, was the national that had initially excluded black people; it naturally tended to subordinate or ignore their needs. Often having no grievance man in the national, the federal locals could not protest against racial differentials in wages and hours. Moreover, if the national subsequently amended its rules to permit the affiliation of black workers even in a segregated status, the AFL, despite the protestations of blacks, transferred the local back to the national.[67]

Racism was rampant in the labor movement in the early decades of the twentieth century, not only in Chicago but across the country. The promise of equality held out by the Knights of Labor and the AFL in its early years had long gone unfulfilled; by 1919 racism was the norm, not the exception. Union delegates in convention referred to "the nigger." And, in 1905, when a delegate rose to a point of order, charging, "There is no such word as 'nigger,' " the chairman replied to great laughter: "There is a word 'nigger,' and it means somebody that is lazy." [68]

Having been barred, segregated, and ridiculed, Chicago's black workers generally could not identify with the labor movement. Excluded black craftsmen often had to seek out unskilled positions, and it would have been unreasonable for them then to unionize with common laborers, especially if they accrued employment benefits as nonunion men. Unfortunately for the stockyards' organization drive, neither all the AFL national unions nor their members followed the progressive lead of the CFL. Black workers were induced to join the federal locals recommended by Gompers, although some overzealous organizers enlisted blacks with the false promise that they would be transferred later to the locals of their respective crafts. A steamfitter expressed the dilemma of many of the black tradesmen in the yards: "I have worked as

[67] Quoted in Booker T. Washington, "The Negro and the Labor Unions," *Atlantic Monthly*, CXI (June 1913), 766; *AFL Proceedings, 1900* and *1919*, 12; 227–28.
[68] Joint Convention of Railway Carmen and Car Workers, *1905 Proceedings*, 18.

a steamfitter at the stockyards for fifteen years and tried to get into [all-white] Local 563, as have others of my race, but we have always been put off with some excuse until we gave up the attempt to get in." Other blacks had become union members during labor disputes, only to be discharged after the strike was over. They felt betrayed, certain that unions were motivated not by a spirit of brotherhood but solely by self-interest. The exclusionist policies of Southern unions had likewise alienated black workers from the labor movement, and some of the migrants to Chicago during the war had traveled there to escape the job control exercised by the unions. Other migrants hesitated to join with whites who, during earlier labor depressions, had replaced them in domestic services, in the operation of barber shops, bootblack parlors, and contractual janitorial services, and in cooking, waiting tables, and dishwashing.[69] Still others had peculiarly individual motives for not unionizing—in some instances because they held life insurance policies that could be voided on grounds of union membership.

Although there were black Chicagoans who recognized the value of the labor movement, they felt that the unions sacrificed the interests of blacks to pacify the racism of white members. And it was the awareness of this inequality that resulted in the creation in Chicago of the 1,200-member Railway Men's International Benevolent Industrial Associ-

[69] Herbst, *Negro in Meat-Packing*, 59–62; E. L. Davis, Macon, Georgia, to T. Arnold Hill of Chicago Urban League, April 21, 1917, in Carter G. Woodson Papers, Library of Congress; Kelly Miller, "The Economic Handicap of the Negro in the North," *Annals*, XXVII (May 1906), 543–50; letter to the editor in *New Majority*, February 15, 1919; see James Weldon Johnson, "Changing Status of Negro Labor," National Conference of Social Work, *Proceedings, 1919*, 383–88; Chicago Commission, *Negro in Chicago*, 426–27, for 1904 waiters' strikes in which black union members felt betrayed; Emmett J. Scott (comp.), "Additional Letters of Negro Migrants of 1916–1918," *Journal of Negro History*, IV (October 1919), 417, 433; the statements of Fannie Barrier Williams, in the *New York Age*, June 15, September 28, 1905; quoted in Alfred H. Stone, *Studies in the American Race Problem* (N.Y.: Doubleday, Page, 1908), 157–58.

ation. It also caused men and women to argue that black workers should federate, thus subordinating the principle of craft affiliation to one of racial solidarity. Just as the Jews had established the United Hebrew Trades, asserted one Chicagoan, so the blacks in all trades should present a "united front" to the AFL in order to have "our rights demanded and adjusted." [70]

On the other hand, the Southern migrants who traveled from the South to work in Chicago's industries brought with them not only a rural psychology but, in many cases, a total ignorance of strikes and unions. Fully 90 per cent of the Northern-born black workers in the yards wore the union button, but few of the migrants did.[71] Other black workers, however, were fully aware of how blacks broke strikes, undermined wages, and reduced the white workers' bargaining power. Strikebreaking presented an opportunity to enter industries which formerly had been closed. Even if a strikebreaker were employed at less than the union scale, he was generally paid more than he was accustomed to earning; and by refusing to go out on strike with whites, blacks received promotions into more highly skilled fields which had not been open to them.

The readjustment from life on the farm to that of industrial wage earner was so immense that the migrants often followed the advice of black leaders, whose advice was understandably more influential that that of white union members. A frequent source of counsel was the Urban League. The most heavily endowed social service agency in the black belt and the main employment bureau there, the Urban League received much of its operating capital from Julius Rosenwald, the president of Sears, Roebuck and a well-known philanthropist. The next

[70] AFL *Proceedings, 1919*, 227–29, 305; NAACP Board Minutes, July 9, 1918, in NAACP Papers, Library of Congress (A-1); Spero and Harris, *Black Worker*, 117–19, 124, 328; *Chicago Defender*, October 13, 1917, May 4, October 12, 1918.

[71] Brody, *Butcher Workmen*, 85; Spero and Harris, *Black Worker*, 271.

largest donor was the Stock Yards Community Clearing House, an organization representing the packers. Other generous contributors to the League's operations were International Harvester, the Pullman Company, several iron works and foundries, and the Illinois Manufacturers Association. This is not to say, however, that large industrial contributors dictated League policy regarding the labor movement; there is no evidence to that effect. The Urban League took a pragmatic view of unions, although the officers of the local branch were clearly cognizant of the danger of postwar labor conflict along racial lines. Robert E. Park, white sociologist and the League's president, feared that all the perplexities of black Chicagoans after the Armistice would be "intimately bound up with" the labor scene, and as early as November 1917 the League announced that it "would welcome any effort tending to an amicable settlement of this vital problem." It met with officers of the Chicago and Illinois Federations of Labor, and it advised the Women's Trade Union League during its campaign to organize black women in the yards, but these efforts accomplished little toward persuading unions to lower their color bars. The dilemma of the League, as of many black leaders, was that though it recognized the exigency of unionizing black workers, it left little doubt that the first move had to be the unions' obliteration of all discriminatory membership policies. The League sought to plot a course between management and organized labor. For two reasons, however, it was more often on management's side: the unions did not lower their color bars, and Chicago's large industries could provide immediate opportunities for the migrants.[72]

[72] Arvarh E. Strickland, *History of the Chicago Urban League* (Urbana: University of Illinois Press, 1966), 48, 50–51, 56–63, 66–67, 72–74, 110; Chicago Urban League, *Annual Report,* I, 10; II, 6; and III, 2; E. K. Jones, "The Negro in Industry," National Conference of Social Work, *Proceedings, 1919,* 438–41; *Chicago Whip,* July 19, 1919; Chicago Commission, *Negro in Chicago,* 365, 366; *Chicago Defender,* March 16, 1918; A. L. Foster, "Twenty Years of Interracial Goodwill through Social Service," in Chicago Urban League, *Two Decades of Service, 1916–1936* (no imprint), *passim;* Julius Rosen-

The attitude of Chicago's most widely circulated black newspaper, the *Defender,* paralleled that of the Urban League. During the war, the *Defender* urged black workers not to "be made a tool or strike breaker for any corporation or firm." But it also warned them to "be sure that you are not put into a SEPARATE UNION; be sure that you are to be treated as other workmen, and if you find that you are to have a union all to yourself, just quit." Several times it asked the unions to recognize the contributions that blacks were making to win the war for democracy by democratizing their membership. "We have arrayed ourselves on the side of capital to a great extent," the *Defender* proclaimed in an editorial in late April 1919, "yet capital has not played square with us; it has used us as strikebreakers, then when the calm came turned us adrift." If it were to the race's "economic, social, and political interest to join with organized labor now, it should not make the least bit of difference what was their attitude toward us in the past, even if that past was as recent as yesterday. If they extend the olive branch in good faith, accept it today." In July, however, after the AFL convention had done little to remove the exclusion clauses of some AFL unions or the segregation clauses of others, the *Defender* complained: "Unwillingly we assume the role of strikebreakers. The unions drive us to it." [73]

Chicago's second leading black newspaper, the *Broad Ax,* reached the same conclusion, but it had always been hostile to the unions. In boosting the qualifications of the black

---

wald Papers: Rosenwald agreed to contribute $1.00 for every $2.00 collected by the Urban League. Whenever the League received enough money to bother Rosenwald for his supplementary contribution, it sent to him a list of the individual contributors and sums contributed. He, in turn, remitted to the Urban League one half of the total on the list. In his papers, in the University of Chicago Library, therefore, is a complete account of the financing of the Chicago Urban League.

[73] *Chicago Defender,* April 21, July 21, October 20, 1917; February 16, 23, March 23, April 27, November 23, 1918; April 12, May 17, June 21, July 5, 1919. The *Whip,* which began publication a few weeks before the riot, supported unionization.

worker, the *Broad Ax* listed industriousness, the willingness
to work "in and out of season," and the fact that "he does not
strike. He is the only industrious worker that is really depend-
able. . . ." [74]

To most leaders in the black belt exclusion and segregation
were the roots of the problem. Also there was a widespread
attitude that employers were the black workers' natural allies,
and that they rather than unions provided security and industrial opportunity. Black people have found, Booker T. Washington wrote in 1913, that "the friendship and confidence of a
good white man, who stands well in the community, are a
valuable asset in time of trouble." For this reason, the black
worker "does not always understand, and does not like an
organization [a union] which seems to be founded on a sort
of impersonal enmity to the man by whom he is employed. . . ." Mary McDowell recalled an example of the
personal relationship which blacks sometimes believed existed between employer and employee. During the campaign
to organize the stockyards, an organizer approached a newly
arrived migrant and explained to him the advantages of union
membership. "It all sounds pretty good to me," the migrant
replied, "but what does Mr. Armour think about it?" [75]

Union leaders accused the packers of subsidizing black
clergymen and other professional people, YMCAs, and welfare
clubs to spread antiunion propaganda. Certain clergymen,
among them unprincipled labor recruiters, did urge their parishioners to spurn union advances. Others, however, endorsed the endeavors of unions that were organizing without
regard to race, arguing that union membership would help to

[74] *Broad Ax,* March 1, 1919.
[75] Washington, "Negro and Labor Unions," 756–57; Spero and Harris, *Black Worker,* 130; Charles S. Johnson, "The New Frontage on
American Life," in Alain Locke (ed.), *The New Negro* (N.Y.:
Atheneum edition, 1968), 291–92; *Chicago Defender,* June 14, 1919;
George E. Haynes, "Negro Labor and the New Order," National Conference of Social Work, *Proceedings, 1919,* 538; Jones, "Negro in Industry," 439.

minimize racial conflict; and among these were two of the city's most eminent ministers, L. K. Williams of the Olivet Baptist Church and John F. Thomas of Ebeneezer Baptist. In addition, black clerical associations invited union organizers to use their groups as forums for outlining labor's views. Other prominent black Chicagoans, including Dr. George Cleveland Hall and Major John R. Lynch, Congressman from Mississippi during Reconstruction, advocated union membership. Speaking at a meeting of Local 651, Hall called for biracial organization "as a means of breaking down prejudice. . . ." For "as soon as the laboring white man was convinced that we were not natural born strikebreakers, but made so by conditions, most of the prejudice would disappear and the two could work side by side. . . ." [76]

The YMCA, where the packers financed "efficiency clubs," was antiunion. The packers helped the organization in other ways as well; Armour, for example, gave an annual membership in the YMCA to each black worker after his first year of employment. Black men at the club meetings, charged J. W. Johnstone, were "lectured and taught that the thing they have to do is to keep out of organized labor." It seems clear, too, that the YMCA's secretary, A. L. Jackson, with his educational background of Phillips Academy at Andover and Harvard College, was intellectually and emotionally sympathetic to the packers, and decidedly hostile to the unions. [77]

[76] Alschuler Hearings, August 13, 1919, 96, in RG 280, 33/864; Dr. Haynes' memorandum to H. L. Kerwin, March 14, 1921, RG 280, 170/1365; Chicago Commission, *Negro in Chicago*, 415, 422, 427–29; Foster, *Great Steel Strike*, 211–12; *Chicago Daily Tribune*, August 1, 1919; *New Majority*, January 11, August 9, 1919; Department of Labor, Division of Negro Economics, *Negro Migration in 1916–17* (Washington: Government Printing Office, 1919), 117, 130; *Chicago Whip*, July 25, 1919; Sandburg, *Chicago Race Riots*, 48–50; Miles Mark Fisher, *The Master's Slave: Elijah John Fisher, a Biography* (Philadelphia: Judson Press, 1922), 189; *Chicago Defender*, February 23, 1918, June 21, 1919; Walter White, "Chicago and Its Eight Reasons," *Crisis*, XVIII (October 1919), 294–95.

[77] Interview with Mr. Jackson, Chicago, June 27, 1969; *Chicago Defender*, June 1, 15, August 24, September 21, October 5, 12, 1918;

It is not quite so difficult to determine the motives of Richard E. Parker, a notorious antiunion propagandist and frustrated politician whom the *Defender* called " 'the second William Jennings Bryan,' as he is always a candidate." Parker admitted that in 1916 he had distributed 20,000 handbills to "All Colored Working Men in the Stockyards," warning them not to "Join Any White Man's Union." He claimed that he had paid for these himself because of his "personal interest" in his race, but he also acknowledged that he had gone to the South in 1916, while working for several packing and steel companies, and had "imported more Negroes than any man in Chicago." Parker edited a newspaper in which he advised black workers not to join the established unions but to join the American Unity Labor Union, which he had founded and of which he was business agent. A card from his union, he boasted, would secure employment for blacks in the building trades, steel mills, and stockyards. Parker was a demagogue and he was doubtless on the payroll of employers, but he might also have been working in the race's interest, as he perceived it. Because "the Negro happened to be born black," he wrote, "the Unions have labeled him inferior." As a result, they barred him not only from membership but also from apprenticeships and the chance to secure work in skilled jobs. "For this reason we formed the American Unity Labor Union," for we could expect "fairness from no local." [78]

Aside from the possibility of Parker, however, were ministers, certain professional men, and other antiunion spokes-

---

Alschuler Hearings, June 21, 1919, 267–77; June 23, 1919, 508–10, 545, in RG 280, 33/864; Chicago Commission, *Negro in Chicago*, 427; Kate J. Adams, *Humanizing a Great Industry* (Chicago: [Armour?], *ca.* 1919), 21.

[78] R. E. Parker to President Harding, March 11, 1921, in RG 280, 170/1365; Parker to Harding, March 14, 1921; and to Secretary of Labor Davis, March 14, 1921, RG 174, 8/102-F; *Pittsburgh Courier*, March 22, 1917, copy in NAACP Papers (C-438); *Chicago Daily Tribune*, March 13, 1921; Chicago Commission, *Negro in Chicago*, 422–23; Spero and Harris, *Black Worker*, 272–73; *Chicago Defender*, February 3, 1917; Herbst, *Negro in Meat-Packing*, 35–36.

men in the black community witting instruments of the packers? Dr. George E. Haynes thought not. It was obvious, he reported after investigating the origins of the race riot, that certain black leaders were adamantly opposed to workers' unionizing, "but there was no evidence that could be obtained that they were influenced to these opinions or used as tools of the employers." Blacks, after all, felt that they had received fair treatment at the hands of Armour, Swift, Sears, and other industries and corporations. The "name of Armour," proclaimed the *Defender,* "has always been a sign of justice, so far as our Race is concerned." These industries hired black people and they contributed conspicuously to charities benefiting the race; in short, their record of friendship and concern, at least in Chicago, far surpassed that of organized labor.[79]

Above all, it was conflict between the white rank and file and their black counterparts that retarded unionization. Labor historians have wasted much energy debating the AFL's attitudes toward black workers, when the truly bitter, and functional, racial animosities were not at the national but at the shop level. Unions have too often directed their recriminations of antiunion blacks, rather than conceding their own inability to control the racial hatreds of white members. In few places was such conflict more pervasive than in the stockyards, where just a month before the race riot of 1919 there was a series of spontaneous walkouts, all racially inspired.

"We are paying the union and wearing the buttons," complained one white member, "and they are getting just as much." Other members echoed this resentment. "Fuck the Union," a black worker had reportedly told one of them. "I am making as much money as you are. What is the use of joining the Union?" Other grievances had to do with charges that black workers received preferential treatment, such as

[79] Haynes' memorandum to H. L. Kerwin, March 14, 1921, RG 280, 170/1365; *Chicago Defender,* July 6, 1918; S. Rogers, "Clearing the Jungle . . . ," *Outlook,* CXXVI (October 6, 1920), 230.

not being docked for reporting late or punished for stealing meat.[80] Overriding everything else, though, was the fact that, for the most part, black men and women in the stockyards were nonunion; and because of it, hundreds of white workers walked out in late June, vowing that they would not return until nonunion blacks were either fired or forced to wear the union button as members.

Black members as well as white accused certain black men who used abusive language and incited violence of being antiunion agitators. The only task of "Heavy" Williams, they said, was to bring new workers from the company employment office to the cattle killing floor, and "he brings up all non-union men and keeps the non-union men from joining the union." " 'Let me tell you,' " he would instruct the new men, " 'when they get after you about this union, don't you join it. . . . You stay out. If you don't you won't be here long.' " Williams also fought with whites, among them "Tubs," whom he threatened to "split open" with a meat cleaver. Williams had been a union member; so had Joseph Hodge, until a black friend of his had been hit over the head with a blunt instrument. Hodge continually cast such vicious and obscene slurs at the union that whites warned he would "agitate a race riot or perhaps . . . get killed." Another antiunion black stabbed a white man on the killing floor after damning the union and branding black union men "a lot of bastards," "a lot of white folks' niggers." [81]

Black workers frequently replaced striking whites in the stockyards that summer. In the hair house, for example, the all-white union of spinners struck, and blacks from various other departments were recruited to fill their jobs. Few whites in the yards could have been unaware of the strike, for, as one man reported, "at the noon hour these colored men are looking out of windows and doors, and these [white] men

[80] Alschuler Hearings, June 20, 114, 176–77, 180; June 21, 307, 389, in RG 280, 33/864.
[81] Ibid., June 20, 148–82; June 21, 220–40, 258–99; June 23, 426.

come out for lunch, and . . . it creates a dis-harmony and hard feelings among the races. . . ." It was also a fact, however, that sometimes blacks joining unions were also discharged.[82]

Organizers and black workers had difficulty communicating with each other, and this was a major cause of friction and of the black workers' unwillingness to unionize. Numerous floor stewards and union committeemen spoke English poorly, if at all. How, a non-English speaking Polish steward was asked by an interpreter, did he expect to explain the benefits of unions to black workers? He did not even try, he said, but there was a black committeeman who "talks the best way he can." Well, then, did he instruct the committeeman? "I don't tell him nothing," he replied. "They have got to get it for themselves." [83]

A black worker who did not "get it," however, would have "it made hot for him," with his "face pushed in" or bricks hurled at him. Frustration as well as racial bitterness provoked these acts of violence. "When I was coming in [to work]," recounted a black man, "six or seven or eight Polocks grabbed a colored fellow out there, and carried him on the [union] wagon, and said, 'you son-of-a-bitch, you will join the union,' and made him go up, and one had him by this arm, and the other by this arm, and one fellow had him by the neck. . . ." [84]

Union leaders claimed that there was no racism involved in this bitterness—that it was simply a labor matter. But it was obviously much more than that by late July 1919; the two issues were inseparably fused. The Irish, Polish, Lithuanian, and other workers who clashed with blacks in other spheres of human relations had their racial antagonisms reinforced if not initiated at the stockyards and in other industries. On the other hand, it could not have been comforting for a black

[82] *Ibid.,* June 20, 182–86; June 23, 525–30.
[83] *Ibid.,* June 20, 103–4.
[84] *Ibid.,* June 21, 241, 320–22; June 23, 476–78.

worker to pick up a copy of the latest Chicago *Labor News* and read about the "patriotism" of the Ragen Colts, who were having a "May Day party." "If you want a real good time, go Saturday evening to Dreamland." [85] Had a black attended, he no doubt would have had his skull cracked. Moreover, labor in Chicago in 1919 was possessed of an intense class consciousness; anyone who was not with it was against it—and the black workers were notoriously not with it. The hostility was so intense that, as in 1905, hatred of black scabs could be generalized into hatred of an entire race.[86] The factors retarding unionization—the black people's distrust of unions and white workers, the economic advantages to be accrued as nonunion workers, the manipulation of black workers by management, and, above all, the hatred of black workers by whites arising from racial antipathy and conditioned by strikebreaking and other antiunion acts—left a long legacy of violence and helped produce the bloody 1919 race riot.

[85] *Chicago Labor News* ("Official Organ, Chicago Trades Union Label League"), May 2, 1919.
[86] Alschuler Hearings, June 20, 83–92, 92–94, 131, RG 280, 33/864.

Contested Neighborhoods
and Bombings

THE EIGHTEENTH BIRTHDAY PARTY given by Mrs. Richard B. Harrison in honor of her daughter," the *Chicago Defender* reported in the late autumn of 1918, was "one of the social events of the season among the younger smart set. . . ." Held at Ogden Grove pavilion, the party featured an orchestra and a grand march. A half-year later, however, in May 1919, there was sadness in the Harrison family, as the front porch of their house on Grand Boulevard lay smoking in ruins, its windows shattered, the victim of a bombing.[1]

Best known for his role of "de Lawd" in *The Green Pastures* in the 1930's, Richard B. Harrison was a black actor whose forte in 1919 was Shakespeare and readings from the poetry of Paul Laurence Dunbar. During World War I he was frequently on the road entertaining, part of the time at Liberty

[1] *Chicago Defender,* November 23, 1918.

157

Loan rallies, and as a result his family was alone in the new house he and his wife had purchased. Mrs. Harrison heard rumors shortly after moving to Grand Boulevard in March that the "colored lady's house would be bombed." Warned by a black janitor that there was a plot to destroy her home, Mrs. Harrison telephoned the police, who casually rebuffed her and characterized her fears as "idle talk." The following evening, a Saturday, the bomber struck. At 11 o'clock, a Yellow Cab pulled up to the curb in front of the Harrison house, the door sprang open, and a man jumped out and ran to the front porch. There he deposited a package before dashing back to the taxicab. An explosion rocked the house just minutes after the taxicab sped away. Anger swept the black community. "This recent explosion could have been easily prevented by the police," exclaimed the *Defender*. But not only did the police seem to be uninterested in protecting the property of blacks; they appeared to the newspaper to have been "giving aid and comfort to a certain element of violators of the law." The police belatedly detailed a squad to protect the family, but the very next night the bombers lobbed explosives from a vacant flat next door onto the roof of the Harrison house. The skylight was destroyed and more windows were shattered. Someone had unlocked the flat to admit the bombers and had locked it afterward, but the police did not question the occupants of the adjacent building or those leaving it after the explosion. "Neighbors Planned Bombing," charged the *Defender*. "The people in the block appeared to have information as to the exact time the explosion would occur." [2]

Nor was this the end of the story. The Harrisons had bought the property from a white realtor, William B. Austin,

[2] *Ibid.*, May 24, 31, June 21, 1919; Arna Bontemps and Jack Conroy, *Anyplace But Here* (N.Y.: Hill and Wang, 1966), 175–76; Chicago Commission on Race Relations, *The Negro in Chicago* (Chicago: University of Chicago Press, 1922), 128–29; *Chicago Daily Journal*, June 17, 1919; *Chicago Herald-Examiner*, June 17, 1919; Richard Bardolph, *The Negro Vanguard* (N.Y.: Vintage Books, 1959), 241, 242–243.

a man who apparently was sympathetic to giving blacks and whites equal access to adequate housing. Anonymous letters began to arrive in Austin's mail after the two bombings, assuring him that police guards would be useless and promising that the bombing campaign had only commenced. The Harrisons moved from Grand Boulevard in mid-June 1919, just a couple weeks after "a man on a bicycle" had ridden by Austin's Lake Shore Drive home and hurled a bomb at it on the way past.[3]

The Harrison and Austin bombings were not isolated occurrences. From July 1917 to the eruption of the Chicago race riot in late July 1919, no fewer than twenty-six bombs were exploded at isolated black residences in once all-white neighborhoods and at the offices of certain realtors who had sold to blacks. Over half of these bombs were exploded during the tense six months leading up to the riot.[4] According to the virulent denunciations by the black press of both the bombers and the police who failed to apprehend them, the single most important cause of the riot was housing. Out of the interracial conflict over housing there arose in the black community a marked lack of faith in the willingness and ability of the police to provide impartial protection. This sentiment, in some cases based on actualities and in others unfounded, led blacks to depend more and more on their own resources for protection. Furthermore, participation in the war, a recently realized and potent political voice in Chicago's affairs, and the self-respect of a courted wage earner had kindled a "New Negro" attitude. The "New Negro" was resolved to defend his family and home with militance.

[3] *Chicago Broad Ax,* June 22, 1918; clipping from *Chicago Post,* June 20, 1919, in NAACP Papers, in possession of NAACP's Middle Atlantic Youth Division, Washington, D.C. (NAACP-2).

[4] Figures and dates of the bombings vary, but see Interchurch World Movement, *The Inter-Racial Situation in Chicago* (no imprint); list of bombings in NAACP-2; Chicago Crime Commission, *Illinois Crime Survey,* part three (Chicago: Illinois Association for Criminal Justice, 1929), 958–59; Chicago Commission, *Negro in Chicago,* 115 ff., 596.

The housing crisis also stimulated the formation of property owners' associations avowedly hostile to blacks. The threats of these organizations and the bombings accentuated the blacks' racial solidarity, thus retarding even further the possibility of interracial accord through mutual interchange.

It is ironic, in light of the strident contention of numerous white property owners that blacks were alien to Chicago's institutions, that the city's first resident was apparently Jean Baptiste Point du Saible, a San Dominican Negro who built a trading post at the mouth of the Chicago River in 1779 and lived there for sixteen years. Despite this beginning, only a few blacks trickled into Chicago before the Civil War, largely because of laws excluding blacks, slave and free, from the state. From 1860 to 1870, however, Chicago's black population rose 285 per cent, although nationwide the race's increase was 9.9 per cent. Most of the new arrivals obtained domestic employment; and, although there was no one black settlement, concentrations of black servants evolved in vicinities near their wealthy white employers. After the Great Fire of 1871, a second fire in 1874, and the dispersal of blacks as well as whites to the undamaged areas, the concentration of blacks and their social institutions on the South Side took vague shape. Chicago was expanding with such rapidity after 1870 that the black influx, though large, little more than kept pace with the flood of white immigrants. New residential districts emerged, but, as these were often segregated, the black arrivals gravitated to their increasingly dense settlements, especially the major concentration on the South Side. Although at the turn of the century blacks' residences were scattered throughout the city, a black man studying in Chicago reported that "no large Northern city shows a greater degree of segregation." [5]

[5] Thomas A. Meehan, "Jean Baptiste Point du Saible, the First Chicagoan," *Mid-America*, XIX (April 1937), 83–92; R. R. Wright, Jr., "The Negro in Chicago," *Southern Workman*, XXXV (October 1906), 554, 557; E. Franklin Frazier, *The Negro Family in Chicago* (Chicago: University of Chicago Press, 1932), 90–97; Robert C.

As evidenced by several incidents in the 1890's and the first few years of the twentieth century, the most effective enforcer of residential segregation in Chicago was organized white resistance. In 1897, for example, Woodlawn property owners met and "declared war" against the small colony of blacks living in the neighborhood. Owners who rented to blacks were angrily denounced as "enemies" who "should be tarred and feathered." Intimidated by threats of violence, blacks often chose to move. Five years later, whites in Woodlawn succeeded in having construction terminated on an apartment house that was being remodeled for black occupancy. Celia Parker Woolley, the founder of a black settlement house, noted at this time that she could not obtain property for the venture. Realtors "were not averse to Negroes living on the premises if they were servants," she reported, "but so soon as they heard that the Negroes were to be considered on a par with white people they refused to lease the property." [6]

By 1906, well over one half of Chicago's black people lived in the South Side black belt, between 12th and 57th Streets, and Wentworth and Cottage Grove Avenues. And while blacks, as one of their leaders wrote in 1905, did "not occupy all the worst streets and live in all the unsanitary houses in Chicago, what is known as the 'Black Belt' is alto-

---

Weaver, *The Negro Ghetto* (N.Y.: Harcourt, Brace, 1948), 14–18; Monroe Work, "Negro Real Estate Holders in Chicago" (unpublished M.A. thesis, University of Chicago, 1903), *passim;* R. R. Wright, "The Industrial Condition of Negroes in Chicago" (unpublished D.B. thesis, University of Chicago, 1901), 7–10; Bessie Louise Pierce, *A History of Chicago* (3 vols., N.Y.: Knopf, 1937, 1940, 1957), I, 186, 413–18; II, 11–12, 33–34, 382–83; III, 480.

[6] Memoranda in "Negro in Illinois" WPA Collection, files in the George Cleveland Hall Branch, Chicago Public Library, quoting from *Chicago Record,* May 5, 1897; and from *Chicago Inter-Ocean,* September 28, 30, 1894; August 19, 1900; February 12, July 25, 1902; December 15, 1904; Allan H. Spear, *Black Chicago: The Making of a Negro Ghetto, 1890–1920* (Chicago: University of Chicago Press, 1967), 21–23; Homer Hoyt, *100 Years of Land Values in Chicago, 1830–1933* (Chicago: University of Chicago Press, 1933), 215–16.

gether forbidding and demoralizing." The next largest settlement was on the West Side, and blacks had filtered into Englewood, the near North Side, and Hyde Park. Between 1906 and 1912, the black belt and satellite areas absorbed almost 10,000 new black residents; by 1912, many of these neighborhoods were saturated.[7] A. P. Comstock, a sociologist who surveyed housing conditions in 1912, particularly in the South Side enclave, outlined the debilitating effects of such human density. On the South Side, he reported, most buildings were of the pre-1902 vintage, that is, before the city ordinances governing the construction of tenements had imposed specific, encompassing restrictions on builders. More toilets were outside the apartments than were inside; they were in hallways, yards, and basements, and included some "privy vaults" which the city had outlawed in 1894. Sleeping rooms were overcrowded, usually because black tenants paying appreciably higher rents than whites took in lodgers to compensate for the differential. Outside stairways and porches were falling apart, and lighting and ventilation were inadequate. The residents complained to Comstock that since black quarters were nearly always tenantable the landlords refused to make necessary repairs. Other social investigators corroborated his findings. "In no other part" of the city, wrote S. P. Breckenridge of the University of Chicago, "was there found a neighborhood so conspicuously dilapidated as the black belt on the South Side. No other group," she added, "suffered so much from decaying buildings, leaking roofs, doors without hinges, broken windows, insanitary plumbing, rotting floors, and a general lack of repairs." This was the

[7] Fannie Barrier Williams, "Social Bonds in the 'Black Belt' of Chicago," *Charities,* XV (October 7, 1905), 40–44; David A. Wallace, "Residential Concentration of Negroes in Chicago" (unpublished Ph.D. dissertation, Harvard University, 1953), 67–69. At the time of the migration, the great majority of blacks still lived in an island between 22nd and 39th Streets and Wentworth Avenue, with scattered settlements to Cottage Grove Avenue. Thus the black belt, as it existed in 1906, absorbed most of the 10,000 blacks without bringing new residential areas into existence.

deplorable state of black housing in 1912, several years before the migration more than doubled the city's black population.[8]

As the migration increased during the war, the disquieting aspects of the housing situation likewise multiplied. Between 1910 and 1920 the expansion of the areas of black residence was negligible, migration resulting instead in the drastically intensified density of the existing areas. On the South Side, for example, the black community almost tripled, rising from 34,335 to 92,501, which was close to 90 per cent of Chicago's black population. None of Chicago's blacks in 1910 had lived in a census tract that was more than 75 per cent Negro; in 1920, 35.7 per cent of the black population did. Only 30.8 per cent in 1910 had lived in one that was more than 50 per cent Negro; in 1920, 50.5 per cent did.[9] Rents soared, moreover, since the demand for housing in the black belt far ex-

[8] Alzada Comstock, "Chicago Housing Conditions, VI: The Problems of the Negro," *American Journal of Sociology*, XVIII (September 1912), 241–57; S. P. Breckenridge, "The Color Line in the Housing Problem," *Survey*, XXIX (February 1, 1913), 575–76; Breckenridge and Edith Abbott, *The Delinquent Child and the Home* (N.Y.: Charities Publication Committee, 1912), 153; *The Colored People of Chicago*, text by Louise de Koven Bowen (Chicago: Juvenile Protective Association, 1913), I, 10–12, 14–16; T. Arnold Hill, "Housing for the Negro Wage Earner," in *Housing Problems in America, 1917* (N.Y.: National Housing Association, ca. 1917), VI, 309–13; Charles S. Duke, *The Housing Situation and the Colored People of Chicago* . . . (Chicago: n. pub., 1919), 8–9; Spear, *Black Chicago*, 23–26, 147–50.

[9] Otis D. and Beverly Duncan, *Negro Population of Chicago* (Chicago: University of Chicago Press, 1957), 92–93; Chicago Commission, *Negro in Chicago*, 106–7. The density in the black belt was more than twice that of white areas; T. J. Woofter, Jr., *Negro Problems in Cities* (N.Y.: Doubleday, Doran & Co., 1928), 79. See also Karl E. and Alma F. Taeuber, *Negroes in Cities: Residential Segregation and Neighborhood Change* (Chicago: Aldine Publishing Company, 1965), 53–54; Paul F. Cressey, "The Succession of Cultural Groups in Chicago" (unpublished Ph.D. dissertation, University of Chicago, 1930), 92–93; Wallace, "Concentration of Negroes in Chicago," 67–69, 408–11; Stanley Lieberson, *Ethnic Patterns in American Cities* (N.Y.: Free Press, 1963), 122; Ernest W. Burgess and Charles Newcomb, *Census Data of the City of Chicago, 1920* (Chicago: University of Chicago Press, 1931), *passim*.

ceeded the supply. As before, rents for blacks were 15 to 25 per cent higher than they were for whites, prompting the *Defender* to protest that "the principal idea . . . of some of these rent vampires is to gouge, gouge, gouge. . . ." [10] In addition to the excessive rents levied by black and white landlords alike, the migration accentuated both the overcrowding and the shabbiness of the facilities; and with lines of migrants waiting to occupy any vacancy, few landlords felt obligated to maintain their buildings in a decent state of repair.

Numerous blacks naturally wanted to escape these surroundings. The black belt was dilapidated, decaying, and overcrowded, and its landlords were obdurate in their refusal to make needed repairs. It was also a breeder of disease and the city's officially sanctioned receptacle for vice. Chicago's medical authorities boasted of the city's low death rate, pointing to statistics which indicated that it was the lowest of any city in the world with a population of over one million. Their statistics told another story as well, however, and it was that Chicago's blacks had a death rate which was twice that of whites. The stillbirth rate was also twice as high; the death rate from tuberculosis and syphilis was six times as high; and from pneumonia and nephritis it was well over three times as high. The death rate for the entire city was indeed commendable, but the statistics indicated that the death rate for Chicago's blacks was comparable to that of Bombay, India.[11]

[10] There is a plethora of evidence on the differential in the rents of whites and blacks: Graham Taylor, "Chicago in the Nation's Race Strife," *Survey*, XLII (August 9, 1919), 696; Leila Houghteling, *The Income and Standard of Living of Unskilled Laborers in Chicago* (Chicago: University of Chicago Press, 1927), 112; "Chicago's Negro Problem," City Club of Chicago *Bulletin*, XII (March 17, 1919), 75; Woofter, *Negro Problems*, 126–27; Elizabeth Hughes, *Living Conditions for Small Wage Earners in Chicago* (Chicago: Department of Public Welfare, 1925), 33; *Chicago Defender*, May 4, 1918; Work, "Negro Real Estate Holders," 29–31.

[11] These figures are from the 1925 Health Department records, but all data indicate that the health of blacks was no better and perhaps even worse in 1919: H. L. Harris, "Negro Mortality Rates in Chicago," *Social Service Review*, I (March 1927), 58–77.

Vice and crime, which were controlled by men of both races, proliferated in the black belt. Such infamous operators as "Teenan" Jones, "Red Dick" Wilson, "Yellow Bill" Bass, "Mexican Frank," Billy Lewis, and Isadore Levin conducted their lurid businesses apparently without restraint before the migration; and, if anything, vice did not abate in the black belt during the war and in 1919. Guides to Chicago's night life boasted of the city's "black-and-tan cabarets," establishments like The Pekin, The Entertainers, Dreamland, and The Panama, where "promiscuous dancing and the intermingling of the races may be observed . . . freely." Reformers, on the other hand, castigated these biracial houses of amusement, bemoaning that "the patrons were Negroes and whites who danced together in a most immoral way." Whether friend or foe of this entertainment, there was no denying the abundance in the black belt of houses of prostitution, saloons, cabarets, billiard rooms, and gambling establishments.[12] Crime, petty and felonious, also abounded. Boys would steal lead pipe and other salvageable items from vacant houses and then sell them to junk dealers. Other crimes like murder, assault and battery, and arson, however, were vicious, and the incidence of felonies in the black belt spiraled during the migration.[13]

[12] Illinois General Assembly, Senate Committee on Vice, *Report, 1916* (n.pl.pub.: n.pub., 1916), *passim;* Junius Wood, *The Negro in Chicago* (Chicago: Chicago Daily News, *ca.* 1916), 25–28, 29–30; Carl Sandburg, *The Chicago Race Riots* (N.Y.: Harcourt, Brace & Howe, 1919), 59–61; Walter Reckless, *Vice in Chicago* (Chicago: University of Chicago Press, 1933), 25–30, 192–95; Louise de Koven Bowen, *The Road to Destruction Made Easy in Chicago* (Chicago: Juvenile Protective Association, 1916), *passim; Clason's Wise Owl Guide to Chicago by Day and Night* (Chicago: Clason's Map Company, 1920), 20; Vice Commission of Chicago, *The Social Evil in Chicago* . . . (Chicago: Gunthrop-Warren, 1911), 38–39; Herbert Asbury, *Gem of the Prairie: An Informal History of the Chicago Underworld* (N.Y.: Knopf, 1940), 275, 306–11; *Illinois Crime Survey,* 847, 852–56.

[13] National Committee on Law Observance and Enforcement, *Report on Crime and the Foreign Born* (Washington: Government Printing Office, 1931), X, 112–15; *Illinois Crime Survey,* 667.

Whether this aggressive and disruptive behavior was a function of overcrowding, or social disorganization, or despair, or perhaps of combinations of all these, the net result was the same: the desire of countless blacks to move away and leave the black belt far behind. Despite a natural ethnic preference to reside near familiar social, economic, and religious institutions, numerous blacks with the financial resources sought sanitary, adequately maintained homes elsewhere.[14] In addition, vacancies in the black belt were practically nonexistent. In the spring of 1917, the Chicago Urban League, which met many of the migrants at the train station and was more instrumental in securing homes for them than any other agency, noted sadly: "It is impossible to do much else short of the construction of apartments for families and for single men." That summer, the Urban League canvassed the real estate dealers who supplied dwellings to blacks to ascertain the seriousness of the shortage. The dealers replied that of 664 black applicants, they were able to assist only fifty. Since the migrants ordinarily could not afford to move into white neighborhoods, and since they were probably apprehensive of direct social contacts with whites, it seems apparent that those who sought to leave the black belt behind them were generally the city's earlier and more prosperous black residents. In a sense, the migrant, whom the more established residents felt to be an undesirable neighbor, and with whom they increasingly identified such distasteful traits as prostitution, gambling, juvenile delinquency, and illegitimacy, was forcing the old settlers out, just as the latter's "invasions" of white neighborhoods would subsequently encourage whites to move.[15]

[14] See the suggestive essay by George M. Carstairs in National Commission on the Causes and Prevention of Violence, *Violence in America,* prepared under the direction of Hugh Davis Graham and Ted Robert Gurr (N.Y.: Signet edition, 1969), 730–42; George E. Haynes, "Conditions among Negroes in the Cities," *Annals,* XLIX (September 1913), 109; Woofter, *Negro Problems,* 77.

[15] E. Franklin Frazier, "The Impact of Urban Civilization upon Negro Family Life," *American Sociological Review,* II (October

The directions in which the black belt could expand were few; it was in "the zone of transition—the interstitial region between residence and industry." [16] To the north were many of the city's light factories and businesses. Although the district was rundown, prices were far beyond the reach of the ordinary househunter because of the industrial potential of the property. To the west, across Wentworth Avenue, were the Irish, whose hostility excluded blacks from that market. This hostility was so intense that the population in one Irish-dominated neighborhood bordering on Wentworth would tolerate only twenty-nine blacks out of 3,762 residents, while in the neighborhood just on the other side of Wentworth, 1,722 out of 3,711 residents were black.[17] To the east the blacks could move into the limited area between Wabash Avenue and Lake Michigan. But as soon as they occupied this, the only direction for sizable expansion was southward—to the neighborhood of Hyde Park and Kenwood.[18]

Being immediately adjacent to the black belt, Hyde Park

1937), 609–18; Chicago League on Urban Conditions among Negroes, *Annual Report,* I (no imprint), 10; Emmett J. Scott, *Negro Migration during the War* (N.Y.: Oxford University Press, 1920), 105; George E. Haynes, "Negro Moves North," *Survey,* XLI (January 4, 1919), 459.

[16] Ernest W. Burgess, "Residential Segregation in American Cities," *Annals,* CXL (November 1928), 108.

[17] *Ibid.,* 111–12. Burgess asserted that "no instance has been noted in the literature where a Negro invasion succeeded in displacing the Irish in possession of a community." See also Burgess and Newcomb, *Chicago Census Data, 1920,* 507, 523; Duke, *Housing Situation and Colored People in Chicago,* 10; Irene J. Graham, "Family Support and Dependency among Chicago Negroes . . . ," *Social Service Review,* III (December 1929), 541–62.

[18] At this time, the Irish were also expanding south, along Halsted Street, which was parallel to and only narrowly separated from the black expansion. Thus the blacks were not able to execute an end run around the Irish southern flank. Some migrants settled in deteriorating neighborhoods in the near North and West Sides: Harvey W. Zorbaugh, *The Gold Coast and the Slum . . .* (Chicago: University of Chicago Press, 1929), 38, 147–49. Also, about 1,000 blacks lived in Robbins, an all-black town incorporated in 1917, near the Calumet area: undated article by Carl Sandburg, "Colored Folk Rule Cook County Town," in Papers of the Chicago Commission on Race Relations, Illinois State Archives, Springfield, Illinois.

was the inevitable destination of numerous blacks. Also important, Hyde Park was a deteriorating neighborhood, one whose homes blacks could afford. Of the over 900 black property owners there in 1920, scarcely ten could have purchased their properties at the original prices. For twenty to thirty years property values had declined because of the odors of the stockyards, the smoke and soot of the Illinois Central trains, the conversion of large homes into apartment buildings and flats, and the fear of an "invasion" of blacks from nearby areas. The residents of Hyde Park had moved away from the neighborhood to escape further depreciat   and in 1916, just as the migration from the South was gaining momentum, an estimated 25 per cent of the buildings in the district stood vacant. The earlier black inhabitants and the few migrants who brought money with them or united with others to purchase properties at the prevailing low prices streamed into Hyde Park to join the few blacks who had moved in earlier, almost unnoticed. Other blacks rented in the neighborhood. This process of expansion continued for nearly two years.[19]

During the war residential construction largely ceased in Chicago as elsewhere. In the early months of 1918 the first effects of a housing shortage, which was soon to be acute, were felt. The demands of whites for dwellings began to exceed the supply. Ugly interracial competition for homes broke out, as enterprising realtors touched off artificial panics with rumors that the blacks were "invading," and then proceeded

[19] Howard R. Gold and Byron K. Armstrong, *A Preliminary Study of Inter-Racial Conditions in Chicago* (N.Y.: Home Missions Council, 1920), 7–8; Thomas W. Allison, "Population Movements in Chicago," *Journal of Social Forces,* II (May 1924), 529–33; Spear, *Black Chicago,* 145–46; Chicago Commission, *Negro in Chicago,* 117, 196–200, 205, 206, 211–13; Charles S. Johnson, *The Negro in American Civilization* (N.Y.: Henry Holt, 1930), 205.

The Chicago Commission defined the general neighborhood of Hyde Park–Kenwood as being from 39th to 59th Streets, and from State Street to Lake Michigan. Hyde Park and Kenwood were often lumped together as simply Hyde Park; to prevent confusion, the author has referred to them compositely as Hyde Park.

to buy the properties of whites at less than their values and to sell to blacks at sizable profits. Many whites soon blamed blacks for the perplexities of property values, the scarcity of housing, and urban decay.[20]

Although blacks seemed to blight the neighborhoods they inhabited, these neighborhoods were generally run-down before their arrival. It was natural, moreover, that black tenants should exhibit a lack of respect for properties upon which their landlords bestowed few improvements, actually allowing them to deteriorate further. In addition, because of excessive rents and exclusion from adjoining vicinities, blacks overcrowded both their abodes and their districts.

To be sure, the migrants were unaccustomed to city dwelling. During the sultry months they paraded without shirts or shoes; they hung their washing on stoops to dry; they loitered on street corners. But no one more fully appreciated the incompatibility between this behavior and the higher aspirations of the race than other blacks. The *Defender,* the black belt's aldermen, churches, and the Wabash Avenue YMCA and other social service agencies staged such events as Clean Up and Grass Seed Weeks in 1918, and a Tin Can Day and Health Week in 1919. Saturday, April 26, was Tin Can Day, and hundreds of boys and girls combed the alleys and back yards. "Old trunks, suitcases, tubs, baby carriages, push carts, and wagons were commandeered for hauling cans," the *Defender* reported. Five dollars in gold was the prize, and the minimum entry was 300 cans. This minimum figure, as it

[20] In 1916, the city issued 8,082 building permits; in 1918, 1,408. *Chicago Daily News,* June 3, 1919; Hugh Reid to Assistant Secretary of Labor, April 24, 1918, Records of Federal Mediation and Conciliation Service (RG 280), 33/1271, Suitland, Maryland; Edith Abbott, *The Tenements of Chicago, 1908–1935* (Chicago: University of Chicago Press, 1936), 272–74; Hughes, *Living Conditions,* 7, 9, 14–15, 26–30; *Abendpost,* March 24, 1919, in Foreign Language Press Survey, University of Chicago Library; Frank A. Randall, *History of the Development of Building Construction in Chicago* (Urbana: University of Illinois Press, 1949), 294, 299; *Housing Problems in America, 1919,* VII, 370–71.

turned out, was superfluous, for the winning entry was 6,840 cans, and altogether 100,587 were turned in.[21] The *Defender* featured a column entitled "Neighborhood Improvements," and the Urban League issued to the migrants a "creed of cleanliness," which sought to appeal to the blacks' national pride. "I AM AN AMERICAN CITIZEN," the creed proclaimed. "I AM PROUD of our boys 'over there' who have contributed soldier service." These soldiers had learned "NEW HABITS OF SELF-RESPECT AND CLEANLINESS," habits which the migrants then vowed to observe for themselves. "I WILL ATTEND to the neatness of my personal appearance on the street or when sitting in front doorways. I WILL REFRAIN from wearing dust caps, bungalow aprons, house clothing and bedroom shoes out of doors. I WILL ARRANGE MY TOILET within doors. . . . I WILL INSIST upon the use of rear entrances for coal dealers, hucksters, etc. . . . I WILL DO MY BEST to prevent defacement of property either by children or adults." Two photographs accompanied the creed, one of a slovenly front porch strewn with articles of clothing, the other of a clean, well-policed front porch. Seated on the first porch were three women in houserobes and kerchiefs, one of whom peeled potatoes while the second combed the third's hair. The four women on the other porch entertained themselves by reading and engaging in polite conversation; they were neatly dressed, all with their buttons buttoned and without kerchiefs on their heads. These efforts at neighborhood and personal improvement persevered despite the steady influx of migrants and the sustained demand for dwellings even approaching habitability. But for many if not most of the migrants, the adjustment to their new status as citizens of the North proved to be herculean. "During their period of absorption into the new life," Walter F. White of the NAACP wrote after the

---

[21] "Elements in the South Side Problem," undated memorandum in NAACP-2; *Chicago Defender,* April 12, 19, 26, May 3, 17, 1919; *Chicago Broad Ax,* June 14, 1918.

riot, many of the migrants tended to be "care-free, at times irresponsible, and sometimes even boisterous," and this "conduct caused complications difficult to adjust." [22]

Several white property owners' associations, most of which had organized initially for responsible community projects and beautification, now focused their efforts on forcing out the blacks already residing in their neighborhoods and on insuring that no others entered. The activities of these associations were conspicuous in the contested districts lying between 39th and 59th Streets, and State Street and Lake Michigan, and they consisted both of mass meetings to arouse the neighborhood residents against the blacks and of the publication in white journals of scathing denunciations of the race. Organized in September 1917, for example, was the Community Property Owners' Protective Association, with its constituency being the district bounded by 39th and 51st Streets, and Cottage Grove and Michigan Boulevard. Its purpose was "keeping 'undesirables' out." "We don't want any gentlemen of color or gentlemen off color in our midst," declared one of the association's organizers, a local realtor.[23]

From early 1917 the property owners' associations and most realtors attempted to restrict the blacks to the black belt. In April 1917, a committee of seven representing the Chicago Real Estate Board, including four realtors in contested neighborhoods, estimated that the "promiscuous sales" to blacks of residences on all-white blocks had brought about immense property depreciation ranging from $5,000 to $360,-000 per block. The committee recommended two courses of action to stop the alleged decline in values.[24] It first of all

[22] National Urban League, "An Idea Made Practical . . . Annual Report, 1919," National Urban League *Bulletin*, IX (January 1920), 20–21; Walter F. White, "Chicago and Its Eight Reasons," *Crisis*, XVIII (October 1919), 293–94.

[23] *Chicago Defender*, September 22, 1917.

[24] On the subject of race and depreciation in Chicago, see Hoyt, *100 Years of Land Values in Chicago*, 97, 124, 312–17; Burgess, "Residential Segregation," 113–14; *Chicago Daily Tribune*, May 10, 1919; "The Housing of Colored People," City Club of Chicago *Bul-*

urged the property owners' associations to build up the solidarity of their neighbors to assure that no more defectors would sell out to blacks. It then called for a meeting with the blacks to discuss the practicability of block-by-block segregation. The same month the Real Estate Board committee met with Jesse Binga, Chicago's leading black banker; Robert S. Abbott, editor of the *Defender*; A. L. Jackson of the Wabash Avenue YMCA, and other leaders of the race, and asked them to persuade the black realtors to "desist" from selling homes to their people in white neighborhoods. To this request the blacks refused. Several months later, the committee of white realtors adopted a resolution calling upon the Real Estate Board to prevent "race hatred, violence, and bloodshed" by appealing to the city council to enact legislation prohibiting further immigration of blacks to Chicago "until suitable provisions are made and such reasonable restriction of leasing or selling be enforced as to prevent lawlessness, destruction of values and property and loss of life." No such legislation received the consideration of the city council, but news of the realtors' appeal did serve to outrage leaders in the black community. "At this time," complained Binga loudly, "when the black men and the white men are asked to do their bit, it is nothing less than a crime . . . for real estate men . . . to begin an agitation on race segregation." Black men would hesitate to enlist in the army if they suspected that their wives and children would be "subject to designing promoters, who are conspiring to develop race hatred in their neighborhood. . . ." [25]

Two obstacles blocked the possibility of legislatively quarantining the blacks. In order for the Chicago City Council to enact zoning legislation, racial or otherwise, it first had to

---

letin, XII (August 18, 1919), 169–70; Egbert Schietinger, "Real Estate Transfers during Negro Invasion" (Unpublished M.A. thesis, University of Chicago, 1948), 4–5 ff.

[25] Chicago **Real Estate Board** *Bulletin,* XXV (April 18, May 15, October 15, November 21, 1917), 313–17, 355, 551, 623–24; *Chicago Defender,* April 14, 21, November 10, 1917.

obtain an enabling act from the Illinois General Assembly, which was dominated by representatives from southern Illinois whose antagonism for Chicago was renowned.[26] The second roadblock was a decision which the United States Supreme Court delivered in 1917. In *Buchanan* v. *Warley,* the court invalidated a Louisville, Kentucky, racial zoning ordinance.[27] As a direct result of this ruling, restrictive covenants came into being, but these efficacious instruments of segregation did not gain currency in Chicago until the mid-1920's.[28] Lacking the voluntary or legal means to isolate the blacks, whites resorted to extralegal or illegal methods—intimidation and bombs.

In November 1917, just days after the Supreme Court handed down the *Buchanan* v. *Warley* decision, the Chicago Real Estate Board reaffirmed the need of founding property owners' associations. The Board resolved to "start a propaganda through its individual members to recommend owners societies in every white block for the purpose of mutual defense." [29] Of these organizations, the Hyde Park–Kenwood Property Owners' Association, which first gained notice in the

[26] After many years of concerted lobbying by Chicago's realtors, the Illinois General Assembly passed an enabling act in late June 1919, which merely allowed the city of Chicago to prohibit the construction of factories in residential areas. It had no black opposition, and was backed by realtors and reformers alike: Illinois General Assembly, *Senate Debates, 1919* (Springfield: Illinois State Journal Co., 1920), 287–89, 312, 1179–80; *ibid., House Debates, 1919,* 716–17, 897–99.

[27] *Buchanan* v. *Warley,* 245 U. S. 60. See "Race Segregation Ordinance Invalid," *Harvard Law Review,* XXXI (January 1918), 475–79; Davis McEntire, *Residence and Race* (Berkeley: University of California Press, 1960), 258.

[28] As early as January 1920, the Hyde Park–Kenwood Association was excluding blacks through the "united action" of white property owners: *Chicago Daily Tribune,* January 10, 1920. By 1925, the bombings, which had plagued blacks and certain realtors, ceased when the restrictive covenants became, as a member of the Chicago Real Estate Board said, "like marvelous delicately woven chain armor . . . [excluding] any member of a race not caucasian": *Hyde Park Herald,* March 20, 1928. Between 1920 and 1930, the black population in Hyde Park–Kenwood even decreased: Duncans, *Negro Population of Chicago,* 96.

[29] Chicago Real Estate Board *Bulletin,* XXV (November 21, 1917), 624.

fall of 1918 for its agitation to "make Hyde Park white," was perhaps the largest and undoubtedly the most vocal. "WE want you to join our organization," began the organization's letter of solicitation. "Hyde Park is the finest residential district in Chicago," and in spite of "the weak-kneed [who] think it is too late . . . WE are going to keep it that way." Joining this "red-blooded organization," the letter continued, would put "big money in your pocket besides preserving our homes for ourselves and children." [30] The Hyde Park–Kenwood Association launched a series of protest meetings at which racial antagonism permeated the speeches, and at which the audiences applauded inflammatory utterances promoting the use of bombs and bullets. "The depreciation of our property . . . has been two hundred and fifty millions since the invasion," one of the association's speakers declared, adding in the spirit of World War I: "If someone told you that there was to be an invasion that would injure your homes to that extent, wouldn't you rise up as one man and one woman, and say as General Foch said, 'They shall not pass'?" The avowed purpose of the organization was the prevention of the alleged depreciation of property by blacks, although from the speeches and editorials it was apparent that the implication of an inferior status for whites residing near blacks grated on the members. The *Property Owners' Journal,* the organ of the Hyde Park–Kenwood Association, inevitably linked aspirations of social equality to the blacks' quest for better housing: "The effrontery and impudence that nurses a desire on the part of the Negro to choose a white as a marriage mate will not result in making the Negro a desirable neighbor. . . ." [31]

[30] In NAACP-2, "By Laws Kenwood Property Owner's [*sic*] Association"; letter from W. H. Schendorf to "Fellow Members," March 24, 1919; and copy of solicitation letter quoted in undated memorandum.
[31] Chicago Commission, *Negro in Chicago,* 118, 119, 590–92; Jesse Binga's article on the association in *Chicago Defender,* March 1, 1919; excerpts from letter from Hyde Park–Kenwood Association to Mayor Thompson, undated, NAACP-2.

As a solution to the black "invasion," bombing might have been viewed as a last resort, but it was attempted early. The first of the bombs arrived in July 1917, when one crashed into the vestibule of the home of Mrs. S. P. Motley near 53rd Street on the South Side. Mrs. Motley and her family had moved into the house in 1913, the first black family on the block, and they had lived there for four years before violence struck. She had purchased the property from a Mrs. Hughes, who, blacks charged, was a "nigger hater" and "an ardent supporter" of the Hyde Park–Kenwood Association. What seemed particularly to rankle Mrs. Hughes, in addition to her hatred of blacks, was that a white agent had negotiated the transaction for Mrs. Motley, and she had not discovered that blacks had been the buyers until the Motleys moved in. When several other black families joined the Motleys on the block in 1917, the white neighbors denounced Mrs. Motley for enticing them there and for operating a rooming house. Fortunately, the bomb claimed no victims, but a family residing in a first-floor flat barely escaped injury when the bomb was detonated, showering plaster, blowing out part of the parlor wall, and demolishing the vestibule and porch.[32]

After an eight-month hiatus, during which the black expansion continued, the bombers returned in earnest. From March 1918 to the outbreak of the riot, twenty-five bombs rocked the homes of blacks and the homes and offices of realtors of both races. Of the eleven bombings in 1918, four were of properties merely held by black real estate agents, while the other seven were of black-inhabited dwellings. Moreover, mobs brandishing brickbats and other weapons and missiles stoned buildings, and intimidation and threats of further violence burgeoned as well. "Look out; you're next for hell," read a "black hand notice." Another was addressed to the black tenants on Vincennes Avenue: "We are going to

[32] A. Clement MacNeal to John Shilladay, April 15, 1920, including four affidavits-case histories of bombings, in NAACP-2; *Chicago Defender,* July 7, 1917.

BLOW these FLATS TO HELL and if you don't want to go with them you had better move at once." [33]

Realtors persisted in commercializing racial antagonism in 1919. Panicky whites focused their wrath on the black race, and blacks, suffering increasingly from the police department's failure to discourage the bombers, viewed the whites with suspicion and made ready to defend their homes and families against further violence. During the first six months of 1919, the bombers struck on fourteen occasions, and one of their bombs killed a six-year-old black girl. In January, explosives damaged the offices of one white and one black realtor, and on March 20 two bombs exploded in the doorways of Jesse Binga's real estate office and an apartment building for which Binga was the agent. [34]

Early the next month explosives tore a gaping hole in the hallway of an apartment building in Hyde Park which a black, J. Yarbrough, had purchased from Binga scarcely three months before. The *Defender* intimated that Yarbrough's white neighbors knew of the bombers' plans, and were possibly conspirators. "It is strange . . . ," noted the newspaper, that even though "the explosion occurred at 2 A.M.," the whites on the block "were up and fully dressed and over to inspect the damage." Since any neighborhood explosion would no doubt rouse the nearby residents out of bed and into their clothes in less than ten minutes, the *Defender* betrayed an understandable bias in its indirect accusation. Yarbrough, however, agreed with the *Defender*'s suspicion, for he filed a $300,000 damage suit against the Hyde Park–Kenwood Association, citing by name four real estate

[33] *Chicago Defender,* May 11, 25, June 1, 8, 15, August 31, September 28, October 26, November 2, 1918; *Chicago Broad Ax,* May 25, 1918; Interchurch World Movement, *The Inter-Racial Situation in Chicago, passim;* Chicago Commission, *Negro in Chicago,* 31, 123–33, 536, 596.

[34] *Chicago Daily Journal,* March 20, 1919; *New York Age,* July 12, 1919; *Chicago Broad Ax,* June 7, 14, July 12, 1919; *Chicago Defender,* June 7, 21, 28, 1919; Bontemps and Conroy, *Anyplace But Here,* 176; Chicago Commission, *Negro in Chicago,* 539; list of bombings in NAACP-2.

Damage done by a bomb thrown into a building at 3365 Indiana Avenue, occupied by blacks. A six-year-old black child was killed.

brokers, including the president, the secretary, and a former secretary of the association. In filing the suit Yarbrough's attorney explained: "We believe the men who placed this bomb are in the employ of real estate men and that the purpose of their work is to frighten Negroes out of . . . the neighborhood." [35]

Possibly there was substance to Yarbrough's claims. The Chicago police arrested only two suspects in connection with the siege of bombings, one of whom was a clerk in the real estate firm of Dean and Meagher in Hyde Park. Both Dean and Meagher were members of the Hyde Park–Kenwood Association, and Dean put up bond for the suspected bomber. White homeowners and real estate dealers of the Hyde Park–Kenwood Association had earlier threatened to "bomb out" blacks residing there. In addition, although two other predominantly white neighborhoods in Chicago were in the "reaction" or conflict stage of residential transition, the agitation against the blacks where there was no Hyde Park–Kenwood Association was unorganized and assumed no more violent form than that of warning letters. As to motive, the association was dominated by realtors who held extensive property in Hyde Park and who affirmed unequivocally that blacks and property depreciation were synonymous. They endeavored, therefore, to preserve their interests by encouraging the blacks to move away and by discouraging any future influxes. Some residences were bombed just after the blacks purchased them, but months before occupancy and before the public learned of the sales; and probably only realtors, along with mortgage bankers, deed registrars, and the principals, could have known of these transactions. Finally, the waves of bombings ensued straightway after, and apparently as a result of, the association's virulent protests against black occupancy.[36]

[35] *Chicago Herald-Examiner*, April 7, July 13, 1919; *Chicago Daily Journal*, April 7, July 12, 1919; *Chicago Daily Tribune*, April 7, 1919; *Chicago Defender*, April 12, 1919.

[36] Walter F. White, "Notes on Chicago of WFW," September 17, 1919, in NAACP-2; Herbert J. Seligmann, *The Negro Faces America*

Whether or not the realtors of the Hyde Park–Kenwood Association conspired to bomb out the blacks, two facts were evident: that the bombings usually occurred shortly after the speakers at the association's meetings had denounced the blacks in vitriolic language (four bombs succeeded the organization's May 5 meeting); and that these denunciations were becoming decidedly more vitriolic in the summer of 1919.

"PREVENT FURTHER INCURSION BY UNDESIRABLES," proclaimed a poster announcing the June 6 meeting of the Hyde Park–Kenwood Association. No doubt the association would have been shocked to discover that blacks, among them the white-skinned, blue-eyed Walter F. White of the NAACP, had infiltrated the meetings, and that White would attend on June 6. White's descriptions of the meeting's "inflammatory and incendiary remarks" were corroborated by Mrs. Meta Harvey, a black who attended the June 20 and 27 gatherings. When she entered the June 20 meeting, which was convened at a bank, she heard the speaker outlining a plan for removing a black hospital from the South Side within the next two months. A voice from the floor interrupted to demand action, not talk; and there were other references to the need for "pep" in forcing the hospital's removal within thirty rather than sixty days. Mayor William H. Thompson and the city's health commissioner were castigated for "their favorable attitude" toward blacks and for "assenting to the location of the hospital where it was." Some voices urged caution, but their advice was ignored. Blacks had armed, said one man; they had bought 800 rifles and buckets full of ammunition at a local department store; there would be bloodshed "if they went at the matter the way they were talking about."

(N.Y.: Harper & Brothers, 1920), 214; *Chicago Daily Journal,* June 13, 1919; *Chicago Whip,* June 24, 1919; *Chicago Daily News,* June 13, 1919; Sandburg, *Chicago Race Riots,* 15–16; Chicago Commission, *Negro in Chicago,* 123, 130–31, 133; Burgess, "Residential Segregation," 112; *Chicago Daily Tribune,* May 10, 1919.

"Bloodshed, nothing!" another man shouted in anger. "Let them step on my corns and I'll show them what I'll do." "If we can't get them out any other way," agreed a voice in the rear, "we are going to put them in with the bolsheviki and bomb them out." Throughout the evening, speakers referred to blacks as "niggers" and "undesirables." One speaker told what he had done to three blacks "hanging around his place." He had put a "bolt" in his fist and knocked one down; "that's the way to treat the niggers," he added. The association's officers, practically all of whom were local realtors and officials of the Chicago Real Estate Board, reported that any real estate agent who did not refuse to rent or sell to blacks would be blacklisted; that block captains had been selected to report any attempts by blacks to move into the district; and, finally, that three hotels in the neighborhood had agreed to cooperate in a plan whereby black employees who did not consent to vacate their residences in the district would be discharged. With these announcements, the meeting was adjourned.[37]

And, in turn, blacks advocated arming themselves in the summer of 1919. The police's flagrant negligence and misperformance of duty had convinced them that they would have to provide their own protection against the property owners' associations and the bombers. Even when blacks reported bomb threats, and the police staked out the dwellings beforehand, no arrests were made after the outrages occurred. A delegation twice attempted to file a complaint with Mayor

[37] In NAACP-2, poster announcing June 6, 1919, meeting; notarized statement by Walter White, January 14, 1920; memorandum by J. R. Shilladay, executive secretary of the NAACP, on "Interview with Mrs. Meta Harvey on Kenwood and Hyde Park . . . Association meetings of June 20 and June 27, 1919," August 3, 1919; and regarding the Lake Park Hospital see *Chicago Defender*, April 19, 1919; *Chicago Broad Ax*, March 15, 22, 1919.

Chicago's white newspapers were split over the commendability of the Hyde Park–Kenwood Association's purposes. The *Herald-Examiner* of July 2, 1919, extolled both Booker T. Washington's 1895 Atlanta address and the association. The *Tribune* of June 30, 1919, felt that a "clash" might follow the association's activities.

Thompson in June 1919, but the mayor's secretary refused to permit the blacks to see him. The *Defender* expressed the consensus of the black community when it protested: "Police activity has been so deliberate and brazenly neglectful that one might construe that they are working in harmony with the bomb throwers." [38] The following week the *Defender* offered the only practicable solution it saw to such one-sided law enforcement when it asked: "Why do these things go on unchecked and the perpetrators not apprehended? . . . Something must be done, and something will be done. If we must protect ourselves we shall do it with a vengeance. . . . This is nature's first law." [39]

The *Whip* also espoused self-defense. A newspaper which commenced publication in the summer of 1919, the *Whip* voiced the attitude of the "New Negro," the militant, intensely race-conscious black who felt acutely the blighted hope of heightened status for the race after the war:

The *Whip* informs you, the whites, that the compromising peace-at-any-price Negro is rapidly passing into the scrap heap of yesterday and being supplanted by a fearless, intelligent Negro who recognizes no compromise but who demands absolute justice and fair play. . . . WE ARE NOT PACIFISTS, THEREFORE WE BELIEVE IN WAR, BUT ONLY WHEN ALL ORDERLY CIVIL PROCEDURE HAS BEEN EXHAUSTED AND THE POINTS IN QUESTION ARE JUSTIFIABLE. . . . THE BOMBERS WILL BE BOMBED.[40]

With the advent of summer the housing situation appeared still gloomier. The shortage in Chicago approached 50,000

[38] *Chicago Defender,* May 31, June 21, July 12, 1919; *Chicago Broad Ax,* June 7, July 12, 1919; *Chicago Daily News,* June 4, 1919.
[39] *Chicago Defender,* June 28, 1919.
[40] *Chicago Whip,* June 28, 1919.

apartments and houses, affecting upwards of 200,000 people. This, in turn, created boosts in rents from 10 to 30 and, in some cases, up to 100 per cent.[41] Returning servicemen aggravated the scarcity. Worse yet, expectations of an enormous summertime construction program to offset at least part of the dearth of dwellings disappeared in mid-July, when Chicago's contractors locked out 115,000 building tradesmen. The race bombings were an accurate gauge of the multiplying housing scarcity; seven explosions punctuated the six sultry weeks preceding the riot. This was the most extensive rash of bombings yet, and it underscored the blacks' distrust of the police and their need for solidarity.

The hostility of the fearful white residents, meanwhile, proceeded to fuse with antipathy to blacks in other spheres, thus creating a more nearly unbroken white front. The property owners' associations, for example, espoused the battle cry of those who denounced the blacks' political power. Undoubtedly reflecting upon the April 1919 mayoralty election, in which William Hale Thompson was reelected although he received only 38 per cent of the total vote, the *Property Owners' Journal* scathingly rebuked the blacks whose bloc support accounted for much of Thompson's plurality. "This vote situation," declared the *Journal,* "is the foundation of the Chicago Negro's effrontery and his evil design against the white man's property." Holding the balance of power, the black vote "can dictate the policy of any administration that happens to be elected by his controlling vote. . . . Wake up, white voters!" [42]

The apex of racial antagonism—the summer of 1919—facilitated the conjunction of varied elements antithetical to the blacks' aspirations. Although the clashes in the political province were less violent than were those for homes, the op-

[41] *Chicago Daily News,* June 3, July 24, 1919; Chicago Real Estate Board *Bulletin,* XXVII (September 25, 1919), 720; *Chicago Defender,* April 19, 1919; *New York Times,* July 25, 1919.
[42] Chicago Commission, *Negro in Chicago,* 591–92.

position was every bit as numerous; and, as in the housing warfare, the animosities engendered by political conflict were, for the most part, an outcrop of the wartime migration. The larger the black community became, the more insoluble appeared the problems.

Politics

THE BLACK BELT OF CHICAGO," Carl Sandburg observed in 1919, when he was a Chicago newspaper reporter, "is probably the strongest effective unit of political power, good or bad, in America." [1] During the years of World War I, Chicago's black vote had twice been decisive in mayoralty elections, and it had installed three black aldermen on the city council. Black people paid a high price for their victories, however, for in several significant ways politics was instrumental in precipitating and sustaining the Chicago race riot. The blacks' voting behavior aroused and reinforced the hostility and racial hatred of numerous groups, certain of which reacted violently. The mayoralty race of April 1919, less than four months before the outbreak of the riot, revived the racial issue as part of an extraordinarily partisan cam-

[1] Carl Sandburg, *The Chicago Race Riots* (N.Y.: Harcourt, Brace & Howe, 1919), 2.

paign. Black votes, in addition, placed in office irresponsible leaders of the race and corrupt white politicians, under whose auspices vice abounded in the black belt. Finally, political factionalism, especially within the Republican party, encumbered functionaries at the city, county, and state levels. The cooperation so necessary to quell the Chicago race riot simply was not forthcoming.

Although the appointment of a black man as town crier in 1837 launched the political history of the black people in Chicago, it was not until 1894 that the race's first effectual political boss emerged. In that year's mayoralty election, Edward H. Wright delivered a sizable vote from the First Ward to the Republican candidate. Wright's election as a county commissioner two years later established him as the most potent political leader of the black electorate. In 1904 the Republican caucus nominated Oscar DePriest, the black lieutenant of South Side boss Martin Madden, for a Third Ward aldermanic post. Although DePriest lost, he was later to be the race's first Chicago alderman and, in the late 1920's, the first black Congressman in the country in almost thirty years. Wright opposed a field of white candidates for the Second Ward's aldermanic vacancy in 1910, but he too was defeated.[2]

The year 1910 marked the beginning of a new history of the black people in politics in Chicago, for it introduced the decade in which the race became a powerful political voice in the city. In 1910, blacks constituted one fourth of the vote of the Second Ward, and the ward's shifting balance of population indicated that before long blacks would dominate its pol-

[2] Bessie Louise Pierce, *A History of Chicago* (N.Y.: Knopf, 1957), III, 48–50; Allan H. Spear, *Black Chicago: The Making of a Negro Ghetto, 1890–1920* (Chicago: University of Chicago Press, 1967), 118–23; Harold F. Gosnell, *Negro Politicians: The Rise of Negro Politics in Chicago* (Chicago: Phoenix Books of University of Chicago Press, 1967), 11–36, 73–74, 81–83, 153–70; Junius B. Wood, *The Negro in Chicago* (Chicago: Chicago Daily News, *ca.* 1916), 13–14; St. Clair Drake and Horace R. Cayton, *Black Metropolis* (N.Y.: Harper Torchbooks, 1962), I, 343–46.

itics. The Second Ward was deteriorating physically, impelling numerous whites to move out, and the black arrivals to the city were concurrently gravitating to that ward. By 1915, a majority of the ward was black, and in the elections of that year it made its political potency known.[3]

In the 1915 primaries, the Second Ward cast 8,633 votes for William Hale Thompson for the Republican mayoralty nomination while his opponent received but 1,870 votes. Thompson's citywide plurality was only 2,508; and it was apparent that "Big Bill's" popularity among the black voters of the Second Ward, his home ward, had provided the margin of victory. Because of a Democratic split, Thompson swept into office in April with the most impressive majority in the city's history. The Second Ward not only added to his total with 15,715 votes to his opponent's 6,345, it also elected Oscar DePriest its alderman to the city council, an event that excited emotions in the ward to "fever heat." For better or worse, the black belt had wedded its immediate political future to the fortunes of William Hale Thompson.[4]

Bill Thompson must be insane, wrote a disgusted reformer. Only insanity could account for the fact that he was "indolent, ignorant of public issues, inefficient and incompetent as an administrator, incapable of making a respectable argument, reckless in his campaign methods and electioneering oratory, inclined to think evil of those who are not in agreement or sympathy with him, and congenitally demagogical." Superpatriots such as Theodore Roosevelt and vocal members of the American Legion and National Security League branded him pro-German and a traitor. Pacifists and radical

[3] Bureau of the Census, *14th Census, 1920* (Washington: Government Printing Office, 1922), III, 274–76; Gosnell, *Negro Politicians,* 74–75.

[4] *Chicago Defender,* April 10, 1915, February 16, 1918; *Chicago Daily News,* July 28, 1919; *Chicago Broad Ax,* December 21, 1918; *New York Times,* April 7, 8, 1915; Harold Gosnell's compilations of election returns in Charles Merriam Papers, University of Chicago Library; Lloyd Wendt and Herman Kogan, *"Big Bill" of Chicago* (Indianapolis: Bobbs-Merrill, 1953), 167–69.

opponents of the war, on the other hand, while conceding that Thompson doubtless possessed limited intelligence, praised him for his open-mindedness and adherence to the guarantees of freedom of speech and assembly. Chicago's Catholics castigated him for being an antipapist. Women registered their disapproval of Thompson's corrupt administration by using their recently acquired franchise in Illinois to vote against him. The United Societies, organized by Anton Cermak and Slavic-American saloonkeepers, distillers, and brewers, marched in huge parades to protest the outrage perpetrated by Thompson when he closed the saloons on Sundays briefly in 1915. Chicago's blacks, however, proclaimed the mayor a second Abraham Lincoln, and predicted that his election to the presidency would herald a new emancipation for the race.

"Big Bill" was indeed a maverick, and one who evoked contradictory responses from different groups. Grandson of a drafter of Chicago's first charter, son of a Civil War hero and wealthy landowner, and inheritor of a substantial fortune as well as of a socially prestigious name in the city, Thompson ran away from home as a teenager rather than attend Yale University. His first job was as a brakeman on the Union Pacific, but he soon donned a cowboy hat and worked as a cook on a cattle ranch in Wyoming, and eventually he became the ranch foreman. Big of frame and with ample jowls that appeared even more ample when they bulged with a wad of tobacco, Thompson never ceased wearing a Stetson—and acting like a cowboy, his critics charged—even after he had to return to Chicago following his father's death. Back in the city, Thompson became interested in football, and, being big and burly, he won national acclaim in 1896 as captain and signal-caller of the championship Chicago Athletic Club team. Four years later he was elected Second Ward alderman.[5]

[5] See biographies of Thompson: Wendt and Kogan, *"Big Bill";* and John Bright, *Hizzoner Big Bill Thompson* (N.Y.: J. Cape & H. Smith, 1930); William H. Stuart, *The Twenty Incredible Years* (Chicago:

Thompson's courtship of the black vote also began in 1900. One of his principal supporters was the Reverend Archibald J. Carey, rector of Quinn African Methodist Episcopal Chapel; and one of his proudest accomplishments as alderman was his sponsorship of Chicago's first municipal playground, which was probably the first in the nation for blacks. Although Thompson was relatively inactive in elective politics in the decade after 1904, he was busy building his political machinery. He continued to exercise influence in the black belt, and by 1915 his political friends on the South Side included the *Chicago Defender,* several fraternal and military organizations, and leading black ministers, realtors, undertakers, insurance agents, and numerous professional men.[6]

For the blacks' overwhelming endorsement of Thompson, there are probably several answers. Above all, "Big Bill" was "right on 'the question' "; that is, he publicly sympathized with the race's aspirations and he recognized the black people by appointing them to political posts. "If you can convince him [the black voter] that you are right on 'the question,' " explained A. L. Jackson of the all-black Wabash Avenue YMCA, "there is hardly anything that you cannot do with him. That is the danger," Jackson added, "and it is also an opportunity if the right leadership can be had." [7] Moreover, the segregated black belt offered a compactness and solidarity that few communities could equal; it was thus easier for a politician, especially one with a flamboyant personality, to stir a large proportion of the voters. And Thompson was an

M. A. Donohue, 1935), 8–10; Lewis H. Hunt, "The Rise and Fall of Thompsonism," *Outlook,* CLVII (April 22, 1931), 562; Charles Merriam, *Chicago: A More Intimate View of Urban Politics* (N.Y.: Macmillan, 1929), 179, 185–90; V. Yarros, "Presenting Big Bill Thompson of Chicago," *Independent,* CXIX (November 5, 1927), 446–48; George C. Hoffman, "Big Bill Thompson of Chicago: His Mayoral Campaigns and Voting Strength" (unpublished M.A. thesis, University of Chicago, 1956), 1–3.

[6] Gosnell, *Negro Politicians,* 93–114, 238–43.

[7] A. L. Jackson, "Chicago's Negro Problem," City Club of Chicago *Bulletin,* XII (March 17, 1919), 76.

expert showman and a bombastic orator. He nearly always wooed his black audiences by denouncing his political foes as "crackers" and by praising heroes of the black race. Jack Johnson was a superb fighter and a "good man," he reminded his black audience at the Pekin Theater in his final speech of the 1915 campaign, and "only a good cowboy" like Willard could have defeated him. "Tomorrow the cowboy will be on your side: Bill Thompson is going to win for you at the polls." Thompson's opponents conceded his talents on the speaker's platform, but they did so normally to question his veracity. "Just before the primaries," complained Robert Sweitzer, his Democratic foe in 1915, "it was 'church, home, and Civil Service' when Mr. Thompson spoke at Hyde Park . . . while down in the First and Second Wards it was 'I am for prize fights and dice games and jobs for you colored boys.'" Thompson portrayed himself as an artless, persecuted defender of the downtrodden. While practically all white politicians were mute, "Big Bill" castigated *The Birth of a Nation* as an abomination and an insult to millions of American citizens. In addition, the fact that several Chicago newspapers, particularly the *Tribune,* seemed to denounce him and the black people in the same breath reinforced his popularity. Noting that Chicago's white press had "for the past few days failed to berate and belittle Mayor Thompson," the *Defender* asked: "What is the matter? Have they lost their pep, or do they feel they are bumping their heads against a brick wall?" To blacks, Thompson was the "angel of the underdog." Finally, the Reverend Carey, Oscar DePriest, Louis B. Anderson, and other black politicians, and George F. Harding, Fred Lundin, and Samuel Ettelson, Thompson's white associates in turning out the black vote, were seasoned bosses of racial and immigrant political blocs; and the 1915 election returns were tributes to their talent.[8]

[8] *Chicago Daily Tribune,* March 13, 1915; *Chicago Defender,* April 15, 1916; see copies of Thompson's personal political organ, *The Republican,* in Chicago Historical Society; *Chicago Defender,* May 1, 22,

Once elected, "Big Bill" did not slight his black supporters. His recognition of the race was immediate and unabashed; he appointed Edward H. Wright and Louis B. Anderson assistant corporation counsels, and he rewarded the Reverend Carey with an investigator's post in the law department. Black people were jubilant, especially after Thompson defended his appointments against the criticism of white Chicagoans: "I am glad to take the full responsibility and the honor for making every one of those appointments, and I want to ask my critics to be as manly and to come out in the open light of day with such un-American sentiments." [9]

In September 1915, at the Half Century Anniversary Exposition commemorating the black people's progress since the Civil War, at which Thompson was the honored guest, Archibald Carey rose to eulogize the mayor before the 22,000 blacks in attendance:

Whatever Mayor Thompson has done, whatever he will do, he will not do out of sympathy for the descendants of a race once enslaved, but for American citizens who have earned their position. By these appointments Mayor Thompson is merely recognizing the worth of a people.

There are three names which will stand high in American history—Abraham Lincoln, William McKinley, and William Hale Thompson.

William Hale Thompson may not be elected president in 1916, but I'm sure he will be in 1920. . . . I present to you . . . your friend and my friend, the biggest man in all Chicago, the biggest man in all Illinois, and the best mayor Chicago ever had—William Hale Thompson.

29, June 12, 1915, April 15, 1916, November 3, 1917; Stuart, *20 Incredible Years,* 14; Wendt and Kogan, *"Big Bill,"* 112; Gosnell, *Negro Politicians,* 37–62.
[9] *Chicago Defender,* July 17, August 7, September 18, 1915.

"Then the storm broke loose," wrote a *Defender* reporter. An elderly black lady, remembering a daily newspaper which after the election had renamed the city hall "Uncle Tom's Cabin," gleefully proclaimed, "if that's the cabin that boy there [Thompson] is one of Uncle Tom's sons in the cabin." [10]

The wartime migration more than doubled Thompson's strength in the black belt. The loyalty of blacks was patently to the Republican party, the party of Lincoln, emancipation, and fighters for equality like Charles Sumner and Thaddeus Stevens. The Democrats, on the other hand, were the "imps of Satan," the party of the "Solid South" and of "the Lynchman's noose and the torchman's fire." Upon the arrival of the migrants, Thompson's machine began to solicit their votes, and observers expressed their astonishment at how eagerly the blacks responded. Scholars who correlated election participation with education and economic status expected a small voter turnout from rural transplants who had had few if any opportunities to vote, who were unfamiliar with Northern racial mores and attitudes, and who often held menial and unskilled positions. To the migrants, however, the ballot box was a symbol of their freedom, and they were eager to exercise the franchise. Blacks wanted to prove their enemies wrong; they wanted to demonstrate that they could govern themselves with honesty and dignity. Robert E. Park, president of the Chicago Urban League, noted that even ward politics, which reformers held in contempt, "assumed at times a dignity and importance it would not otherwise have had because it has been associated with the Negro's struggle for fundamental civil and political rights." Moreover, black Chicagoans felt that politically the Second Ward was the capital of black America. The "whole country," boasted the *Defender*, "is looking for Chicago to be the one place that can be depended upon to send a [black] man to Congress to speak for

[10] *Ibid.*, September 18, 1915; *Chicago Broad Ax*, September 18, 1915.

them." The results of this enthusiasm and this feeling of responsibility were high voter turnout and political participation. In the Second Ward in 1920, for example, 72 per cent of the eligible blacks registered, compared to 66 per cent of the city's other citizens, and this vote was at least 10 per cent of that of all Chicago's registered Republicans. And proportionately there were more eligible blacks than whites in Chicago, for the migrants were generally in the prime of life; proportionately there were fewer black people arriving in Chicago who had not attained voting age than whites, and blacks, unlike foreign-born whites, arrived as American citizens. Thus, in 1920, blacks were 4.1 per cent of the city's population, but they were 6 per cent of its adult population. Also at that time, the black people were over 75 per cent of the Second Ward's vote, almost 30 per cent of the Third Ward's, and their votes were of decisive importance in close contests in the First, Sixth, Fourteenth, and Thirtieth Wards.[11]

"Thompson is a good advertiser," noted Victor F. Lawson, progressive Republican and editor of the *Chicago Daily News,* "but of bad wares." [12] And, indeed, in several ways, the mayor's actions represented a poor return for the black people's political investment in him. During his first term, Chicago's vice was resegregated in the black belt, and many whites south of the black belt feared, as a result, that immoral activities were a natural concomitant of black residential expansion. Prodded for years by reformers and social workers, Thompson's predecessor, Carter H. Harrison II, had finally

[11] Harold F. Gosnell, "The Chicago Black Belt as a Political Battleground," *American Journal of Sociology,* XXXIX (November 1933), 329–41; Gosnell, "How Negroes Vote in Chicago," *National Municipal Review,* XXII (May 1933), 238–43; *Chicago Defender,* January 5, February 16, May 11, 18, 1918; Gosnell, *Negro Politicians,* 15–37, 41n; Bureau of the Census, *14th Census,* III, 274–76; Robert E. Park, *Race and Culture* (Glencoe, Illinois: Free Press, 1950), 174; Charles Merriam and Harold Gosnell, *Non-Voting* (Chicago: University of Chicago Press, 1924), 139–41, 199–200.
[12] Victor F. Lawson, Chicago, to Arthur Brisbane, New York, March 13, 1919, Lawson Papers, Newberry Library, Chicago.

driven much of Chicago's vice outside the city limits, but under "Big Bill's" "wide-open town" policy most of the illicit activities filtered back and congregated in the black belt. Also during the first Thompson administration, the beer garden, revue, and public dance hall merged to form a notable Jazz Age institution, the "black-and-tan cabaret." [13] As a pacifying gesture to reformers, Thompson ordered saloons to close on Sundays, and he revoked the licenses of certain cabarets. But within weeks, the saloons were again bustling on the Sabbath; and when the indignation against the cabarets subsided, their licenses were quietly returned. One of the most infamous of the cabarets was the Panama Cafe, which the police force twice closed and reopened within six months.[14] For no apparent reason other than its efficiency, Thompson rendered impotent the police squad responsible for suppressing the city's depraved operations; "going reform" was not the key to promotion in the Chicago police department.[15] In 1918, the city council enacted anti-cabaret legislation which shut down the resorts; thereafter, cabarets could permit dancing but they

[13] Merriam, *Chicago*, 20–21; Louise C. Wade, *Graham Taylor: Pioneer for Social Justice, 1851–1938* (Chicago: University of Chicago Press, 1964), 197, 200–2; Herbert Asbury, *Gem of the Prairie: An Informal History of the Chicago Underworld* (N.Y.: Knopf, 1940), 243–47, 275, 289, 306–11; Lloyd Wendt and Herman Kogan, *Lords of the Levee* (Indianapolis: Bobbs-Merrill, 1943), 282–88.

[14] Walter Reckless, *Vice in Chicago* (Chicago: University of Chicago Press, 1933), 76–79, 84–85, 90–95, 101–3, 109–10, 192; *Chicago Herald-Examiner*, August 15, 1916; *Chicago Daily Tribune*, March 3, 1916; *Chicago Defender*, August 26, 1916; "Civic Issues in the Chicago Primaries," *Survey*, XXXV (March 18, 1916), 713; Wendt and Kogan, *"Big Bill,"* 127–32, 139, 143–48; "Murder, Politics and Vice in Chicago," *Survey*, XXXII (August 8, 1914), 476–77; Chicago Crime Commission, *Illinois Crime Survey*, part three (Chicago: Illinois Association for Criminal Justice, 1929), 847, 851–56, 890–92; Stuart, *20 Incredible Years*, 19–20; Virgil W. Peterson, *Barbarians in Our Midst: A History of Chicago Crime and Politics* (Boston: Little, Brown, 1952), 99.

[15] "Vice as a Nuisance," *Survey*, XLII (June 21, 1919), 464; Reckless, *Vice in Chicago*, 76–78; "Chicago 'The Cleanest City,'" *Survey*, XLI (November 9, 1918), 164; Citizens' Association of Chicago, *45th Annual Report, 1919* (no imprint), 6.

could sell only soft drinks to the dancers. Before the 1919 elections, however, the lid was lifted, the black-and-tans were reopened and were "ablaze with light," and the black belt was again the focus of the city's night life.[16] That there was a direct connection between the Thompson regime and vice in the black belt was incontrovertible. "Crime conditions among the colored people," declared the judge of Chicago's morals court, "are being deliberately fostered by the present city administration. . . . Disorderly cabarets, thieves, and depraved women are allowed in the section of the city where colored people live." And, he added, the black people were being "exploited" not just by whites but also "for the sake of men in politics who are a disgrace to their own race." [17]

Following the 1915 election, the Second Ward sent Louis B. Anderson to the city council to replace DePriest, and in 1918 it selected another black politician, R. R. Jackson, to join Anderson. Too often, though, black politicians proved to be poor representatives of the race's long-term interests. "The colored people have simply been sold out by the colored leaders," complained the black surgeon and former Progressive, Dr. George Cleveland Hall, in castigating the Second Ward aldermen. "Our leaders are in the hands of white politicians," even though what the black people most "need [are] representatives who are strictly representative, who are responsible first of all to the people of the ward." [18]

Hall obviously was not alone in his criticism. The Municipal Voters' League censured DePriest after his first term. Not only had he voted against almost every reform measure proposed, but "no alderman in Chicago's history [has] piled up a more notorious record in so short a time," the League asserted. Making allowances for the organization's self-righteousness and abhorrence of machine politics, the fact is

[16] *New York Times*, August 3, 1919; *Chicago Defender*, March 30, April 6, May 11, November 9, 1918.

[17] Quoted in Wood, *Negro in Chicago*, 29–30.

[18] *Chicago Daily News*, July 28, 1919; *Chicago Defender*, February 16, 23, March 2, 1918.

that, in January 1917, DePriest was indicted by a grand jury for "conspiracy to allow gambling houses and houses of prostitution to operate and for bribery of police officers in connection with the operation of these houses." Indicted and charged with DePriest were Chief of Police Stephen K. Healey, three police lieutenants, a cabaret owner, and several underworld figures who allegedly were "collectors and payers of 'graft' money." The Democratic State's Attorney, Maclay Hoyne, had initiated this crusade against the South Side resorts at least in part to discredit the Republican administration, but the evidence of corruption which he disclosed was alarming. The police had permitted houses of ill fame, assignation hotels, and gambling parlors to operate for cash payments. "Fixers" also effected the restoration of saloon licenses, and for bribes the police were "partial" in their enforcement of the Sunday closing law. Both Chief Healey and "Teenan" Jones, owner of the Elite No. 2, a cabaret and gambling den at 35th Street and South State, turned state's evidence, confessing their guilt and charging that DePriest had accepted funds from gangsters and had represented gambling clubs with the police. Jones testified to paying DePriest $2,800 for "protection" in 1916. Although DePriest was acquitted, primarily because his lawyer, Clarence Darrow, convinced the jury that the gifts were not for protection but were campaign contributions, the evidence tended to support the indictment. In any case, the trial was disastrous to his immediate political career, and he did not offer himself for reelection to the city council.[19]

[19] Municipal Voters' League, *Twenty-Second Report, 1916* (no imprint), 15–16; *Chicago Daily News*, January 19, 1917; *Chicago Daily Tribune*, June 5, 12, 1917; Sandburg, *Chicago Race Riots*, 59–61; Wood, *Negro in Chicago*, 25–29; Citizens' Association of Chicago, *43rd Annual Report, 1917*, 5–6; *44th Annual Report, 1918*, 6, 10; Citizens' Association *Bulletin* No. 35 (January 20, 1917), 1–3; Merriam, *Chicago*, 144–47; George W. Ellis, "The Chicago Negro in Law and Politics," *The Champion Magazine*, I (March 1917), 349–51, 358–359; Reckless, *Vice in Chicago*, 30; *Chicago Defender*, January 5, 19, February 3, March 3, 24, June 2, 16, 1917.

The other black aldermen did not establish much more savory reputations in the eyes of reformers. The Voters' League rebuked Louis B. Anderson, DePriest's successor, for his "bad record," especially for his failure to support ordinances "regulating dry cabarets" and "prohibiting owners and drivers of taxicabs from using them for immoral purposes. . . . Quite as bad as his predecessor, DePriest," the League concluded. On R. R. Jackson alone did reformers bestow modest praise, not for his independence, but for his "good personal reputation." [20] But the Voters' League did not appreciate that the black constituents of these aldermen had at least the feeling and sometimes the experience of being represented. The Second Ward aldermen received the recognition of the city's most powerful officials, and they were powerful in their own right. Louis Anderson was "Big Bill's" floor leader in the city council; he was "the man," stated a reporter, "who holds up Mayor Thompson's hoop for the aldermen to jump through." Anderson and Jackson saw to it that racial slurs by policemen and other city employees were investigated, and that victims of false arrests were released. Streets were cleaned after they registered protests with the sanitation department. When the city closed the Stanton Avenue Police Station at 35th Street, the *Defender* complained that the Second Ward, "with its 15,000 voters of the Race, is denied the prestige of a police station." Several months later, after strenuous and persuasive efforts by Anderson and Jackson, the city reopened the facility.[21]

Perhaps these were token and short-run benefits, but the black electorate hailed them as victories, and it increasingly identified the race's political progress with the continuance in office of the black aldermen and William H. Thompson. In 1918, for example, Perry Howard, a black politician in Mis-

[20] Municipal Voters' League, *Twenty-Fourth Report, 1918* (no imprint), 12–13; *Twenty-Fifth Report, 1919,* 14.

[21] See newspaper clippings in Merriam Papers; *Chicago Defender,* July 7, 1917, March 30, April 13, May 11, 25, June 8, July 6, 27, August 3, 1918.

sissippi, was voted off the Republican National Committee by its members. Thompson had assured Anderson, Jackson, Edward H. Wright, *Defender* editor Robert S. Abbott, and George W. Ellis, a lawyer, that if elected Illinois' national committeeman, he would endorse Howard; and when the committeemen voted 25–23, Thompson cast his lot with the minority. Although it had been a defeat for the race, Thompson's vote, the *Defender* asserted, was evidence once again that he was "the greatest friend the Race has had in high office since the days of Lincoln." [22] Also in 1918, "Big Bill" ran unsuccessfully in the primaries for the Republican senatorial nomination, and again the black belt mobilized its political resources behind him. He was the new emancipator, Ed Wright reminded black voters, and "every colored man who refused to shout or vote for Mayor Thompson should be run into the Lake." He was "the best friend politically we have ever had," added the *Defender*. And once again Thompson proclaimed that he was not only proud of his black friends, but that he was even proud to be "bitterly criticized in some quarters for having too much regard and solicitude for your people." [23]

Criticism of the Thompson administration was usually no more than verbal, such as that voiced by the Danish-Americans who organized the "We Can't Stand Thompson Club." [24] Other groups reacted violently, however, especially the Irish-Americans. As far back as 1915, the Irish had castigated Thompson for his alleged anti-Catholicism. Just before that year's mayoralty primary, leaflets were distributed charg-

[22] See Frank O. Lowden Papers, University of Chicago Library; *Chicago Defender*, February 2, 16, 23, March 2, 23, May 4, 1918; William F. Nowlin, *Negro in American National Politics* (Boston: Stratford, 1931), 56, 59, 116, 121–22.

[23] *Chicago Defender*, April 13, May 11, 25, June 1, July 6, 20, 27, September 7, October 9, November 2, 9, 1918; *Chicago Broad Ax*, September 14, 1918; *Chicago Daily News*, August 28, September 5, 1918.

[24] *Revyen* (Chicago), October 16, 1915, in Foreign Language Press Survey (FLPS), University of Chicago.

ing that because the wife of Harry Olson, Thompson's opponent, was Catholic, Olson would subvert the public school
system. The allegation was repeated after the primaries, only
this time the accused culprit was the Democratic candidate,
Robert M. Sweitzer, a Catholic and the brother-in-law and
protégé of Democratic boss Roger Sullivan. *Save the Public
Schools* was the title of an anti-Catholic pamphlet circulated
in Protestant neighborhoods, and the members of a secretive
club, the Guardians of Liberty, went from door to door in the
same neighborhoods explaining that the Pope would govern
Chicago if Sweitzer were elected. In most cities, such documents and gossip might merely have been dismissed as forg-
eries and fabrications, but not in Chicago. For in that city,
which was about half-Protestant, half-Catholic, religious ri-
valries had had bitter political ramifications for years. Protestants in particular feared an imminent Catholic take-over of
the Board of Education for the purpose of abolishing the public schools, and even after corruption in Thompson's city hall
had been exposed, Protestants justified their continued endorsement of the mayor by explaining that before "Big Bill,"
the "city hall was filled up with Catholics" and the Pope had
been "the real power in Chicago." Sweitzer deplored Thompson's raising of the "religious issue" in 1915, charging that he
had used it "to prejudice some people against me. . . . This
is nothing new for the scurrilous Thompson crowd." But
Thompson responded by labeling Sweitzer a bigot.[25]

Whatever the truth was in this muddled controversy, one
result was evident: the Irish and certain other Catholic
groups harbored resentment and even hatred of Thompson
and whoever supported him, particularly if those supporters

[25] Merriam, *Chicago,* 130, 158, 189; Hoffman, "Big Bill Thompson," 8, 11; Wendt and Kogan, *"Big Bill,"* 95, 97, 100–3, 107–8; William L. Chenery, "The Protected Sex at the Polls," *Harper's Weekly,*
LX (May 8, 1915), 439–40; *New York Times,* March 21, April 7,
1915; Stuart, *20 Incredible Years,* 15; Charles Merriam's Walgreen
Lectures, in Merriam Papers; George S. Counts, *School and Society
in Chicago* (N.Y.: Harcourt, Brace, 1928), 229–40, 250.

were black. During Thompson's campaign parades in 1915, Catholic gangs on the curbs shouted: "G'wan, you lousy Protestants. Down with the A.P.A.'s [American Protective Association, an anti-Catholic organization powerful in the 1890's]." Moreover, when the votes were tabulated, Thompson polled only 18.3 per cent of the Irish vote, while his total among blacks was 73 per cent. From other political issues, too, it was evident that these groups were scarcely ever in agreement. On bond measures in the stockyards district from 1915 to 1917, for example, the Irish and the immigrants from Southern and Eastern Europe usually voted in the negative, while blacks were always in the affirmative. Much more ominous, though, was another development that was at least partly political in origin—the proliferation of assaults on black people by Irish gangs and "athletic clubs" as the year 1918 merged into 1919.[26]

"Hit me and you hit two thousand," was the motto of the best known of the gangs, the Ragen Colts, whose territory was the "back-of-the-yards" district extending south of 43rd Street to 63rd. Organized in 1902 as the "Morgan Athletic Club," the Colts were sons of Irish laborers in the stockyards. Their "patron saint" was Frank Ragen, a Democratic Cook County Commissioner who paid the rent on the clubhouse and made financial donations to their other enterprises. Among the activities of the eighteen-to-thirty-year-old kids were baseball, football, and rugby teams, picnics and dances, and an annual minstrel show. Boxers and wrestlers also represented the Colts in citywide competition, and the cups and trophies which lined the shelves of the clubhouse testified to their success. But the Colts also engaged in "slugging" and political intimidation. "In the days before machine-gun politics," reported a criminal investigator, "the knuckles of the club members made themselves so felt that, in the words of a

[26] Wendt and Kogan, *"Big Bill,"* 111; Hoffman, "Big Bill Thompson," 14–15; C. O. Gardner, *The Referendum in Chicago* (Philadelphia: n.pub., 1920), 35, 49.

member, 'When we dropped into a polling place everyone else dropped out.' " It was apparent that the Colts and other clubs could not have survived had they had to rely solely on the contributions of their own members, but it was also evident that their financial patrons realized profits from their investments on election day.[27]

Thompson ran for reelection in 1919. He swept the February primary, and the black electorate turned out in full force. The Second Ward cast 12,143 votes for Thompson, while his two Republican opponents received only 1,492 and 319. The April election, however, promised to be a vastly tougher contest. In "Big Bill's" four years as mayor he had alienated both the antisaloon and liquor interests, and both management and labor. His espousal of neutrality even after the United States' entry into the war further diminished his waning popularity. Reformers charged that he had wrecked the schools and the civil service. In addition, all of Chicago's daily newspapers labored against his reelection. Although Thompson's prospects were exceedingly dim, two rays of hope stood out: the possibility of a Democratic split and the votes of a pair of unpopular minorities, the Germans and the blacks.[28]

The Democratic nominee was again Robert Sweitzer, whose intimate dependence upon Sullivan's tainted machine so vexed good government Democrats that they welcomed the candidacy of an independent Democrat, Maclay Hoyne. Organized labor had earlier deserted the Democrats to form the Labor party, whose nominee was John Fitzpatrick, president of the Chicago Federation of Labor. With four candidates in

[27] Frederic M. Thrasher, *The Gang: A Study of 1,313 Gangs in Chicago* (Chicago: University of Chicago Press, 1927), 15–19, 455–460; *Illinois Crime Survey*, 1001–3, 1005.

[28] See William Chenery, "Politics in Chicago," *New Republic*, XVIII (March 15, 1919), 213–14; Chenery, "The Fall of a Mayor," *ibid.*, VII (May 13, 1916), 36–38; Counts, *School and Society*, 6–7, 11–12, 68–69; *Chicago Daily Tribune*, March 22, 27, 1919; *Chicago Defender*, March 1, 1919; *Chicago Daily News*, March 29, 1919; Glen Edwards, "Schools and Politics in Chicago," *Survey*, XLII (August 16, 1919), 724–26.

the race, Thompson's stock soared; if his support held firm, a plurality was possible.

The campaign was perhaps the most acrid ever waged in Chicago. One political reporter put his finger on the basis of the bitterness: "All the prejudice tom-toms were sounding furiously." Only Fitzpatrick, possibly because he was no threat, seemed to escape the urge to inveigh against the other candidates. Hoyne hurled broadsides at Thompson for his exploitation of the black vote, and he similarly railed against Sweitzer for playing on the fears and sentiments of the foreign-born. Sweitzer supporters, in turn, had handbills distributed questioning Thompson's national loyalty. The mayor retaliated in late March by filing a $250,000 damage suit against the libelous Democratic boosters. In addition, the athletic clubs stepped up their terrorization of black people in the spring of 1919. Other foes of Thompson publicized him as "a 'nigger lover' who kissed black babies, and his black cohorts were blamed for the decline of South Side real estate values, for putting white men out of jobs, and for the deterioration of South Side schools." [29] Propaganda and lies punctuated the campaign, but at its termination no candidate was nearer victory than at the beginning. On election eve Thompson and Sweitzer were neck and neck, and the gamblers had not even the confidence to offer odds. For the first time in years all bets were at even money.[30]

On April 1, election day, nearly 700,000 citizens swarmed to the polls, and, as often happened in Chicago, fistfights and brawls marked the final hours of what the *New York Times* called "the wildest mayoralty campaign in Chicago's history."

[29] Gosnell, *Negro Politicians,* 369; "The Chicago Elections," *Public,* XXII (March 1919), 201–2; Stuart, *20 Incredible Years,* 26; Wendt and Kogan, *"Big Bill,"* 167–71; "Mayor Thompson of Chicago: Side Issues in His Election," *Outlook,* CXXI (April 16, 1919), 636; *Chicago Daily News,* March 5, April 1, 1919; *New York Times,* March 27, 1919.

Regarding the increasing terrorization of black people by Irish gangs in the spring of 1919, see Chapter VII.

[30] *Chicago Daily News,* April 1, 1919.

By nightfall Thompson's reelection was conceded, even though his opponents had polled over 62 per cent of the vote. Thompson's unprecedented margin in 1915 of 150,000 votes had ebbed in 1919 to a plurality of 21,622, and the only vote that boosted his strength over 1915 was in the black belt. A Democratic spokesman promptly imputed his slim triumph to fraud in the black belt. Other Democratic party leaders insisted that, at the very least, the black vote alone had elected Thompson. Thompson's total in the Second Ward was 15,569 to Sweitzer's 3,323, and he had overwhelmingly captured the numerous black precincts in the First, Third, Sixth, Fourteenth, and Thirtieth Wards. "Big Bill's" tally in the black belt more than provided his plurality, but one cannot assert that it alone elected him any more than one can declare that either Thompson's substantial German bloc or his cultivated Swedish vote was the sole basis of his victory. Without the black people, or the Germans or the Swedes, however, Thompson would not have been reelected. And the primary Democratic organ, the *Chicago Daily Journal,* boomed out at dusk on election day in bold front page headlines: NEGROES ELECT BIG BILL.[31]

Such partisan criticism did not seem to alarm black voters. Reveling in the Democratic recognition of black political potency, the *Defender* proclaimed: "If this was intended as a criticism of our action, we cheerfully accept it." The *Defender*, moreover, patted itself on the back for its role in the triumph. Rationalizing that since all the daily newspapers had opposed Thompson and the *Defender* alone had zealously advocated his reelection, it boasted: "Modesty prevents us from

[31] The Democrats claimed that the city police had detained the returns in the Second Ward until the Republicans determined how many votes Thompson needed; that many blacks then voted. *Chicago Daily Journal,* April 1, 1919; *Chicago Daily News,* April 2, 1919; *Chicago Daily Tribune,* April 2, 1919; John M. Allswang, "The Political Behavior of Chicago's Ethnic Groups, 1918–1932" (unpublished Ph.D. dissertation, University of Pittsburgh, 1967), 39, 199; Hoffman, "Big Bill Thompson," 26–29; "The Chicago Vote," *Survey,* XLII (April 12, 1919), 83–84; *New York Times,* April 1, 2, 6, 1919.

claiming that 'The World's Greatest Weekly' wields more political influence than all the Chicago dailies combined, but
results are what count." A black dentist caught up in the jubi-
lation wired the mayor that the race had higher aspirations
for him: "I congratulate you upon victory. If our people are
to blame, as papers indicate, we are not ashamed of it.
Twelve million of us will help make you President." [32]

Yet Thompson had polled only 38 per cent of the vote, and
his election was counter to the voting exhibited for other city
posts. Democrats captured well over 60 per cent of the city
council vacancies, in addition to the four major elective
offices next in importance to the mayor's job. And "the white
people of Chicago," as one of them explained, "greatly resented" the power of the black electorate, and "the way in
which the colored vote put Mayor Thompson into office again
at this last election." Whites, and particularly the Democrats,
who for four years had aspired to control city hall, were an-
tagonized not just by the behavior of the black voters but even
more by "the preference given to the colored people by the
Thompsonites" in return for their votes. "The colored people freely talk of their power over the whites through their
hold over 'Big Bill' Thompson—their equality with the
whites . . . ," and some whites so resented this imputation of
equality that they would fight to demonstrate their superiority.[33]

"Why did Mayor Thompson and Governor Lowden," the
Chicago Daily Journal asked in 1919, "refrain for three days
from using troops to put down the rioting which has disgraced
and damaged Chicago?" The state militia had intervened
during riots in Springfield in 1908 and East St. Louis in 1917,
when people were being murdered and property was de-

[32] *Chicago Defender,* April 5, 12, 19, 1919.
[33] Ellis C. Dow to F. W. Shepardson, August 2, 1919, Chicago
Commission on Race Relations Papers, Illinois State Archives, Springfield; see also a right-wing Chicago journal, *Weber's Weekly,* No. 20
(August 9, 1919).

stroyed. Troops had even intervened in Chicago in 1917 when there was no riot and the threat of a disturbance was minimal. "Why were troops not used in Chicago at least by Monday night, instead of waiting till Wednesday night?" [34] This was a question numerous Chicagoans were asking as the death toll topped ten, then twenty, while mobs roamed the streets unrestrained by police. Frank O. Lowden and William H. Thompson were the officials responsible for summoning the militia, a move that was so imperative in the early stages of the race riot but that was not executed until the pendulum of mob violence was on the downswing. By the summer of 1919, however, discord between the two men was so marked that cooperation in subduing the rioting that erupted on a South Side beach on July 27 was, while not impossible, simply not forthcoming.

"Why was the mayor so reluctant to call for troops?" The answer given by *The Messenger,* a radical black periodical, was politics, and it was an answer with which many observers, radical and otherwise, agreed. Thompson hesitated because he "evidently considered [such a request] a reflection upon his administration not to be able to cope with the situation." Thompson did not want martial law, which, the governor's administration contended, was a precondition for the ordering of the militia out of the armories and into the streets. But as the violence spread and the fatalities mounted, the mayor was "compelled to effect a compromise by asking the governor to send troops to 'assist' [the] police force. . . . Perhaps you have heard of the difference[s] between Mayor Thompson and Governor Lowden." [35]

Thompson and Lowden had not always headed warring factions within the Republican party. As early as 1901 Lowden had supported Thompson in an unsuccessful race for mayor, and in 1916 Thompson's machine had vigorously

[34] *Chicago Daily Journal,* July 31, 1919.
[35] "A Report on the Chicago Race Riot by an Eye-Witness," *The Messenger,* II (September 1919), 12.

aided Lowden in the Illinois gubernatorial contest, apparently in return for the national committeeman's post. With Lowden's election the era of concord ended, for the governor so ignored the mayor in matters of patronage that, as Lowden's biographer has remarked, an "indorsement from Thompson seemed almost equivalent to a blackball." [36]

Their open split occurred dramatically during the first year of the war. Early that fall Thompson, whose espousal of neutrality was so frequent that his enemies tabbed him "unser Bill," invited a pacifist organization, the People's Council of America for Democracy and Terms of Peace, to meet in Chicago. The council had already been banned from Minneapolis and a small Wisconsin town. Unable to contact Thompson to dissuade him from permitting the assembly, Lowden, who believed that the council was using freedom of speech as a subterfuge for treason, ordered Chicago's chief of police to dissolve the gathering. He was "satisfied," Lowden told reporters, "that this meeting was designed for the purpose of bringing on draft riots and obstructing the Government in other respects." Incensed, Thompson invited the council back, this time under police protection. The governor retaliated by dispatching the adjutant general and a trainload of several companies of Illinois National Guardsmen to drive the council out of Chicago once and for all. By the time the troops had debarked, the council had adjourned, but the split between the mayor and the governor was irreparable. Moreover, the Chicago city council voted 42–6 to commend Lowden, and it sought a formula whereby it could impeach Thompson, who was also hanged in effigy by irate Chicagoans. It should be noted, though, that in 1917, unlike 1919, Governor Lowden had ordered the militia to Chicago; and he had done so not only without a request from the mayor for

[36] William T. Hutchinson, *Lowden of Illinois* (Chicago: University of Chicago Press, 1957), I, 104, 308; Stuart, *20 Incredible Years*, 26–32; Peterson, *Barbarians in Our Midst*, 112–13; Wendt and Kogan, *"Big Bill,"* 144, 177–79.

troops, but indeed much to Thompson's displeasure. Two years later, Lowden maintained that he was constitutionally powerless to act without such a request.[37]

Having vowed to swing his downstate machine behind the candidacy of the Republican who would be the "strongest opponent" of Thompson for the senatorial nomination, Lowden endorsed Medill McCormick in 1918. McCormick handily outran the mayor, especially in Lowden's district.[38] After the Armistice, Lowden was promoted for the presidency; his prospects were partly contingent upon leading a solid Illinois delegation, that is, one rid of Thompsonians, to the Republican convention. The mayor's reelection in 1919, however, quashed this hope. "Big Bill," too, had presidential aspirations, and had had ever since 1915.[39]

A further and historically divisive factor in Illinois Republicanism, and one for which Thompson and Lowden were not responsible, was Chicago's perennial tussle with the downstate-dominated legislature for home rule. Thompson particularly desired to transfer the power to regulate franchises from the state public utilities commission to the city. When the legislature debated the issue in 1919, Lowden and the down-

[37] Hutchinson, *Lowden of Illinois*, 378–80; Stuart, *20 Incredible Years*, 47–51; *The Republican*, September 15, 22, 1917; *Chicago Daily Tribune*, August 20, September 1–3, 1917; *New York Times*, September 3–5, 1917; Wendt and Kogan, *"Big Bill,"* 158–59; Andrew J. Townsend, *The Germans of Chicago* (n.pl.pub.: n.pub., *ca.* 1932), 103–4. Lowden apparently was also ready to send the state militia into Chicago on July 4, 1919, if violence erupted during the general strike called by the Tom Mooney Central Strike Committee: *New Majority*, June 14, 1919; Richard H. Frost, *The Mooney Case* (Stanford: Stanford University Press, 1968), 331; *Daily Jewish Courier*, July 8, 1919, FLPS.

[38] *Chicago Daily News*, August 28, 1918; Charles Merz, "Tammany in Illinois," *New Republic*, XXIV (September 29, 1920), 123–25.

[39] *Chicago Daily Journal*, April 2, 4, 11, 1919; *Chicago Defender*, July 5, 12, 1919; *New York Times*, July 22, 1915, April 11, June 21, July 14, 15, 20, 1919. Lowden's Chicago supporters had attempted to defeat Thompson by aligning with the independent candidate and even the Democratic choice. After his reelection in April, Thompson immodestly informed a news reporter that "no man is big enough to refuse a nomination for President if it is offered him."

staters prevailed, with the assistance of Roger Sullivan, gas magnate and Democratic boss of Chicago. The franchise strife entered a new phase in the summer of 1919. One of "Big Bill's" most frequent campaign promises had been maintenance of the nickel carfare, but when a labor dispute arose among the street car and elevated car employees, and the state public utilities commission determined to mediate, wage increases and a consequent rise in fares were imminent. Lowden even led the commission's team of arbitrators to Chicago, and he remained with it, much in opposition to Thompson's wishes, until the day the race riot broke out and throughout most of the hectic days that followed.[40]

Minor irritants widened further the gulf between the state's two highest officials. The governor, for example, did not send Thompson a congratulatory message upon his reelection in April, and this reportedly rankled the mayor. Although Thompson invited Lowden and his party to join him on his reviewing stand in June, to applaud Illinois' returning Prairie Division of troops, Lowden and his retinue chose to review the soldiers from a grandstand. "Big Bill," meanwhile, occupied his private stand a mile away.[41]

These two irreconcilable men were the public officials to whom Chicago's citizens looked for the restoration of order during the frenetic, bloody days of late July and early August 1919. They not only did not work together to provide it; they scarcely spoke to each other.

[40] *Chicago Daily Journal,* June 5, July 21, 1919; *Chicago Daily News,* April 1, 1919; Merriam, *Chicago,* 13; Albert Lepawsky, *Home Rule for Metropolitan Chicago* (Chicago: University of Chicago Press, 1936), 10–13, 116–19; diary of Mrs. Frank O. Lowden, July 25, 1919, to August 9, 1919. Mrs. Lowden's diary was made available to the author by her daughter, Mrs. C. Phillip Miller of Chicago.

[41] *Chicago Daily Journal,* April 11, June 18, 1919; Governor's secretary to W. H. Thompson, June 14, 1919, Lowden Papers.

The "New Negro," the Police, and Militant Self-Defense

If we must die—let it not be like hogs
Hunted and penned in an inglorious spot,
While round us bark the mad and hungry dogs,
Making their mock at our accursed lot.
If we must die—oh, let us nobly die,
So that our precious blood may not be shed
In vain; then even the monsters we defy
Shall be constrained to honor us though dead!

Oh, Kinsmen! We must meet the common foe;
Though far outnumbered, let us show us brave,
And for their thousand blows deal one death blow!
What though before us lies the open grave?
Like men we'll face the murderous, cowardly pack,
Pressed to the wall, dying but fighting back! [1]

[1] *Liberator,* II (July 1919), 21. Although it is sometimes asserted that McKay wrote this poem after, and probably in response to, the

SO WROTE A BLACK POET, Claude McKay, in the
summer of 1919. And his was not a solitary voice calling for self-assertion, manliness, and resolute self-defense. In
the forefront of this firmness of purpose was the returning
black soldier, who, as one veteran put it, "knows past all
doubting how to be unafraid in the valley of the shadow and
how to die splendidly defending his own." [2] Black veterans,
the NAACP's W. E. B. Du Bois told an overflow audience at
Chicago's Wendell Phillips High School, "will never be the
same again. You need not ask them to go back to what they
were before. They cannot, for they are not the same men any
more." [3] "I went to war, served eight months in France,"
recalled one of Chicago's ex-soldiers. "I wanted to go, but I
might as well have stayed for all the good it has done me.
. . . No, that ain't so," he added bitterly, "I'm glad I went.
I done my part and I'm going to fight right here till Uncle Sam
does his. I can shoot as good as the next one. . . . I ain't
looking for trouble, but if it comes my way I ain't dodging." [4]

In addition to the soldiers who had steeled their courage in
the crucible of war, countless thousands of other blacks were
of one voice in their condemnation of nonviolence. Only
twice in the twentieth century, August Meier and Elliott Rudwick have written, have there been major periods when black

---

Washington race riot, it is apparent that he wrote it earlier. The issue
of the *Liberator* in which the poem appeared was published before
the Washington riot. For similar expressions of the blacks' fierce determination to retaliate, see "The Remedy for Mob Violence," *The
Veteran* (June 28, 1919), in 66th Cong., 1st Sess., U. S. Senate, *Investigation Activities of the Department of Justice*, Doc. No. 153
(Washington: Government Printing Office, 1919), 165; Carita Owens
Collins, "Be a Man," in *ibid.*, 163; *Cleveland Gazette,* September 6,
20, 1919; Robert T. Kerlin, *The Voice of the Negro, 1919* (N.Y.:
Dutton, 1920), *passim.*

[2] W. H. Jordan, *With "Old Eph" in the Army* (Baltimore: H. E.
Houck, 1919), 47–48.

[3] *Chicago Broad Ax* and *Chicago Defender,* both May 24, 1919.

[4] Chicago Commission on Race Relations, *The Negro in Chicago*
(Chicago: University of Chicago Press, 1922), 481.

intellectuals have advocated retaliatory violence and masses of black citizens have committed dramatic acts of social violence. One was the period of the mid-1960's, the other was 1919. Reports drifted north from Tennessee, Mississippi, Texas, and other Southern states in the spring of 1919 that "Negroes were arming" there as well as in the North. They would "not make trouble unless they were attacked," said R. R. Church, a black leader in Memphis, "but in that event they were prepared to defend themselves." Obviously, some of these reports were the result more of the panic of whites who feared that blacks were arming to impose "social equality" than they were of personal observation. Yet others were authentic. Robert T. Kerlin, in 1919 a student of current black newspapers, wrote that with but one exception, "Self-defense is applauded and advocated . . . by the entire colored press. . . ."[5]

Black men and women in 1919 were imbued both with pride in their race and with a fierce determination to possess the rights pledged to Americans by the Constitution. As an upshot of the migration and the race's contributions to the Allies' victory—as soldiers, industrial workers, purchasers of Liberty Bonds—black people felt they had earned the enjoyment of these guarantees. They were resolved also to defend their life, liberty, and property against white aggressors; consequently, numerous would-be lynchings became race riots when blacks fought back.[6] And perhaps nowhere was this

[5] Meier and Rudwick, "Black Violence in the 20th Century," in National Commission on the Causes and Prevention of Violence, *Violence in America,* prepared under the direction of Hugh Davis Graham and Ted Robert Gurr (N.Y.: Signet edition, 1969), 380–85; report of investigation of Herbert J. Seligmann, May 18–25, 1919, in NAACP Papers (C-74), Library of Congress (NAACP-1); Fuller Williamson to A. G. Whittington, August 25, 1919, in Papers of U. S. Railroad Administration (RG 14), Suitland, Maryland; Kerlin, *Voice of the Negro,* 23; E. Franklin Frazier, "New Currents of Thought among the Colored People of America" (unpublished M.A. thesis, Clark University, 1920), 39–41; Chicago Commission, *Negro in Chicago,* 488–90.

[6] Rollin Hartt, "The New Negro," *Independent,* CV (January 15, 1921), 59–60.

determination to retaliate more evident than in Chicago during the city's race riot.

Personifying the attitudes of this "New Negro" was W. E. B. Du Bois, a founder of the NAACP, a leader of the black intelligentsia, and as editor of the *Crisis* a foremost articulator of the protests of black people. There was a chasm separating his immediate goals and doctrines from those of Booker T. Washington, the acknowledged leader of his race until his death in 1915; and the growing popularity of Du Bois' writings by 1919 was evidence of the long road the New Negro had traveled in just a few years. Washington had advocated patience, accommodation, and social, economic, and political "uplift" through economic development. Du Bois, on the other hand, preached assertiveness, and he rejected Washington's prediction that with vocational training and the acquisition of property would come the vote and an end to the race's subordinated status. He urged black people to claim their rights. Gradualism and satisfaction with "half a loaf" were patently contrary to the aspirations and expectations of the New Negro. Declaring that Washington was "a compromiser between the South, the North, and the Negro" and thus not a true leader of the race, Du Bois first disputed his teachings at the turn of the century. "So far as Mr. Washington preaches Thrift, Patience . . . ," wrote Du Bois, "we must hold up his hands and strive with him. . . . But so far as Mr. Washington apologizes for injustice, North or South, does not rightly value the privilege and duty of voting, belittles the emasculating effects of caste distinctions . . . so far as he, the South, or the Nation, does this,—we must unceasingly and firmly oppose them. By every civilized and peaceful method we must strive for the rights which the world accords to men. . . ." [7]

After the Springfield, Illinois, race riot of 1908 had dramatically revealed the intolerable status and vulnerability of

[7] W. E. B. Du Bois, *The Souls of Black Folk* (Chicago: A. C. McClurg, 1903), 41–59.

blacks, Du Bois and a group of sympathetic whites established the NAACP. In this organization, Du Bois felt, he had an effective instrument with which to contest Washington's philosophy. Through its periodical, the *Crisis,* he put forth monthly the precepts of rebellion against lynchings, of stout objection to the countless inequities that black people had to endure, and of the use of protest for the righting of these wrongs. During the war the size and receptivity of Du Bois' audience mounted; from an annual circulation in 1915 of 385,000, the *Crisis* sold 560,000 copies in the first six months of 1919 alone. Other New Negro periodicals and newspapers likewise proliferated in size and number. In Chicago, the circulation of the *Defender* boomed from 10,000 to 93,000 during the war years; and in the summer of 1919, the *Whip,* the city's most militant black weekly, initiated publication. More than simply reflecting the rapidly increasing literacy of the race, this upsurge signified that black people enjoyed and agreed with what they were reading.[8]

The New Negro did not reject all of Washington's teachings. In fact, many of the assertive race journals praised his contributions; certainly thrift, the acquisition of property, and qualification in a trade were desirable goals. Yet there was one tenet that the New Negro generally could not bear: nonresistance to physical aggression. After the Atlanta race riot of 1906, Washington had urged "the colored people . . . to exercise self-control and not make the fatal mistake of attempting to retaliate, but to rely upon the efforts of the proper authorities to bring order and security out of confusion. If they do this," he said, "they will have the sympathy of good people the world over." [9] But it was self-defense, not self

[8] For *Crisis* circulation figures, see NAACP Board minutes, July 11, 1919, in NAACP-I (A-1); for the increase in NAACP branches during the war, see NAACP, *8th and 9th Annual Reports, 1917 and 1918* (no imprint), 17, 55; and *ibid., 10th Annual Report,* 7, 64.

[9] *New York Age,* September 27, 1906; quoted in Frederick G. Detweiler, *The Negro Press in the United States* (Chicago: University of Chicago Press, 1922), 138.

control, that was the byword of the New Negro; if attacked, he would oppose his enemy with resolute militance.

Had Washington not died in 1915, he would still have witnessed the repudiation of his teachings, especially by Northern blacks.[10] For two forces were undermining his kind of conservative dominance: the migration of over 450,000 black people to the North, and black soldiers' participation in the war. These dynamics, even more than the preachments of Du Bois and the other advocates of rebellion and protest, were the immediate progenitors of the New Negro.

Of its very nature the migration was a rejection of Washington's counsel to Southern blacks to "cast down your bucket." Much more significantly, patience and accommodation were woefully inadequate guidelines for the black people who had come North. For the migration was not just a matter of physical relocation; it was the abrupt transformation of a feudal peasantry into an urban proletariat. Conservative Southern ministers, disciples of Tuskegee, and other beneficiaries of Washington's patronage could not influence the Northern masses as they had the Southern; the exigencies of Northern city dwelling often demanded adjustments from the selfsame doctrines that they were preaching. On the other hand, the New Negro press and spokesmen were in general attuned to the needs, attitudes, and goals of black people in the cities of the North.

The migration also meant psychological liberation from the chronic trauma of caste. Being powerless in a hostile society had frequently caused black men and women to adopt avoidance and denial mechanisms. They had begun to believe what white people told them—that they were inferior; the self-fulfilling prophecy had become a reality. They had also sup-

[10] Kelly Miller, *Radicalism and the Negro* (Washington: Murray Bros., 1920), 11; Horace M. Bond, "Negro Leadership since Washington," *South Atlantic Quarterly*, XXIV (April 1925), 115–30; E. Franklin Frazier, "The American Negro's New Leaders," *Current History*, XXVIII (April 1928), 56–59; V. F. Calverton, "The New Negro," *Current History*, XXIII (February 1926), 694–98.

pressed their anger, sometimes turning it against themselves in destructive acts, other times projecting it onto fellow blacks and being hostile to them rather than to the white oppressor. For many, the migration, accompanied by such benefits as higher wages, the franchise, and decent schools, meant an end to or at least a subsidence of self-hatred.[11]

"I have talked with some about leaving," reported a white railroad official in Mississippi, "and they say they are equal to a white man in the North. . . ." Moreover, merely being able to pack up his belongings and depart for the North with some expectation of finding a job made the migrant conscious of his control over his own destiny. For a sharecropper, with his tradition of dependence on and obedience to the orders of the landowner, this was liberating indeed. Upon arriving in the North, the migrant found not only that he could obtain work, but even on occasion that he could demand equal pay with whites for equal work and nondiscrimination in shop conditions. Because of the migration, noted Dr. George E. Haynes of the Labor Department's Division of Negro Economics, the black man "is coming to a consciousness of himself as a man among men." He was becoming an independent agent who could "look the world in the face and . . . make no apologies because God made his skin black and his hair curly." And upon arriving in Chicago, the migrant usually received advice which reinforced the exhilarating feeling of liberation. Do not call the foreman "boss," warned the *Defender*. "Leave that word dropped in the Ohio river. Also captain, general and major. We call people up here, Mister This or Mister That." Also do not tip your hat to white workers; ". . . treat them as you want them to treat you—AS A MAN. . . ." Liberation could, as Walter F. White of the NAACP observed in Chicago, result in "irresponsible" and "boisterous" conduct. But it also resulted in heightened self-

[11] See James P. Comer's highly suggestive essay, "The Dynamics of Black and White Violence," in Graham and Gurr, *Violence in America,* 423–40.

esteem, and this could mean black people redirecting anger from themselves and their race and focusing it on the whites they saw as the oppressors.[12]

Apparently the composition of the migration was also significant. Neither very many children nor very many old people journeyed to Chicago. The migrant was typically an unattached male, whether he was unmarried or had left his wife and family behind until he could get established; single males, of course, could leave home with greater ease than entire families when job opportunity beckoned from Chicago. A preponderance of the migrants, moreover, was of young adult age, usually between the years of twenty and forty-four. Of black males and females in the city in 1920, 60.2 and 59.6 per cent, respectively, were between twenty and forty-four, while the corresponding figures for native-born whites were 40.6 and 40.9 per cent. Just under one fourth of Chicago's black males were in their twenties. Although the significance of these data is open to debate, there seem to be several possible correlations between them and the emergence of both the New Negro and retaliatory violence in Chicago. Young adult males furnished the bulk of the self-defense and black violence during the riot. Being unattached, living in boarding houses or as lodgers, and not feeling the restraints of family obligations, many were free to participate in this racial warfare. It was to this age group, too, that the doctrines of the New Negro had great appeal. For in at least

[12] Letter from Hattiesburg, Mississippi, May 18, 1917, in Files on East St. Louis, in U. S. Department of Labor Papers (RG 174), Box 205, National Archives; George E. Haynes, "Negro Labor and the New Order," National Conference of Social Work, *Proceedings, 1919*, 531–38; Charles S. Johnson, *Shadow of the Plantation* (Chicago: Phoenix Books of University of Chicago Press, 1966), 3–4; Frazier, "New Currents of Thought," 12–13, 16–19; Charles S. Johnson, "The New Frontage on American Life," in Alain Locke (ed.), *The New Negro* (N.Y.: Atheneum edition, 1968), 287–88; George E. Haynes, "Effect of War Conditions on Negro Labor," *Proceedings of Academy of Political Science*, VIII (1918), 174–76; *Chicago Defender*, April 21, 1917; Walter White, "Chicago and Its Eight Reasons," *Crisis*, XVIII (October 1919), 293–94.

one respect these young men were unlike their fathers, who had been of comparable age during the immediate aftermath of slavery. The sons had encountered fewer whites who had taken even a paternalistic interest in them; as a result, their distrust and hatred were often more acute, and they "found it difficult," as Allan Spear has pointed out, "to live with whites on the terms accepted by their fathers." [13]

As weighty an immediate source of the New Negro as the migration was participation in the war. Black men had clamored to enlist, just as white Americans had. In addition to national allegiance, a most pervasive reason for the unflagging support of black people was the intense hope that one of the fruits of world democracy would be the fulfillment in the United States of the principle of equality of rights, opportunity, and treatment. It was in this spirit that the *Crisis* implored blacks, "while this war lasts, [to] forget our special grievances and close our ranks shoulder to shoulder with our white fellow citizens." Expressions of this purpose highlighted practically every discussion of the war by black men and women. Forget "all the injustice for the time being," exclaimed speakers at Chicago's Bethel African Methodist Episcopal Church in April 1917, and be "as one man ready to stand by the government in this crisis. . . ." Just before embarking on a tour of cantonments in France, Julius Rosenwald received a letter from Emmett J. Scott, the black special assistant to the Secretary of War. Tell the black soldiers, Scott had written, "that the DEMOCRACY for which they

[13] Ernest W. Burgess and Charles Newcomb, *Census Data of the City of Chicago, 1920* (Chicago: University of Chicago Press, 1931), 9–10; E. Franklin Frazier, *The Negro Family in Chicago* (Chicago: University of Chicago Press, 1932), 262, 270 ff.; Irene J. Graham, "Family Support and Dependency among Chicago Negroes: A Study of Unpublished Census Data," *Social Service Review,* III (December 1929), 541–62; Elizabeth Hughes, *Living Conditions for Small Wage Earners in Chicago* (Chicago: Department of Public Welfare, 1925), 11; Louise V. Kennedy, *The Negro Peasant Turns Cityward* (N.Y.: Columbia University Press, 1930), 135–40; Allan H. Spear, *Black Chicago: The Making of a Negro Ghetto, 1890–1920* (Chicago: University of Chicago Press, 1967), 137–38.

have gone forth is an idealism as holy as ever [a] Crusader went forth to battle for, and that their struggles shall not be in vain." [14]

Even Southern racists acknowledged that black soldiers, by serving, would earn for their race a stake in democracy—and this prospect alarmed them. Arguing against conscription for blacks, Senator James K. Vardaman and other politicians asserted that it would be a contradiction of the color-line creed; that it would place firearms in the hands of black men; that it would expose these men to social equality in France, thus "Frenchifying" and ruining them. But the government proceeded to draft blacks, more than 340,000 of them; and including volunteers, regular Army units, and the National Guard, upwards of 400,000 served in all. In addition, 200,-000 of these men served in France, 42,000 as combat troops.[15]

Of the black combat units that served heroically, the 8th Illinois was the only regiment commanded wholly by blacks for much of the war. Officered and manned primarily by Chicagoans, the unit was one of which the black community was immensely proud. Called the "Black Devils" by the Germans

[14] "Close Ranks," *Crisis*, XVI (July 1918), 111; *Chicago Defender*, April 7, 1917; E. Scott, Washington, to J. Rosenwald, Washington, July 31, 1918, Julius Rosenwald Papers, University of Chicago Library. For perhaps the best poetical treatment of this theme, see Roscoe Jameson, "Negro Soldiers," *Crisis*, XIV (September 1917), 249; and Joseph S. Cotter, Jr., "Sonnet to Negro Soldiers," in Walter C. Jackson and Newman I. White, *An Anthology of Verse by American Negroes* (Durham, N.C.: Trinity College Press, 1924), 182.

[15] Memorandum from Emmett J. Scott to Grosvenor B. Clarkson, Director, National Council of Defense, March 26, 1919, in RG 174, Box 17, 8/102; Rufus E. Clement, "Problems of Demobilization and Rehabilitation of the Negro Soldier after World Wars I and II," *Journal of Negro Education*, XII (Summer 1943), 533–34; Moorfield Storey, *The Negro Question, An Address . . . before the Wisconsin Bar Association* (N.Y.: NAACP, n.d.), 5; *Chicago Defender*, April 28, 1917; *Congressional Record*, LV, 6062–63; "American Negro in the World War," *Negro Year Book, 1925–26* (Tuskegee Institute, Alabama: Negro Year Book Publishing Co., 1925), 250–53; and *ibid., 1919–1921*, 188–93.

because of their fierce fighting at St. Mihiel, the Argonne Forest, and the Meuse, and called the "Partridges" by the French because of their proud military bearing, the 8th Illinois fought the last battle of the war in the final drive against the Germans. Suffering 20 per cent casualties, the regiment surrendered only one prisoner to the Germans and was one of the most abundantly decorated of American outfits. The United States awarded the Distinguished Service Cross to twenty-one of the regiment's heroes, while the French government pinned the *Croix de Guerre* on sixty-eight of them.[16]

Photographs of the 8th Illinois adorned shop windows in Chicago's black belt, and surrounding the pictures were the helmets, rifles, and canteens that the troops had sent back from France. Black officials returning from the battlefield praised the regiment, and there was scarcely a public meeting in the black belt that was without a prayer or a cheer for the 8th. "Our boys are just natural bayonet fighters," boasted Franklin Denison, the former colonel of the regiment who had become ill in France. The black troops, he said, were "cheerful and earnest"; they were happy to be fighting for democracy, "and they believe that their fighting will provide a fuller measure of equality for you and for them when it is over—that the democracy for which they are fighting will include the American Negro when peace is signed in Ber-

[16] *Heroes of 1918* (no imprint), in stacks, Library of Congress; Walter White, "Notes on Chicago of WFW," September 17, 1919, NAACP Papers located in Washington, D.C., at the Middle Atlantic office of the NAACP's Youth Division (NAACP-2); *Complete History of the Colored Soldiers in the World War* (N.Y.: Bennett & Churchill, 1919), 93–105; W. Allison Sweeney, *History of the American Negro in the Great World War . . .* (Chicago: Crineo-Henneberry, ca. 1919), 183 ff.; Emmett J. Scott, *Scott's Official History of the American Negro in the World War* (Chicago: Homewood Press, 1919), 214–30; Major Warner A. Ross, *My Colored Battalion* (Chicago: pub. by author, 1920), 83–119; "Soldiers" file in the WPA's "Negro in Illinois" project, files in George Cleveland Hall Branch, Chicago Public Library; William S. Braddan's history of the 8th Illinois, in *Chicago Broad Ax,* May 3, 10, 17, 24, 31, June 7, 14, 21, 1919; *Chicago Defender,* December 22, 1917, January 5, August 10, 1918.

lin. . . ." Chicago's black soldiers, he added, were "not complaining now"; "their complaint will come when it is all over. . . ." [17]

The 8th Illinois returned to Chicago in mid-February 1919; and, according to the *Defender*'s reporter, it was greeted with "a maelstrom of joy and wonderment." It was "a day of wild rejoicing," awaited for months, for the 8th was "the first of the city's fighters to come back as a unit." Four hundred thousand cheering people lined Michigan Avenue as the 8th marched by the reviewing stand filled with white and black dignitaries. Offices and stores had closed for the day, and 60,000 exuberant Chicagoans had jammed the Coliseum to welcome the unit. The speakers included the 8th's black officers, who thanked their friends for coming; but in the midst of the speeches Mayor Thompson, "who just couldn't miss the fun," burst into the hall amidst much applause. For "your devotion to our country and your heroism in battle," he shouted happily, "I bespeak for you that justice and equality of citizenship which shall . . . enable you and your posterity . . . as a living truth, to sing in a mighty chorus, 'My Country 'Tis of Thee, Sweet Land of Liberty.' " [18]

Black people had been active on the home front, too, pitching in across the country by purchasing an estimated $250,-000,000 worth of thrift stamps and Liberty Bonds. And in Chicago, aside from succoring the Allied armies by laboring long days in essential war industries, black men and women had donated countless hours of volunteer work. Auxiliaries of the Red Cross had knitted sweaters, caps, and socks, while other ladies had greeted soldiers at the railroad stations with refreshments and had packed Christmas boxes for shipment to France.[19]

[17] *Journal of Illinois State Historical Society,* XI (January 1919), 606–12.

[18] *Chicago Defender* and *Chicago Broad Ax,* both February 22, 1919.

[19] Elinora Manson, "War Activities among the Colored Women of Chicago," in *Chicago Broad Ax,* December 21, 1918; *Chicago De-*

With the Armistice, men and women in the black belt eagerly awaited prompt payment for their contributions; caught up in the validity of their supplications, most asked for no more than justice. Such was the moderate entreaty of a black poet, Chicago's Fenton Johnson:

> For we have been with thee in No Man's Land,
> Through lake of fire and down to Hell itself;
> And now we ask of thee our liberty,
> Our freedom in the land of Stars and Stripes.[20]

Less idealistic blacks knew that the superordinate white community would grant justice grudgingly, if at all.

Despite their warm welcome home, the veterans of the 8th Illinois returned to Chicago with "a very widespread dissatisfaction bordering on bitterness."[21] Having fought on the Mexican border in 1916, the 8th Illinois had been ordered back to the Southwest in 1917, this time to Houston's Camp Logan. One company had just detrained at Houston when a race riot erupted in that city. Black troops of the 24th Infantry, goaded by white civilians, had taken up their weapons and killed seventeen of the local citizens. After a farcical trial, thirteen of the troops were hanged for murder and mutiny, and forty-one were imprisoned for life. These trials, reported a sergeant from the 8th, "caused many days of anxiety to our boys. . . . Uneasiness akin to despair swept our ranks." Because of the post-riot hysteria, the rest of the unit did not leave Chicago for Texas until October. But the city was still in "a state of frenzy" when the regiment arrived, and

---

fender, April 19, 1919; Ira De A. Reid, "A Critical Summary: The Negro on the Home Front in World Wars I and II," *Journal of Negro Education,* XII (Summer 1943), 515; *Congressional Record,* LIX, 7482; Monroe Work (comp.), "Negro Patriotism," *Southern Workman,* XLVIII (October 1919), 510–11.

[20] Fenton Johnson, "The New Day," in William S. Braithwaite (ed.), *Victory!* (Boston: Small, Maynard, 1919), 30–31.

[21] Report from Director, Division of Negro Economics, to Secretary of Labor, September 12, 1919, RG 174, 8/102-E.

the city council redoubled its efforts to ensure that the city's accommodations were segregated. The atmosphere in France was decidedly different, but the racial attitudes of the American military hierarchy apparently were not. Bitterness swept the 8th when a white officer replaced Colonel Denison as commanding officer in France. The white colonel, charged the unit's chaplain, Major William S. Braddan, was "one of the worst enemies of the colored soldiers." He allegedly branded the soldiers of the 8th as "a bunch of thieves," adding that he had "never seen as many ruffians outside of prison." Braddan also quoted the colonel as saying: "You are not fit for a combat unit, you are nothing but an armed mob, unfit for ought save a labor battalion." Whatever the truth of these allegations, it is evident that numerous black troops abhorred the colonel, and that he in turn had contempt for many of them.[22]

Postwar hostility to the aspirations of blacks was intense and widespread. In the early months of 1919, lynchings proliferated, several of them of black soldiers still in uniform. Moreover, white people misconstrued these aspirations as overweening exertions for social equality; and as expectations of equality collided with the general determination of whites to reestablish prewar subserviency, bitter disillusionment set in upon the black community. The war, however, and its concomitant, the migration, had helped to form the New Negro, who would persevere with intensified militancy in spite of and perhaps even because of the opposition. Black people had endured oppression when there seemed to be no other alternative; but once the war had suggested the possibility of escape, oppression became intolerable. It was thus not a case of absolute deprivation but of relative deprivation, especially for the

[22] Sgt. Oscar Walker, "The Eighth Regiment in France," in *Heroes of 1918*, not paginated; *Chicago Defender,* July 28, August 25, September 22, October 13, November 10, 1917; *Champion,* I (September 1916), 7–9, 39–40 ff.; Edgar A. Schuler, "The Houston Race Riot, 1917," *Journal of Negro History,* XXIX (July 1944), 300–38; Ross, *My Colored Battalion,* 9–10; *Chicago Broad Ax,* May 3–June 21, 1919.

migrants who had usually arrived in Chicago with higher expectations and lower skills than Northern blacks. For the migrants in particular, the obdurate resistance of whites could be psychologically more disruptive in a dynamic urban setting than in a traditional area of the South. And, of course, there were the aspirations, embittered though they were, of the black soldier. He "is coming back," A. L. Jackson told a group of white business and professional men, "with a consciousness of power hitherto unrealized, a sense of manhood, and a belief in his ability to carry responsibility. He believes," Jackson added, "that his strength is the same as that of other men." This assertion of independence and manliness was a sentiment with which much of Chicago's black community seemed to agree in 1919. For many blacks, the period of patient endurance was past. Sparked by persistent antagonism or by a dramatic racial incident, they might well retaliate against whites, and the tinderbox of race relations would burst into flames.[23]

Other indispensable facets of the New Negro attitude were race pride and heightened race consciousness. Culturally as well as politically and economically, both were useful as antidotes for the fever of race hatred in the United States, and in its cultural aspects the New Negro attitude had been evolving since at least the turn of the century. "Race prejudice," white sociologist Robert E. Park wrote in his introduction to the Chicago Urban League's 1917 report, "in so far as it has

[23] Chicago Urban League, *Annual Report,* II (no imprint), 3–4; Loraine Green, "The Rise of Race-Consciousness in the American Negro" (unpublished M.A. thesis, University of Chicago, 1919), 49 ff.; Lewis A. Coser, "Violence and the Social Structure," in Shalom Endleman, *Violence in the Streets* (Chicago: Quadrangle, 1968), 74–75; Ralph H. Turner (ed.), *On Social Control and Collective Behavior* (Chicago: University of Chicago Press, 1967), 173; report of Brandeis University's Lemberg Center for the Study of Violence, in *Washington Post,* June 27, 1967; Neil J. Smelser, *Theory of Collective Behavior* (N.Y.: The Free Press, 1962), 243; "Returning Soldiers," *Crisis,* XVIII (May 1919), 14; A. L. Jackson, "Chicago's Negro Problem," City Club of Chicago *Bulletin,* XII (March 17, 1919), 75.

compelled him to think always and everywhere in racial terms, has given the Negro a cause, and created a solidarity and unity of purpose which might not otherwise exist." This observation was indeed pertinent to the world of black culture. Years before the war, with its migration and accelerated urbanization for blacks, the impulse toward cultural autonomy and ethnocentrism had been evident. Parents started to buy black dolls for their children, even spending a little more for them. "Lift Ev'ry Voice and Sing," written in 1900, became the "Negro National Anthem." Unashamed racial themes began to distinguish the art and literature of black intellectuals. A further cultural example of race pride and consciousness involved the color of the Lord. A *Crisis* editorial in 1914, intimating that Jesus was "not a white man," touched off the profitable issuance of such pamphlets as *Jesus Was Born Out of the Black Tribe, Jesus Christ Was Part Negro,* and *The Black Man, the Father of Civilization, Proven by Biblical History.* And in 1915, to explode the myths of black history, Carter G. Woodson, aided by Dr. George Cleveland Hall, A. L. Jackson, and several other men, organized the Association for the Study of Negro Life and History at Chicago's Wabash Avenue YMCA. The Association's *Journal of Negro History* first appeared in January 1916, beginning what John Hope Franklin has called perhaps "the most far-reaching and ambitious effort to rewrite history that has ever been attempted in this country." It was also significant, Franklin has written, as "a remarkable attempt to rehabilitate a whole people" and "to develop self-respect and self-esteem." [24]

[24] Chicago Urban League, *Annual Report,* I (no imprint), 4; August Meier, *Negro Thought in America, 1880–1915* (Ann Arbor; Ann Arbor Paperbacks of University of Michigan Press, 1966), 256–78; Green, "Rise of Race Consciousness," 3–9, 40–44; Robert E. Park, *Race and Culture* (Glencoe, Illinois: Free Press, 1950), 87; W. Lloyd Warner, *Color and Human Nature: Negro Personality Development in a Northern City* (Washington: American Council on Education, 1941), 16; "The Color of the Lord," *Crisis,* VIII (June 1914), 73; Miles Mark Fisher, "The Negro Church and the World War," *Journal*

Although the beginnings of this cultural rebirth antedated the war and the migration, these latter events were powerful stimulants to its emergence. Perhaps its leading edge during and after the war was the New Negro poetry. "A people that is producing poetry . . . ," asserted a professor of English at the time, "is not a people that is perishing. On the contrary, it is a people that is astir with vital impulses, a people inspired by life-giving visions." Robert Park even felt that the New Negro poetry not only reflected a new dynamism in black culture but that indeed it was "a transcript of Negro life" itself. Even while treating such racial and literary categorizations with skepticism, the scholar still must view the black poetry of 1919 as an invaluable source. For it was, among other things, the poetry of rebellion and protest, and it mirrored the predisposition of black men and women to identify white skin with oppression.[25]

It was "the stirring year 1917," the black scholar and writer William Stanley Braithwaite has noted, "that heard the first real masterful accent in Negro poetry." That September the *Crisis* published Roscoe Jameson's "Negro Soldiers," and the next month, in *The Seven Arts,* appeared Claude McKay's "The Harlem Dancer." Glorifications of black beauty and courage, these works seemed to touch off a poetic interest in being black, thus reversing the prewar art with its imitation of white values and customs and its suppression of black individuality. Moreover, with the bitter disillusionment of the immediate postwar months, the pathways to cultural assimila-

---

of Religion, V (September 1925), 494; Carter G. Woodson, "Ten Years of Collecting and Publishing the Records of the Negro," *Journal of Negro History,* X (October 1925), 598–606; John Hope Franklin, "The New Negro History," *Journal of Negro History,* XLII (April 1957), 93–94.

[25] For the characteristics of race consciousness, see W. O. Brown, "Nature of Race Consciousness," *Social Forces,* X (October 1931), 90–97; Robert E. Park, "Negro Race Consciousness as Reflected in Race Literature," *American Review,* I (September-October 1923), 505–6; Park, *Race and Culture,* 299; Frazier, "American Negro's New Leaders," 58–59.

tion were impeded, and, as if by reflex, literary race pride in 1919 was dramatically heightened. Some black writers, trying to breach the caste barrier, still sought to erase racial distinctions, cultural and otherwise. But other writers, and especially the younger ones, glorified the selfsame characteristics disdained by those who aspired to become "whiter and whiter" with every generation. In "The Mulatto to His Critics," for example, a poet earnestly identified with being black, spurning the urge to "pass" for white, while another black poet placed his pagan African heritage on a plane superior to his Christian American environment. These men and women no longer wanted to imitate white America; they were proud of what they were.[26]

Although in a real sense positive contributions, race pride and heightened race consciousness did more than build up self-respect. They militated against nonviolence. As lynchings and other forms of oppression abounded early in 1919, black poets increasingly condemned the white perpetrators of the crimes. In July 1919, for example, Claude McKay's "A Roman Holiday" appeared:

'Tis but a modern Roman holiday;
Each state invokes its soul of basest passion,
Each vies with each to find the ugliest way
To torture Negroes in the fiercest fashion.
Black Southern men, like hogs await your doom!
White wretches hunt and haul you from your huts,
They squeeze the babies out your women's wombs,
They cut your members off, rip out your guts!

[26] Braithwaite, "The Negro in American Literature," in Locke, *New Negro*, 38–40. For a discussion of the origins and manifestations of the "Negro Renaissance," see Robert A. Bone, *The Negro Novel in America* (New Haven: Yale University Press, 1958), 61–64; Park, "Race Consciousness in Race Literature," 509, 511–12; Bond, "Negro Leadership since Washington," 116–17; Georgia D. Johnson, "The Octoroon," *Liberator*, II (August 1919), 10; Countee Cullen, "Heritage," in Locke, *New Negro*, 250.

Other poems, nearly as inflammatory, were also published at this time. Undoubtedly several of these descriptions of the horrors of hangings and burnings were true, but the poems indicted the white race as a whole; the object of bitterness had been generalized from the "cracker" to all whites. The black press likewise railed indiscriminately against an entire race over the depredations of a few fiends. In this respect, Chicago's *Defender* and *Whip* were prime offenders.[27]

Chicago's black community in 1919 identified white skin more and more with oppression. In this teeming metropolis, impersonality bred stereotypes and mutual distrust, especially along racial lines. A. L. Jackson warned a gathering of white men in March 1919: "Young men among the negroes . . . are growing up with a suspicion against anything that is white. . . . We cannot afford to let this attitude grow." [28] Stanley Norvell, a black ex-officer of the American Expeditionary Force, similarly explained to Victor F. Lawson, editor of the *Chicago Daily News,* that "Negroes have become highly suspicious of white men, even such white men as they deem their friends ordinarily." [29]

Considered with the New Negro's fierce determination to defend himself, this stereotype of the white oppressor was portentous. A single instance of aggression could be ascribed by blacks to all white Chicagoans; in massive retaliation against all available whites for the immediate misdoings of a few, a race war would surely result.

[27] *Liberator,* II (July 1919), 21; see Georgia D. Johnson, "Prejudice," *Crisis,* XVIII (May 1919), 14; Walter Hawkins, "A Festival in Christendom," in Robert T. Kerlin (ed.), *Negro Poets and Their Poems* (Washington: Associated Publishers, 1923), 234–35; G. R. Margetson, "The Fledgling Bard and the Poetry Society," in Newman I. White, "Racial Feeling in Negro Poetry," *South Atlantic Quarterly,* XXI (January 1922), 22; Eugene Gordon, "A Survey of the Negro Press," *Opportunity,* V (January 1927), 8.

[28] Jackson, "Chicago's Negro Problem," 75–76.

[29] S. Norvell, Chicago, to V. Lawson, Chicago, August 22, 1919, Rosenwald Papers; also in William M. Tuttle, Jr. (ed.), "Views of a Negro during 'the Red Summer' of 1919," *Journal of Negro History,* LI (July 1966), 209–18.

* * *

Outspoken government officials generally could see only a
Bolshevik plot behind the retaliatory violence of a people
they thought they knew as docile and cheerful. Behind the
Chicago race riot, there is "more than the smouldering antagonism of race feeling," a British intelligence officer authorita-
tively reported. The riot was the result of "a vicious and well
financed propaganda" campaign. But who would finance such
unrest and why would they want to promote bloodshed? His
answer was simple enough: "Revolutionary agitators [who
seek] to stimulate a sympathetic unrest among the coloured
races in order to make the breakdown of the Capitalist system
universal." Without agitators, an American Army intelligence
officer agreed, there would have been no racial violence that
summer. The "inspiring parties," he reported, were members
of the "Boule," a secret society in West Africa. The "Boule,"
or "Bowl," as some people called it, was anarchistic, and it
made its members take an oath swearing "to die defending
their brothers and to exterminate white rulers." The New
York State Senate's Lusk Committee was another governmental endeavor to impute to radicalism the race pride of black
men and women and their determination to retaliate against
aggression. Also in 1919 Representative James F. Byrnes of
South Carolina followed this lead and declared that the race
riots "were part of a general scheme of that 'Little Russia'
[which] is being established in the North." Partly as a consequence of Byrnes' accusation, the Justice Department initiated an investigation of radicalism and sedition among black
people. The report of the Attorney General's investigation
not only assailed blacks for their "ill-governed reaction
toward race rioting" and for recommending "retaliatory
measures in connection with lynching," but also cited as seditious the blacks' "political stand . . . toward the present
Federal administration, the South in general, and inciden-
tally, toward the peace treaty and the league of nations." A
further criterion of black radicalism was apparently the de-

nunciation of Booker T. Washington's racial philosophy; those who condemned it were not to be trusted. The report intimated, moreover, that an end to black subserviency was a threat to law and order.[30]

The New Negro attitude was a radical departure from the doctrines of Washington, but it was manifestly not Bolshevistic. Even Attorney General A. Mitchell Palmer, before his antiradical operations shifted into high gear, admitted that the Washington and Chicago race riots were "due solely to local conditions." [31] Although certain newspapers and periodicals such as the *Challenge, Crusader, Messenger, Negro World,* and *Veteran* did seize upon radical economic and political solutions for racial problems, the overwhelming majority of black men and women were too race conscious to embrace extreme class consciousness.

Chicago's leading black weeklies emphatically denounced Bolshevism. The *Defender,* in fact, published a cartoon in July 1919 which pictured four vultures perching on a tree limb; these "Birds of a Feather" were the "Lyncher," "Bomber of Our Homes," "Segregation," and "Bolshevism." The *Broad Ax* was likewise in adamant opposition to all shades of radicalism.[32]

After the Chicago race riot an Army intelligence officer

[30] W. F. Elkins, " 'Unrest among the Negroes': A British Document of 1919," *Science and Society,* XXXII (Winter 1968), 68–79; *Chicago Daily News,* November 5, 1919; Arthur I. Waskow, *From Race Riot to Sit-In, 1919 and the 1960s* (Garden City, N.Y.: Doubleday, 1966), 77–79, 186–96; Chicago Commission, *Negro in Chicago,* 574–575; *New York Times,* October 5, 1919; Major H. A. Strauss, USA, to Director, Military Intelligence, Subject: Negro Agitation, July 1, 1919, in Glasser Files, Justice Department (RG 60) Papers, National Archives; State of New York, Joint Legislative Committee Investigating Seditious Activities, *Revolutionary Radicalism* (Albany: J. B. Lyon, 1920), II, 1210–11, 1312–13, 1464–66, 1476–1520; *Congressional Record,* LVIII, 4302 ff.; 66th Cong., 1st Sess., U. S. Senate, *Investigation Activities of the Justice Department,* 162, 164.

[31] *New York Times,* July 31, 1919.

[32] *Chicago Defender,* May 10, July 12, 1919; *Chicago Broad Ax,* July 12, 1919.

submitted a report to the Chicago Commission on Race Relations charging the Industrial Workers of the World with responsibility for the bloodshed. The officer compiled a list of "inflammatory" meetings at which the IWW supposedly propagandized blacks. Several of the Commission's members, however, had attended the same meetings and "were able to report personally the entire absence of any of the features described in the report." [33]

Many white Americans were groping in the dark for the origins of the New Negro. As often happens they came up with a simple answer to a complex phenomenon. They did not perceive that race pride and the readiness to retaliate were the offspring of such dynamics as the war and the migration.

Other government officials could not perceive, or perhaps would not admit it if they could, that the readiness of black people to retaliate was also born of their profound lack of faith in all levels of government. Their disillusionment with the administration of Woodrow Wilson was both bitter and widespread. As a presidential candidate, Wilson had solicited their votes; and his campaign pronouncements, although probably influencing few blacks to transfer party allegiance, had fostered the race's trust in him. Writing to a leading black clergyman in 1912, Wilson had expressed his desire to "assure my coloured fellow citizens of my earnest wish to see justice done them in every matter, and not mere grudging justice, but justice executed with liberality and cordial good feeling." But once elected, he failed to nominate a black politician for the ministerial post to Haiti and he did not fully endorse his black nominee for the Register of the Treasury, both slots traditionally held by black men. Worse yet, the Bureau of Printing and Engraving, the Post Office Department,

[33] Minutes of the Chicago Commission on Race Relations, December 4, 1919, in Rosenwald Papers, and in Papers of Chicago Commission on Race Relations (CCRR), Illinois State Archives, Springfield, Illinois.

and offices of the Treasury Department segregated dining and toilet facilities and certain working areas. As a consequence of federal segregation, Booker T. Washington dejectedly observed: "I have never seen the colored people so discouraged and bitter as they are at the present time." [34]

Wilson was out of touch with the race's needs and aspirations, as various incidents of his first administration revealed. For example, the first motion picture to be shown at the White House was *The Birth of a Nation*. Wilson not only did not respect the protests of blacks, he retaliated. In late 1914 he remarked after a siege of criticism: "If the colored people made a mistake in voting for me, they ought to correct it." The black supporters of Wilson in 1912 generally swung back to the Republican party in 1916.[35]

The President's inaction during the East St. Louis, Illinois, race riot of the summer of 1917 was one more reason for opposing him. It was also the event which more than any other destroyed the faith of Chicago's black people in their

[34] See NAACP-1 (C-272, 411); Meier, *Negro Thought in America*, 186–89; Arthur S. Link, "The Negro as a Factor in the Election of 1912," *Journal of Negro History*, XXXII (January 1947), 81–99; R. S. Baker, *Woodrow Wilson, Life and Letters: Governor, 1910–1913* (Garden City, N.Y.: Doubleday, Doran, 1931), III, 387–88; other assurances by Wilson included a paid advertisement in the *Crisis*, V (November 1912), 44–45; and a friendly statement to a delegation headed by William Monroe Trotter in July 1912, see *Crisis*, IV (September 1912), 216–17; Henry Blumenthal, "Woodrow Wilson and the Race Question," *Journal of Negro History*, XLVIII (January 1963), 1–21; "Segregation in Government Departments," *Crisis*, VII (November 1913), 343–44; "Federal Segregation," *ibid.*, 331–34; Oswald Garrison Villard, "The President and Segregation at Washington," *North American Review*, CXCVIII (December 1913), 800–7; Kathleen L. Wolgemuth, "Woodrow Wilson and Federal Segregation," *Journal of Negro History*, XLIV (April 1959), 158–73; Nancy J. Weiss, "The Negro and the New Freedom: Fighting Wilsonian Segregation," *Political Science Quarterly*, LXXXIV (March 1969), 61–79.

[35] Lewis Jacobs, *The Rise of the American Film* (N.Y.: Harcourt, Brace, 1939), 175; *New York Times*, November 13, 1914; Gosnell, *Negro Politicians*, 27–28; the *Chicago Defender* was particularly hostile to Wilson's reelection; see the issues of October 7, 14, 21, 28, 1916, in which the *Defender* put down "Wilson's Ideal Negro" as an "Old Uncle Tom."

state government's ability and willingness to protect them. The toll of about forty blacks dead and hundreds wounded was ominous, since the tensions which precipitated the tragic riot—job competition, housing, politics—were building in Chicago. During the violence the state militia and local police had connived and often united with the white mobs in shooting, burning, and hanging blacks. Chicago's black community believed it had abundant justification for arming itself.[36]

The shameful dereliction of the state militia and the police touched off an explosion of indignation among Chicago's black people. They were, as a migrant informed his pastor in Alabama, "very much torn up about East St. Louis." The Negro Fellowship League and several AME churches sent burning protests to President Wilson and Governor Lowden. At a gathering of 100 black men in July 1917, Ferdinand L. Barnett, an attorney, advised the audience to fall back upon its own resources for protection.

> Arm yourselves now with guns and pistols. . . . Don't buy an arsenal, but get enough guns to protect yourselves. You may be victims in Chicago within a fortnight of such murders and outrages as have taken place in East St. Louis. And when trouble starts let us not hesitate to call upon our Negro militiamen to defend us. . . . Protect yourselves. And let no black man permit a policeman to come in and get those guns.

At the same meeting, A. H. Roberts, a black state senator, called for divine vengeance; he hoped that "God would de-

---

[36] 65th Cong., 2nd Sess., U. S. House of Representatives, Committee on Rules, *East St. Louis Riots* (Washington: Government Printing Office, 1918), 6, 8–10, 15–16, 18; "The Massacre of East St. Louis," *Crisis*, XIV (September 1917), 219–38; Graham Taylor, a Chicago social worker, and others reported that "East St. Louis sounded the alarm," impelling blacks to establish "private arsenals," Graham Taylor, "Chicago in the Nation's Race Strife," *Survey*, XLII (August 9, 1919), 695; Elliott M. Rudwick, *Race Riot at East St. Louis, July 2, 1917* (Carbondale: Southern Illinois University Press, 1964), *passim.*

mand 100,000 white lives in the war for each Negro slaughtered in East St. Louis." [37]

The stories of mass racial murder in East St. Louis were too horrible to blot out of one's memory overnight. Meeting in Chicago seven months later, the AME's midwestern bishops reminded Governor Lowden of the inconsistency of hastily sending troops to Chicago in September 1917 to prevent a group of pacifists "from discussing an academic political question," while it "took three long days to get a battalion of troops from Springfield to East St. Louis, Illinois, to quell the slaughter of scores of Race men, women, and children. . . ." "All this credit or discredit, as you like it," concluded the *Defender*, "belongs exclusively to Governor Frank O. Lowden." [38]

If East St. Louis shattered the trust of black men and women in the state's capacity to protect them, the behavior of Chicago's police only intensified their insecurity and readiness to furnish their own protection. Black people had long complained of insufficient billets in the police department, and it was not until the Thompson administration that the city government was responsive to these entreaties; it doubled black representation on the force between 1915 and 1919. Even in that latter year, however, blacks, while comprising over 4 per cent of the city's population and at least 6 per cent of its laboring force, still made up less than 2 per cent of the police establishment. But it was not just representation; it was a matter of protection. Throughout the late spring and early

[37] Unpublished autobiography of Mrs. Ida B. Wells-Barnett, 352–365, in possession of Mrs. Barnett's daughter, Mrs. Alfreda Duster, in Chicago; [?] Cooper to [?] Hayes, November 6, 1917, in E. J. Scott Papers in War Department Papers, National Archives; Chicago Commission, *Negro in Chicago*, 544; *Chicago Defender*, July 7, 14, 21, 1917; *Crisis*, XV (January 1918), 116–21; Emmett J. Scott, "Additional Letters of Negro Migrants of 1916–1918," *Journal of Negro History*, IV (October 1919), 463; *Congressional Record*, LV, 5410–11; *Chicago Daily Tribune*, July 5, 24, 1917.

[38] *Chicago Defender*, February 23, 1918. See also Spear, *Black Chicago*, 202–3.

summer of 1919, as white mobs wantonly murdered several black men and beat numerous others, the residents of the black belt were so anxious about their security that they pleaded with the city administration for much more than black increments to the police force; since certain white officers were conspicuously sympathetic to the mobsters, the black people begged that every white patrolman in the black belt be replaced with "a colored bluecoat." [39]

Although decades of race friction in Chicago had antedated World War I, it was not until the wartime influx that the proliferation of gang assaults on isolated blacks, pitched battles between teenagers, and other outbursts of racial violence helped to precipitate a full-scale riot. In July 1917, for example, a gang of angry white youths, having heard that a local white saloonkeeper had been murdered by a black man, boarded an automobile, located a streetcorner gathering of blacks, and fired their weapons into it. The saloonkeeper had actually died of a heart attack. Racial violence also erupted that summer and fall on streetcars and elevated trains, at transfer points, in the parks, and along Wentworth Avenue. Clarence Kelly was riding a southbound elevated train in July, when a mob of whites forced him off the train. But the "cheap ruffians," as the *Defender* described them, alighted with Kelly and started to chase him. Hearing the uproar, a nearby white policeman slipped behind the pursued black man and hit him over the head with his pistol. When Kelly tried to rise, the officer fired a shot into his body. Lying in a pool of blood, Kelly was finally taken to a hospital, but he died two hours later. Bitterness frequently originated in the schools. Black students leaving the school grounds after ad-

[39] *Chicago Defender,* July 6, 1918; Chicago Commission, *Negro in Chicago,* 490; Bureau of the Census, *14th Census, 1920* (Washington: Government Printing Office, 1923), IV, 1078; Harold F. Gosnell, *Negro Politicians: The Rise of Negro Politics in Chicago* (Chicago: Phoenix Books of University of Chicago Press, 1967), 250; Spear, *Black Chicago,* 35–36; clippings from *Brooklyn Daily Eagle* and *Brooklyn Standard Union,* both August 25, 1919, in NAACP-2.

journment encountered brickbats as well as brutal taunts and epithets, and black and white youths, screaming "nigger," "Mick," and "white trash," had rock fights, which, as one participant recalled, were "out of this world." Usually there were no serious injuries, just "hickies and things like black eyes," but on one occasion a black youngster lost an eye, and on another, one broke an arm.[40]

Black people deplored these attacks and insults. But what probably disturbed them just as much were the inactivity and occasional collusion of the police. Stories of alleged brutality, of "white skunk officers," studded practically every page of local news in the *Defender*. Whether this reportage was entirely accurate was not so important as the fact that this was the way the black press, and probably the vast bulk of the black population, perceived the white arm of the law. Just as whites had generalized beliefs about blacks as being immoral, criminal, and emotional, among other things, so blacks had generalized beliefs about whites that caused them to distrust and even to hate them. And the most visible, and at times hateful, of the whites were white policemen. "White scum" not only beat defenseless women without provocation, they also were agents of segregation. In October 1917 the captain of the precinct which was situated to serve 70 per cent of Chicago's blacks ordered an end in cabarets of "the MINGLING of Colored and white patrons of both sexes. . . ." Although the captain's stated purpose was "to avoid the starting of disputes or quarrels which may terminate in serious race riots," his order nevertheless offended blacks, who argued that the police force was racist, brutal, and "for Irish alone." "Why," the *Defender* asked, "is the dark brother on the police force put in plain clothes as soon as he is promoted? We see no [black] police sergeants, no [black] lieu-

[40] Interview with Mr. John Turner Harris, Chicago, June 26, 1969; *Chicago Defender,* March 17, July 7, August 11, October 6, November 17, December 29, 1917, January 19, 1918; Chicago Commission, *Negro in Chicago,* 595–96.

tenants in uniform on duty . . . ," only Irish. If such "skunks
. . . don't want to associate with honorable men," they
should be discharged. "A dismissal of one or two Irish brats
would make the rest sit up and take notice." Moreover, if a
black read or heard of an instance of alleged brutality, the
name of the officer involved was usually Irish—McCarthy,
Healey, Murphy, McGuire. Headlines in the black press proclaimed that innocent black men and women were either
"beaten by Irish Officers" or assaulted by them "with abusive
language." [41]

The summer of 1918 was even more uneasy than that of
the year before, with increased attacks in the schools and
parks, at the beaches, and on public conveyances. Clashes
frequently broke out at Washington Park, which disgruntled
whites had begun to call "Booker T. Washington Park." Chicago's beaches were "FREE TO ALL," the *Defender* had
reminded its readers for months; they "belong to the citizens
of Chicago," "there are no certain places designated" for
blacks. But when black people tried to enjoy these public facilities, lifeguards prohibited them from entering the water
and white mobs chased them off with rocks. Biracial amusement, or even what appeared to be biracial amusement, also
continued to ignite violence. Julian Valdes, a black man, was
in the company of four black women, when two police officers, thinking that two of the women were white, and probably prostitutes, began to flirt. Valdes protested, trying to explain, when one of the officers bellowed: "Nigger, what in the
hell are you doing with these white women? Let's beat this
darky's brain out. It makes my blood boil to see a nigger
anywhere around a white woman." Again Valdes protested.
But then the officer, swearing that if this were Georgia he
would see Valdes lynched, struck him in the eye, causing a
bloody gash. "The situation has become serious in the Second
Ward," complained the *Defender,* with white policemen ac-

[41] *Chicago Defender*, October 20, 27, November 3, 10, December
8, 1917, January 19, February 16, 23, 1918.

costing and insulting black women and abusing respectable citizens. And tension mounted as the morals squad raided certain of the South Side's cabarets and alleged whorehouses in the summer and autumn of 1918; what seemed to unsettle law authorities even more than the illegal acts themselves was the fact of a biracial clientele committing them. Observers predicted that if a race riot broke out in Chicago, it would probably be a barroom incident that would be the immediate precipitator. "ALL SOUTH SIDE SLEEPING OVER A VOLCANO," proclaimed the *Broad Ax,* adding with apparent prohibitionist sentiments that rioting would strike Chicago just as it had East St. Louis, "unless the saloons are gotten rid of." [42]

Chicago's deteriorating race relations in 1919 were in almost inverse ratio to the rising temperatures and seething labor unrest. Minor affrays in April, May, and early June excited the black community, and the *Chicago Evening Post* noted that the black belt was "a potential stick of dynamite. What happened in Springfield and East St. Louis—not to [mention] outside of the bounds of our own state—can and may happen in Chicago." But these were relatively minor symptoms of the illness. It was not until the murder of two black men on the evening of June 21 that racial hatred leaped to fever pitch, and that the plummeting faith of blacks in the police struck bottom.[43]

[42] *Chicago Defender,* August 4, 1917, March 23, June 8, 27, August 3, September 21, October 19, November 2, December 28, 1918; Arna Bontemps and Jack Conroy, *Anyplace But Here* (N.Y.: Hill and Wang, 1966), 179; *Chicago Broad Ax,* August 17, 1918; interview with Mr. A. L. Jackson, Chicago, June 27, 1969.

[43] *Chicago Daily Tribune,* April 23–24, May 4, 6, 9, 10, 14, 1919; and *Chicago Evening Post,* quoted in St. Luke *Herald* (Richmond, Virginia), June 7, 1919, all clippings in NAACP-2; *Chicago Broad Ax,* May 3, 1919; Kerlin, *Voice of the Negro,* 82. On April 25, the *Defender* indicted the police for not arresting white rowdies; one of its front page headlines was "White Policemen Cause So. Side Riot," but the article dealt with minor scuffles, not a riot. On May 27, a white gang with revolvers, reportedly part of Ragen's Colts, began a bar fight with a black man. On June 13, a black father assaulted the white

White and black gangs had collided near the black belt on June 13, and two days later another clash erupted, this time in Washington Park. These gang fights were inconclusive; the evening of June 21 was to be the occasion of "the big battle," and the showdown was scheduled to be waged in Washington Park. Shortly before midnight, warfare erupted near a grade school where white students had recently terrorized their black classmates with rocks. From that point, incidents of violence burst forth in rapid succession. At 12:30, an anonymous telephone voice informed the Stock Yards Police Station that a white mob was "out to kill all the blacks." Two hundred policemen hastened to Washington Park, but the mob had decided to split up and seek out isolated blacks to assault, and apparently to avoid the park. The first murder victim fell with a bullet in his stomach a few minutes before midnight. Although an alert bystander hastily seized one of the armed assailants and summoned a policeman, the officer neither arrested the white mobster, notwithstanding the revolver in the accused's hands, nor did he examine the weapon to determine whether or not it had been discharged. Another unprovoked attack killed a second black man that night. A white gang stormed out of a poolroom, shot and stabbed the man, and assured his demise by beating him over the head with billiard cues.[44]

The bloodshed of June 21 inflamed the black community, while the lack of arrests practically assured future clashes. At the nucleus of this white lawlessness, as everybody seemed to know, was the Irish athletic club, the Ragen Colts. "RAGAN'S [*sic*] COLTS START RIOT," was the *Defend-*

---

principal of a grade school near the black belt, apparently because the principal had not stopped white students who had hurled rocks at their black classmates: *Chicago Herald-Examiner,* June 15, 1919; *Chicago Defender,* April 26, June 7, 21, 1919.

[44] *Chicago Herald-Examiner,* June 23, 1919; *Chicago Daily Tribune,* June 23, 27, 1919; Chicago Commission, *Negro in Chicago,* 56–57, 595–96; *Chicago Broad Ax,* July 26, 1919; *Chicago Defender,* June 21, 28, 1919; *Chicago Daily News,* August 2, 1919; various reactions from the black press, in NAACP-2's newspaper clippings.

er's banner headline after the night of June 21; "Gang of Hoodlums Riddle Man's Body With Bullets." But only infrequently did the police interfere with the Colts' violent activities. Many of the members, as the *Defender* observed, were "sons and relatives of a number of the policemen of the Stock Yards station and, as a result, their depredations seldom occasioned an arrest." The Colts received an added measure of protection as the political underlings of a local Democratic machine. Obviously feeling that the government of William Hale Thompson was not safeguarding their vital interests, the Colts resorted to vigilante action against blacks. The Colts, moreover, felt increasingly threatened in 1919, as they watched black workers walk through the gates at the stockyards, as they heard of their foe Thompson's overwhelming electoral victories in the Second Ward, as they saw black families picnicking and relaxing in Washington Park. In early summer, the Colts had paraded down an isolated street in the black belt, smashing street lights and windows; by midsummer, they were ready to commit murder. As they perceived the threat from black people intensifying during the sultry days of 1919, the Colts' solidarity likewise intensified —and with it their race hatred and violent behavior.[45]

The violence of June 21 had purged no emotions. Nine days later two black brothers, James and Charles Jackson, battled a mob of nearly fifty whites. Riding a streetcar with several inebriated white passengers, the brothers had hotly objected to being jostled. Tempers and angry voices rose. James leaped from the streetcar at the next stop, but so did the white men, and they pummeled him brutally to the street. Charles fled, too, firing a pistol over his shoulder and wounding several of his pursuers as he ran; but the mob finally chased him over a railroad embankment, and he fatally broke his neck. Police officers then arrested James Jackson, evi-

[45] *Chicago Whip,* June 24, 1919; *Chicago Defender,* June 28, July 12, 1919; Robert E. Park *et al., The City* (Chicago: University of Chicago Press, 1925), 9–10; Frederic M. Thrasher, *The Gang: A Study of 1,313 Gangs in Chicago* (Chicago: University of Chicago Press, 1927), 15–17, 454–60, 472–73.

dently to shield him from further injury, but the *Defender* was nevertheless astounded. Their action was not only "reprehensible" in this fracas, the newspaper charged, but it "often savors a disposition on their part to sympathize with the mob."[46]

Race relations deteriorated further as Independence Day approached. The police received anonymous telephone messages threatening to run the black people out of Chicago and asserting that arrests of white rioters would produce "Rescue Parties." Following the murders of June 21, fliers were posted in or near the black belt announcing: "We will get you July 4." Blacks prepared to defend themselves. Black women who had to travel on public transportation began to carry knives and razors. The Reverend Archibald J. Carey incorporated into his sermons Matthew 24:44, "be ye also ready," as part of his warning to his parishioners to "arm their homes." By the Fourth, the long-awaited race war seemed at hand, and black people were prepared. The "July 4 picnic baskets," a social worker reported, "contained weapons which were regarded as more of a necessity of life than lunches." The holiday passed without any reported violence, causing the *Defender* to quip, "NO 'RACE RIOTS' on the Fourth of July, what do you know about that?" But tension still hung heavy in the air.[47]

Contemporaneous with the depredations of the white mobs

[46] *Chicago Daily Journal,* July 1, 1919; *Chicago Herald-Examiner,* July 1, 1919; *Chicago Defender,* July 5, 1919. *Defender,* July 5, 1919, maintained that Charles was killed not by a fall but by the blows of the mob. It added that he "did not die without leaving the impression that he was filled with 'Race consciousness' and intended to enjoy some of that democracy that he had fought for in France."

[47] *Chicago Daily Tribune,* June 23, 1919; Taylor, "Chicago in the Nation's Race Strife," 695; *Chicago Defender,* June 21, July 5, 12, 1919; Joseph A. Logsdon, "The Rev. Archibald J. Carey and the Negro in Chicago Politics" (unpublished M.A. thesis, University of Chicago, 1961), 70–71; J. Arthur Davis, "Chicago Rebellion: Free Black Men Fight Free White Men," *The Messenger,* II (September 1919), 31–32; White, "Notes on Chicago of WFW," in NAACP-2; interview with Mr. Chester Wilkins, Chicago, June 25, 1969; *Topeka Plaindealer,* August 8, 1919.

were, of course, the bombings both of blacks' residences and the offices of realtors whom black people patronized. As with the gang violence, the police arrested few of the bombers, and none was convicted. Black people such as the militant Ida B. Wells-Barnett, director of a recreation center, exhorted the city administration to enforce the law without regard to race. "Will no action be taken to prevent these lawbreakers until disaster has occurred?" the fiery Mrs. Barnett asked. "An ounce of prevention beats a pound of cure. And in all earnestness I implore Chicago to set the wheels of justice in motion before it is too late, and Chicago be disgraced by some of the bloody outrages that have disgraced East St. Louis." But the city took no action; and Chicago's black people prepared for the worst, knowing beyond doubt and from unhappy past experience that in the event of racial violence there would be only the flimsiest external police control to shield them from white mobs.[48]

July 1919 was a sultry month. Most days the temperature reached the nineties. People were restless and uncomfortable in the steaming heat. And to add to this discomfort, on the first day of July the wartime prohibition act went into effect, banning the manufacture or sale of whiskeys and other distilled spirits, wines, and beers containing more than one half of 1 per cent alcohol. Most Chicagoans thought the war was over; and just two months before, in a public referendum, the city's wets had outvoted the drys by 400,000 to 150,000. Legally, however, the war was not over, and the "wartime" prohibition would remain law "until the conclusion of the present war and thereafter until the termination of demobilization." Through a technicality, people complained, government would deny the popular will; and it seemed evident that prohibition had added to the general unrest. "It is folly," said

[48] Letter to the editor, *Chicago Daily Tribune*, July 7, 1919. See also minutes of the meeting of directors of the Chicago Law and Order League and the Hyde Park Protective Association, July 10, 1919, Papers of Hyde Park Protective Association, Chicago Historical Society.

John Fitzpatrick of the Chicago Federation of Labor, "to believe that wage disputes are solely responsible for these strikes in Chicago." Another potent cause, he explained, was the denial of beer and wine to the working class, while "the wealthy have their cellars full." [49]

During those sweltering days, one of the few events that the black community had to celebrate was the arrival home on Friday morning, July 25, of the 1,800 black troops of Illinois' 803rd Pioneer Infantry. Carrying their rifles, the black soldiers paraded down Michigan Avenue toward Grant Park, where friends had laid out a bountiful picnic, featuring "luscious kisses, jazz music, home folks an' fried chicken." At midafternoon, the troops entrained for demobilization processing at Camp Grant, an hour's ride from Chicago.[50]

July's abnormally high temperatures, averaging close to thirteen degrees above normal, caused interracial contacts to increase many-fold as Chicago's inhabitants sought relief at beaches and parks. The *Defender* and the *Whip* both recommended escape to the waters of Lake Michigan at 25th Street. In addition, swarming the streets were masses of people, including tens of thousands of workers on strike, teenagers out of school for the summer, and, on front stoops, the men and women who could no longer tolerate being in their hot and stuffy flats and apartments. Chicago was hot, frustrated, and angry that July. Worse yet, it was sitting atop the volcano of a race war, and that volcano was about to erupt. And, on July 27, it did.

[49] *Chicago Defender,* July 5, 1919; *New York Times,* April 2, July 1, 21, 1919.

[50] *Chicago Daily Tribune,* July 25, 1919; *Chicago Daily Journal,* July 24, 1919; *Chicago Daily News,* July 24, 1919; Taylor, "Chicago in Nation's Race Strife," 696.

Racial Violence in Chicago and the Nation: The Future, Immediate and Distant

THIRTY-EIGHT DEAD, 537 wounded, hundreds homeless—this was the toll, and an awesome one it was. Walter Lippmann, writing in 1919, deplored the Chicago race riot as "an event infinitely more disgraceful than that . . . Red Terror about which we are all so virtuously indignant. . . ." [1] Black and white Chicagoans also deplored the city's racial bloodshed. Some white people expressed astonishment at the news of the violence. Why Chicago? the incredulous asked. Chicago was a dynamic city, they said, a little rough perhaps, but at least its diverse ethnic, religious, and racial groups had been able to coexist for years without resorting to such rioting. Amazement and disbelief did not strike the black community, just sadness and a reaffirmation of self-defense. The riot, a black man recalled many years

[1] In the preface to Carl Sandburg, *The Chicago Race Riots* (N.Y.: Harcourt, Brace & Howe, 1919), iii.

later, brought Chicago's black people "closer together than they had ever been before," and it accelerated the trend toward arming for future danger.[2]

The riot in Chicago should have surprised few people, black or white, for it was well within the context of two modern historical phenomena: twentieth-century urban racial violence in America, and the frenzy of the year 1919. Added to these, of course, were the many peculiarities of Chicago's troubled history of race relations. In fact, the surprising thing to a historian studying the riot is not that it happened, but that it did not happen time and time again, especially in the tense and potentially explosive months after July 1919. For if the historian, working as a social scientist, were to have fed the facts of Chicago's post-riot racial unrest into a computer, that machine, having digested the pre-riot history of Chicago's race relations, would in all likelihood have predicted renewed eruptions of racial bloodshed.[3]

Not surprisingly, the Chicago race riot of 1919 marked no surcease to that period of transition between war and peace; it was just the midpoint in a year of unrest and violence that had several months yet to run.[4] Not only was the nation still in the throes of the Red Scare, but in the succeeding months it became even more haunted by the specter of radicalism, Bolshevism, and revolution. Worse yet in terms of deaths, racial warfare continued to erupt in America.

After Chicago, the next major riot of the Red Summer

[2] Interview with Chester A. Wilkins, Chicago, June 25, 1969.

[3] Regarding the following pages of this chapter, if the historical data in this study fit into any sociological construct, it would most closely resemble the framework of Neil J. Smelser's *Theory of Collective Behavior* (N.Y.: Free Press, 1962). Also helpful to the historian are H. O. Dahlke, "Race and Minority Riots—A Study in the Typology of Violence," *Social Forces*, XXX (May 1952), 419–25; and to a lesser degree, Stanley Lieberson and Arnold R. Silverman, "The Precipitants and Underlying Conditions of Race Riots," *American Sociological Review*, XXX (December 1965), 887–98.

[4] See Dahlke, "Race and Minority Riots," 423–25; Smelser, *Theory of Collective Behavior*, 12–21.

erupted in Omaha, Nebraska. A meat-packing center like Chicago, Omaha had also attracted thousands of Southern black men and women to its stockyards during the war, and by 1919 its black population had doubled to well over 10,000.[5] As in Chicago, too, racial tensions in Omaha had mounted with its rising black population. And when the fires of racial hatred had flared out of control in Chicago in July and August, their ugly glare had made Omaha's black people uncomfortable and fearful for their lives. Black workers in South Omaha's packing plants had congregated in small groups on July 29 to discuss arming themselves; and before the chief of police could issue an order the next day banning the sale of firearms, black people had purchased scores of weapons and ammunition. Also at the time of the Chicago bloodshed, Mayor Edward P. Smith, realizing the precarious state of race relations in his city, had ordered a local movie house to cease showing *The Birth of a Nation* or to remain closed until aroused racial feelings had subsided. Unlike Chicago, however, white Omaha believed it was suffering from an epidemic of black criminality and especially of sex crimes. And when on September 28 police arrested William Brown, a black man accused of molesting a young white girl, a mob of whites began to assemble at the courthouse, angrily demanding that the authorities release the alleged rapist to them for the execution of quick justice. When Mayor Smith mounted the courthouse steps in an effort to persuade the whites to disperse peacefully, he was taunted and heckled as a "nigger lover"; for to these people, the mayor, whose law firm was then in the employ of the NAACP to defend two black men accused of assaulting white women, represented the enemy. His appeal for calm unheeded and abused, Smith was then

---

[5] Omaha's black population was slightly in excess of 5 per cent of the total population. Along with Omaha, the other "jailhouse" riot in 1919 was in Knoxville, Tennessee, in late August and early September; see Arthur I. Waskow, *From Race Riot to Sit-In* (Garden City, N.Y.: Doubleday & Co., 1966), 105–10.

seized by the mob, which placed a rope around his neck, and had nearly succeeded in hanging him from a trolley pole when police cut the rope and rescued him. Still undeterred, and indeed even angrier, the mob lit a fire in the courthouse. Beginning on the first floor, the flames quickly lept up to the higher floors, but when the fire department arrived to extinguish the fire, the men in the mob cut the hoses. Still the flames rose, and, fleeing from them, the prisoners climbed to the roof, and there, to escape death themselves, several of them tried to throw Brown down to the mob. Finally, several men pushed past policemen and entered the building to capture Brown. Once the mob had him, Brown was shot, hanged from a lamppost, and his body burned, riddled with hundreds of bullets, and mutilated beyond recognition. Dreading another Chicago race riot, the state of Nebraska wired for federal assistance, and the War Department responded by dispatching troops from various forts in the region. Yet it was not just the Nebraska authorities who were apprehensive. In Springfield, Illinois, Mrs. Frank O. Lowden recorded in her diary that the governor had read the "sensational [newspaper] accounts of a mob in Omaha yesterday and of mob violence done. . . . Such actions," she noted, "stir up more trouble or are liable to elsewhere and Frank feels uneasy and so has decided to go to Chicago this evening." No race riot erupted in Chicago; and in Omaha, assisted by a downpour so torrential that the city's streetcars had to stop operations for a half hour, the soldiers were able to restore order. But by then four people were dead and fifty injured.[6]

[6] *Chicago Defender,* July 12, 1919; *Chicago Daily Journal,* July 30, August 1, 1919; *Chicago Herald-Examiner,* August 3, 5, 1919; diary of Mrs. Frank O. Lowden, September 29, 1919, in possession of Mrs. C. Phillip Miller, Chicago; Waskow, *From Race Riot to Sit-In,* 110–120; numerous newspaper clippings and much correspondence regarding the Omaha riot in Papers of the NAACP (NAACP-2), in the possession of the Middle Atlantic office of the Youth Division, Washington, D.C.; *New York Times,* September 29, 30, 1919; *Omaha Daily Bee,* September 30, October 1, 1919; Robert T. Kerlin, *The Voice of the Negro, 1919* (N.Y.: E. P. Dutton, 1920), 87; U. S. House of Repre-

On October 1, while federal troops were patrolling the streets of Omaha, news came from east central Arkansas of an armed insurrection of blacks against whites. In Phillips County, Arkansas, as in many cotton producing regions of the South, black farmers were not landowners but tenants or sharecroppers, working for a percentage of the cotton crops they cultivated. Much injustice plagued these black farmers. They could purchase provisions only at the "plantation" or other specified stores; and being continually in debt, they purchased goods on credit and in anticipation of a percentage of the sale price of their crops. They not only paid more than the average retail prices, but they were unable to obtain from the stores itemized statements of their indebtedness. Nor was this all. When the landowner sold the cotton, he customarily would not show the bill of sale to his tenants and sharecroppers, so they, of course, could not know the dollar value of the portion to which they were entitled. But an incident in mid-June 1919 warned the local black citizens of the futility and danger of protesting against such a system. A black farmer in Star City, Arkansas, who objected by refusing to work, was lynched and "a sign reading 'this is how we treat lazy niggers' was tacked to his head." [7]

Yet black farmers in Phillips County, singing "Organize, oh organize!" established a union, the Progressive Farmers and Household Union of America, through which they intended to protest to the landowners. Sixty-eight sharecroppers at a plantation near Ratio commissioned a white law firm in Little Rock to plead a test case. If the landowner would not produce an itemized statement of account, they would prosecute; failing that, they would refuse to pick cotton then in the field or to sell cotton belonging to them for less than the market price. Realizing the potential impact of this demand for

sentatives, 66th Cong., 2nd Sess., Committee on the Judiciary, *Hearings on H.J. Res. 75; H.R. 259, 4123, and 11873* [*Antilynching Hearings*] (Washington: Government Printing Office, 1920), 58.

[7] *Chicago Defender,* June 21, 1919; *Antilynching Hearings,* 58.

their rights, black farmers in the county armed themselves. Then, on October 1, a special agent of the Missouri Pacific Railroad was shot to death outside a black church in Hoop Spur, and a deputy sheriff with him was wounded. There were two versions of the shootings, one stating that the white detective fired "promiscuously" into the church, where a chapter of the Progressive Union was in session, and that the blacks returned the gunfire. The Little Rock *Arkansas Gazette* reported the other version, which was that the white men had parked near the church at Hoop Spur "to repair a puncture, and while working on the car the party was fired upon by unidentified persons," presumably black.[8]

News of the clash at Hoop Spur spread rapidly throughout the county and to towns across the Mississippi River. Armed white men sped to Helena, Arkansas, from Clarendon, Marianna, and Marvell on the Arkansas side of the river, and from Lula, Tunica, Friars Point, and Clarksdale on the Mississippi side. Emergency posses, totaling 500 men and including a detachment from the American Legion post at Helena, inundated Elaine, Arkansas. Frightened for their lives, black men fled into the woods and canebrakes; and white men, motivated in part by reports that the Progressive Union was advocating "social equality" and by rumors that the blacks had scheduled "a general slaughter of white people in the locality" for October 7, pursued them and massacred them. Martial law was declared on October 2, and the violence abated as soldiers of the regular Army were ordered from Camp Pike to Phillips County at the request of Governor Charles Brough.

"The white citizens of the county," Governor Brough declared on October 3, ". . . deserve unstinted praise for their action in preventing mob violence." It is scarcely possible to conceive of a statement so hideously ludicrous. For at least twenty-five black people, and probably many, many more,

[8] Little Rock *Arkansas Gazette,* October 2, 1919.

had been hunted down by white mobs and slaughtered like animals, and at least five white men had been killed as well.[9]

Other factors also make it difficult to explain why there was not a recurrence of race rioting in Chicago. In addition to the continuing presence of the year of transition, 1919, with its Red Scare and Red Summer, the fact of migration to Chicago was still abundantly evident. Not only did Southern blacks and demobilized soldiers continue to settle in Chicago, but efforts by recruiters to entice black people to the South after the riot were almost totally unsuccessful. Advertisements appeared in Chicago's newspapers, both black and white, after the riot. "TO COLORED LABOR SEEKING HOMES," read the statement in the *Broad Ax* of the Coahoma, Mississippi, Chamber of Commerce. Its purpose was to inform Chicago's black people that Coahoma "offers a home and great opportunities to those who care to

[9] A thorough study of the Elaine, Arkansas, riot is needed, one that would explore the relationship between the 1919 union and the Southern Tenant Farmers' Union of the 1930's, as well as the relationship between the Arkansas riot and the Longview riot and between labor conflict and racial violence in general. Beginning points for such a study would be Waskow, *From Race Riot to Sit-In*, 121–74; in NAACP-2, legal briefs re the riot; "Arkansas Riot," undated story; [U. S. Bratton?] to Senator Charles Curtis, November 8, 1919; Robert L. Hill to NAACP, November 26, 1919; [?], Marvell, Arkansas, to Emmett J. Scott, November 12, 1919; "The Story of a Southern White Man"; and undated statement of George Washington Davis, Pine City, Arkansas, in General Records of the Justice Department (RG 60), Glasser Files, Major Eugene E. Barton to Acting Intelligence Officer, Chicago, October 9, 1919; and report on riot from Captain Edward P. Passailaigue to Assistant Chief of Staff, G-2, 3rd Division, October 13, 1919; Little Rock *Arkansas Gazette*, September 27, October 2–4, 6, 1919; Walter F. White, "The Race Conflict in Arkansas," *Survey*, XLIII (December 13, 1919), 233–34; White, " 'Massacring Whites' in Arkansas," *Nation*, CIX (December 6, 1919), 715–16; Kerlin, *Voice of the Negro*, 88, 89; Mary White Ovington, *The Walls Came Tumbling Down* (N.Y.: Harcourt, Brace, 1947), 154–64; *Congressional Record*, LVIII, 8818–21; *Crisis*, XIX (December 1919), 56–62; O. A. Rogers, Jr., "The Elaine Race Riots of 1919," *Arkansas Historical Quarterly*, XIX (Summer 1960), 142–50; J. W. Butts and Dorothy James, "The Underlying Causes of the Elaine Riot of 1919," in *ibid.*, XX (Spring 1961), 95–104.

come. . . ." Kentucky advertised for coal miners and loaders, with its inducements being modern buildings, "commissary the best," steady work, and, perhaps above all, "NO LABOR TROUBLES." Recruiters also came to the city from Louisiana, Tennessee, and other parts of Mississippi, and they all seemed to be agreed on one thing. "I want the southern Negro, who is familiar with the South's general attitude on the race question," said a Mississippian who was looking for cotton pickers. A Louisianian added that he wanted 1,000 families, but not "colored people who have always lived in the north. . . ." They wanted the migrants to come back, but the recruiters found few takers. "The colored people in Chicago feel this is their last ditch," explained banker Jesse Binga. "Here is something to look forward to, [while] in the South they know there are Jim Crow cars, segregation, humiliation and degradation." "The colored people see that if they can't make it in Chicago," noted A. L. Jackson of the Wabash Avenue YMCA, "then it's no use to try somewhere else. Of all places they don't want to go back South." [10]

In addition, as the residents of Chicago's black community well knew, the hostility of the surrounding white ethnic groups had not diminished since the riot. Chicago's racial bloodshed had been the "ideal-type" or "type-case" of Northern urban racial violence, with the riot involving direct "ecological warfare" between the residents of white and black neighborhoods. After the riot, the stereotypes and generalized beliefs, which the nearby Irish- and Polish-Americans and various other ethnic groups held about black people, continued to be invariably deprecating and hostile. The black

---

[10] Report from Director, Division of Negro Economics, to Secretary of Labor, covering the period August 1–31, 1919, in General Records of the Labor Department (RG 174), 8/102-E; *Chicago Broad Ax,* August 16, 1919; *Chicago Herald-Examiner,* August 8, 1919; *Chicago Daily Tribune,* August 31, 1919; T. Arnold Hill, "Why Southern Negroes Don't Go South," *Survey,* XLIII (November 29, 1919), 183–185; and in NAACP Papers, Library of Congress (NAACP-1), numerous newspaper clippings, all in (C-373).

skin not only served as a symbol arousing distinctly unfavorable feelings toward black people, it also helped to redefine ambiguous and anxiety-producing situations; how easy it was to identify and condemn the despised black people as the source of one's anxiety and as the threat to one's economic security and social status. Moreover, Chicago's press did not cease reporting the news of black people in a disparaging manner, frequently indulging in minority baiting. And, finally, white people continued to disdain black men and women as undesirable competitors—in the labor market, in politics, in contested neighborhoods, and in public accommodations.[11]

With even greater frequency after the riot than before, bombs demolished windows, porches, vestibules, and other portions of the homes of black people residing in contested neighborhoods. Also damaged were the residences and offices of the realtors of both races who sold and rented to them. One in August and five in December 1919; and in 1920, six in February, one each in March, April, September, and December, and two in October—this was the toll of bombings.[12] Other realtors, politicians, and even the coroner's jury investigating the deaths of riot victims advocated the residential segregation of the races as the solution to unrest in the city.[13]

[11] Smelser, *Theory of Collective Behavior,* 8–9, 81–82, 101–9, 222 ff.; Allen D. Grimshaw, "A Study in Social Violence: Urban Race Riots in the United States" (unpublished Ph.D. dissertation, University of Pennsylvania, 1959), 155, 209–12; Dahlke, "Race and Minority Riots," 423–25; Waskow, *From Race Riot to Sit-In,* 10, 58–59.

[12] Minutes of the meeting of Executive Committee, February 20, 1920, in Papers of the Chicago Commission on Race Relations (CCRR), Illinois State Archives, Springfield; Waskow, *From Race Riot to Sit-In,* 51, 53–55, 74–75; *Real Estate News,* XV (August 1919, January, February 1920), 3; 3; 1, 4–6; *Crisis,* XXI (March 1921), 213–15; and in *ibid.,* XXII (August 1921), 158; Chicago Crime Commission, *Illinois Crime Survey,* part three (Chicago: Illinois Association for Criminal Justice, 1929), 958–59; *Chicago Daily News,* August 29, 1919; list of bombings in NAACP-2; Interchurch World Movement, *The Inter-Racial Situation in Chicago* (no imprint), *passim.*

[13] *Chicago Daily Tribune,* August 7, 12, 1919; Chicago Commission

The property owners' associations were more vocal than ever before. "EVERY WHITE PERSON" was the addressee of a poster which the Hyde Park–Kenwood Association had nailed on trees and poles in the district. There would be a meeting, "the most important meeting ever held in the history of Hyde Park," the poster announced, on the evening of October 20, 1919. "Protect your property. . . . Shall we sacrifice our property for one third of its value? And run like rats from a burning ship?" the poster asked. "Or shall we put up a united front and keep Hyde Park desirable for ourselves?" The meeting drew 2,000 people, who at the end rose "with one accord," and shouted their intention "to free the district of Negroes." Pamphlets circulated in contested neighborhoods after the riot. One of them, "An Appeal of White Women to American Humanity," told of the "horrible conduct of [black] French Colonials on the Rhine and the abuse of German white women." [14] Yet the police did little or nothing to protect black residents, despite the public threats of realtors and property owners' associations to rid certain areas of the "invaders." "Property is being destroyed and life endangered by bomb throwing," Francis W. Shepardson, a white member of the Chicago Commission on Race Relations, complained to Governor Lowden in February 1920. "The facts are known to all. They are reported in the papers. But," he added, "there seems to be no authority interested in the protection of Americans whose skins are black. The condition is a disgrace to American citizenship"; and, Shepardson predicted, "Unless something is done soon another riot is certain." [15]

---

on Race Relations, *The Negro in Chicago* (Chicago: University of Chicago Press, 1922), 51.

[14] In NAACP-2, a typescript copy of poster distributed to Hyde Park–Kenwood districts; excerpts from a letter to Mayor Thompson from the association, undated; *Chicago Herald-Examiner,* October 21, 25, 1919; Herbert J. Seligmann, *The Negro Faces America* (N.Y.: Harper & Bros., 1920), 212–17; Waskow, *From Race Riot to Sit-In,* 51, 53–55, 74–75.

[15] Shepardson to Lowden, February 2, 1920, CCRR Papers.

In the labor market, too, race relations during the aftermath of the riot were bitter.[16] In the stockyards, for example, the unions and the packers angrily denounced each other as the instigators of the racial bloodshed.[17] Once again, the black worker was the man in the middle, for he could not align himself with one side without alienating the other; and by March 1921 it seemed that racial violence would once again erupt in the stockyards. A strike threatened; and if there were a strike, D. E. Northam, a newspaperman and former company official in the stockyards, notified the Labor Department, "it will immediately develop into a race war, blinding the real issue by appealing to race hatred." Union officials agreed; a strike would precipitate the "bloodiest and most disastrous race war this country has ever known." [18] There was no strike at that time, but it was evident that labor conflict and racial violence in Chicago were still inextricably bound up with each other.

Acrid recriminations also marked Chicago's post-riot politics; and the scapegoat of these shouting matches often proved to be the black voter. The chief cause of the recent bloodshed, contended Mayor Thompson's bitter foe, State's Attorney Maclay Hoyne, was "black belt politics." The culprits were "City Hall organization leaders, black and white, [who] have catered to the vicious elements of the negro race for the last six years, teaching them that law is a joke and [that] the police car can be ignored if they have political backing." Had it not been for black gamblers, panderers, and grafters, with their involvement with "Big Bill" Thompson's

[16] For racial tension in the Chicago area during the 1919 steel strike, see *Chicago Daily Tribune,* October 30, 1919; *Chicago Herald-Examiner,* October 4, 1919; Seligmann, *Negro Faces America,* 206–7.

[17] *New Majority,* August 2, 9, 1919.

[18] In Records of Federal Mediation and Conciliation Service (RG 280), Suitland, Maryland, D. E. Northam to Secretary of Labor James J. Davis, March 22, 1921, in 170/1365; telegram from Starick Epworth League, Chicago, to Secretary Davis, March 20, 1921, in 170/1365-A.

machine, there probably would have been no riot.[19] Like Hoyne, the supporters of Mayor Thompson also engaged in the cynical exploitation of the bloodshed for political profit. With hyperbole and distortion, they, too, indicted the opposition for responsibility for the riot. "The recent regrettable disorders in Chicago," asserted the Thompson organization's *The Republican,* "fortunately nipped in the bud by the firm and prompt action of Mayor William Hale Thompson, were largely the logical and inevitable outcome of the encouragement given to violence and mob rule by newspapers like the Chicago Tribune. . . ." In World War I, as during the pacifist rally which Thompson had permitted to convene in Chicago in 1917, "papers of the Tribune stamp boldly and unblushingly encouraged lawlessness and disorder of every kind, in the sacred name of 'patriotism.'" *The Republican* also took issue with the *Tribune*'s statement that Chicago had "had the most horrible race riots of American history." This was a "contemptible falsehood"; Chicago had not had the worst riot in American history, for "hundreds" had been murdered in East St. Louis. The statement was but one more example of the *Tribune*'s eagerness, "in its insane desire to discredit Mayor Thompson . . . to blacken the reputation of Chicago and to start dissension among its people. . . ." [20]

Despite these massive threats to the accommodative structure of race relations in Chicago, and the possibility of renewed violence, the city's police department seemed to be no better prepared, and no more willing, to enforce justice equitably than before the riot. Perhaps the best example of this was the intensification of residential bombings, with the continued total absence of arrests and convictions. The attitudes

[19] In NAACP-2, Walter F. White to John R. Shilladay, August 26, 1919; "Lull after the Storm," *Survey,* XLII (August 30, 1919), 782; in *ibid.* (September 6, 1919), 826; *Chicago Daily News,* August 25, 1919.

[20] *The Republican,* August 9, 1919; and "Memorandum Re Conference with James Minnick . . . Chicago," Arthur B. Spingarn Papers, Library of Congress.

of hostile white policemen had not measurably improved, either, if the statement of Officer Daniel Callahan is any example. One year after the riot, Callahan—who had been suspended for his negligent conduct at the 29th Street beach and subsequently reinstated—offered his opinion that "the black people have since history began despised the white people. . . . It wouldn't take much to start another riot, and most of the white people . . . are resolved to make a clean-up this time." If a black person should talk back to him, Callahan declared, "or should say a word to a white woman in the park, there is a crowd of young men of the district . . . who would procure arms and fight shoulder to shoulder with me if trouble should come. . . ." [21] Certainly Chicago's black people had as little faith as ever in the police.[22] The memory of the department's behavior during the bloodshed was a bitter one, and it rankled in the black community. The twenty-four jurors on the all-white grand jury also expressed their amazement at the partiality of law enforcement during the riot. After hearing over thirty consecutive cases involving black defendants, the grand jury not only denounced State's Attorney Hoyne, it even staged a strike, refusing to hear further cases until Hoyne came forth with evidence against white rioters. "What the —— is the matter with the state's attorney?" the jurors grumbled. "Hasn't he got any white cases to present?" [23]

[21] Chicago Commission, *Negro in Chicago,* 451.

[22] Regarding faith in the police and the importance of police control as perhaps "the crucial factor" in determining whether or not a riot erupted, see Allen D. Grimshaw, "Actions of Police and the Military in American Race Riots," *Phylon,* XXIV (Fall 1963), 271–89.

[23] Report of the grand jury, undated, in CCRR Papers; memorandum re "Action of Chicago Branch, N.A.A.C.P. in re Legal Defense Chicago Riots," October 4, 1919, Arthur Spingarn Papers; *Chicago Daily Journal,* July 30, August 4, 1919; *Chicago Defender,* August 9, 1919; in NAACP-2, "Summary of Chicago Riots Cases in Report Submitted by A. Clement MacNeal," December 31, 1919, plus much correspondence, many reports, press releases, and memoranda re legal defense of riot victims and defendants; *Chicago Daily Tribune,* August 7–9, 1919; *Chicago Herald-Examiner,* August 9, 1919; Waskow,

It was not the lack of a precipitating incident that saved Chicago from another race war. For, indeed, there were enough incidents in 1919 and 1920 to have precipitated a half-dozen riots.[24] In late August 1919, for example, rumors swept the South Side of "a repetition of the recent riots, only much more serious." The violence would erupt on Labor Day; the "gangs of white hoodlums," Walter White notified the NAACP, "are planning to break out then." [25] No violence erupted on Labor Day, and, despite further rumors, the night of Halloween was also devoid of a race riot.[26] Rumors, however, can have a logic and reality of their own; often it is not fact that precipitates a riot, but what people perceive to be fact. Rumors, like stereotypes and generalized beliefs, can redefine ambiguous situations by predicting what will happen, and sometimes it does.[27]

"We are standing on the brink of another such disaster as occurred last July," Dr. George Cleveland Hall, a black member of the Chicago Commission on Race Relations, predicted in February 1920.[28] Two months later, Walter White echoed this prediction, adding specifically that the causes of the riot would be bombings and the black belt's lack of faith

---

From *Race Riot to Sit-In,* 45 ff.; Allan H. Spear, *Black Chicago: The Making of a Negro Ghetto, 1890–1920* (Chicago: University of Chicago Press, 1967), 217–18; Chicago Commission, *Negro in Chicago,* 46–49.

[24] For the significance of precipitating incidents, see Smelser, *Theory of Collective Behavior,* 12–21, 247 ff.

[25] Walter White to John R. Shilladay, August 26, 1919, NAACP-2.

[26] Castle M. Brown to Military Intelligence Branch, October 28, 1919, in Glasser Files; and Major Thomas B. Crockett to Director of Military Intelligence, October 30, November 26, 1919, in *ibid.; New York Times,* December 21, 1919; Chicago Commission, *Negro in Chicago,* 572–73.

[27] Smelser, *Theory of Collective Behavior,* 81–82, 247–48; Gordon W. Allport and Leo Postman, *The Psychology of Rumor* (N.Y.: Henry Holt, 1947), 193–96.

[28] Minutes of the meeting of the CCRR, February 25, 1920, copies in both CCRR Papers and Julius Rosenwald Papers, University of Chicago.

in the police. Black people feel "that they will have to depend upon themselves for proper defense," a "feeling" which, White added, had "developed to the point of martyrdom." It was "a dangerous and serious matter to have so large a percentage of Chicago's population in this frame of mind." [29] There were numerous other predictions of a riot that spring, many of them designating May 1 as the date. Then, on June 20, short-lived violence did erupt.

Sometime earlier in 1920, R. D. Jonas, a white man, and Grover Cleveland Redding, a black man who claimed to be a prophet and a native of Ethiopia, established Chicago's Star Order of Ethiopia and Ethiopian Missionaries to Abyssinia. Apparently the organization was an illegitimate offspring of Marcus Garvey's Universal Negro Improvement Association, and Jonas and Redding fostered the notion that their movement, like Garvey's, would facilitate the return of black people to Africa. On Sunday, June 20, Redding gathered a small group of "Abyssinians." Wearing the toga of an Abyssinian prince and sitting astride a white horse, Redding led the others in parade. An automobile filled with rifles was also in the procession. At 35th Street the parade stopped in front of a biracial café at 35th Street. Redding drew out of his robe an American flag, and, after dousing it with gasoline, he set it afire. Two white policemen argued with the Abyssinians, but fled after being intimidated with threats and loaded revolvers. A black patrolman arrived as a second American flag was being burned. He also remonstrated with the men, accusing them of disloyalty; and they shot him. A protesting white sailor was also shot; he staggered into the doorway of a cigar store and collapsed with fatal wounds. Before they escaped temporarily, the Abyssinians had fired twenty-five shots, injuring several people and killing two. Had the police not been vigilant and impartial, this conflagration could easily have escalated into unrestrained and generalized violence. The Chi-

[29] Statement prepared by Walter F. White, *ca.* April 15, 1920, NAACP-2.

cago Commission on Race Relations praised the police and the press for their "careful handling of the matter." [30]

Further rumors cited Labor Day 1920 as the date of the race riot; yet there was none. And there was no riot in September of that year, when three black men stabbed a white man to death in the stockyards district, nearly severing his head from his body.[31] As late as August 1921 three members of the Chicago Commission on Race Relations sent an urgent telegram to Governor Lowden, warning him that "Chicago still faces possibility of another race riot . . . unless importance of spirit of cooperation is magnified." [32] Yet again there was no riot. It was not that the antagonists were not organized; if anything, they were more tightly organized than they had been before. The black people, as one of their number recalled, had had a new feeling of togetherness since the riot.[33] The same was true of the hostile white groups. In fact, one of the supreme ironies of 1921 was that the Ragen Colts were not only "mobilized for action," but that the gang's target at that time was not Chicago's black people, but rather the Ku Klux Klan, for its anti-Catholicism. In September, 3,000 people from the stockyards district watched as the Colts hanged in effigy "a white-sheeted Klansman." [34]

Why, then, was there no riot? Perhaps the answer lies in

[30] In *ibid.,* "Defender of the Abyssinian Name and Mission: My Duty: Statement of R. D. Jonas," undated; and T. Arnold Hill to Walter White, June 24, 1920; material from Cook County coroner's jury investigating the incident in RG 60 (158260–2); interview with Mr. Wilkins; "Abyssinia and America," *Survey,* XLIV (July 3, 1920), 491; *Chicago Daily Tribune,* June 21, 23, July 24, 1920; Graham R. Taylor to Francis W. Shepardson, June 21, 1920, CCRR Papers; Chicago Commission, *Negro in Chicago,* 59–64, 480, 521, 537–38.

[31] Chicago Commission, *Negro in Chicago,* 64–67, 572–73.

[32] Telegram from Julius Rosenwald, Harry Eugene Kelly, and Francis W. Shepardson, Tuskegee, Alabama, to Frank O. Lowden, Chicago, [August?] 1921, Lowden Papers, University of Chicago.

[33] See A. Clement MacNeal to John R. Shilladay, March 10, 1920, NAACP-2; *Crisis,* XXII (August 1921), 158.

[34] Smelser, *Theory of Collective Behavior,* 253 ff., re mobilization for action; and Kenneth T. Jackson, *The Ku Klux Klan in the City, 1915–1930* (N.Y.: Oxford University Press, 1967), 95.

such rays of hope as the Chicago Commission on Race Relations, which Governor Lowden had appointed to survey the causes of racial violence in Chicago.[35] But few people in authority took its conclusions seriously. Perhaps the answer lies in a widespread but unexpressed revulsion, shared by black and white alike, at the excesses of the 1919 bloodshed. Perhaps the riot was a cathartic, purging people of some of their anger for a time. It is a fact that throughout American history major race riots have seldom recurred in the same city within a short period of time. Most probably, the answers lie in some such intangible factor, something that cannot be programmed, something that might forever escape detection by the historian or social scientist, but something that might be worth more than all the studies and surveys of riots and violence put together.

People used to think of "The Long Hot Summer" as the movie version of a William Faulkner novel. Beginning in 1964, with outbursts of racial violence in Harlem, Rochester, Jersey City, Paterson, Elizabeth, the Chicago suburb of Dixmoor, and Philadelphia, these words came to mean fear, hatred, bloodshed, death, even apprehension about America's ability to survive as a nation. "Will this be another long hot summer?" news commentators asked in 1965 and every year thereafter. The answer was always in the affirmative, and it took the form of a succession of place names—Watts in 1965, Chicago and Cleveland's Hough section in 1966, Tampa, Cincinnati, Atlanta, Newark and other New Jersey cities, and Detroit in 1967, and scores of cities in the spring of 1968, following the assassination of Dr. Martin Luther King, Jr. These names conjured up a plethora of disturbing scenes: wounded black men and women, their faces covered with blood, lying unconscious or sobbing with pain; helmeted firemen using tear gas, club-swinging policemen, phalanxes of

[35] For the operations of the CCRR, see CCRR Papers, and the extensive account in Waskow, *From Race Riot to Sit-In,* 60–104.

marching soldiers, their rifles extended, their bayonets unsheathed; overturned and burning police cars; block after block of flaming buildings; looters climbing through smashed windows into grocery, liquor, clothing, and appliance stores and emerging with their arms filled.

By 1968 racial distrust and anger divided the nation as it had not been divided for 100 years. "Arming for Armageddon," as one writer observed, were countless people, including the white ladies in the suburbs who practiced assiduously with their pistols until they could hit the target every time; if there were to be a "second Civil War," they would be ready. White vigilantes and self-proclaimed black revolutionaries were also armed and prepared to shoot to kill. Patrolling certain communities in northern New Jersey, for example, were white members of an organization known as People's Rights Enforced Against Riots and Murders; its acronym was thus PRE-ARM, and its purpose was to guard against the "rising tide of [black] insurrection."

Governments, too, succumbed to the unrest and even to the hysteria. Jittery politicians, along with cynically ambitious ones, enacted state and federal antiriot laws. While broadening police powers in New York State, legislators also debated authorizing policemen or private citizens to shoot suspected arsonists, even if the suspects were not trespassing on the property involved. "Law and order," with or without justice, became a political rallying cry in that presidential election year, and its appeal was not confined to the South. Police agencies in 1968 stockpiled tear gas grenades, shotguns and high-powered rifles, mace spray guns, and other antiriot equipment. They also bought armored cars and helicopters, weapons not designed to help apprehend the individual law violator, but lethal weapons with the potential for indiscriminate destruction. Moreover, the police enlisted white civilians for reserve duty in the event of race riots. In Cook County, Illinois, for example, the sheriff announced his intention to recruit a riot control unit of 1,000 volunteers to act with full authority as deputy sheriffs if mobilized. And that spring the U. S. Army announced that it would conduct weekly courses in riot control at Fort Gordon, Georgia, for any police departments and National Guard units that wished to enroll.

What had caused these eruptions of urban racial violence with their resultant outpouring of fear, distrust, and hostility? Why had the high hopes for racial equality and brotherhood of the earlier 1960's degenerated into bloodshed? These were questions to which various local, state, and federal commissions sought answers.[36] With more honesty than most of these commissions, the National Advisory Commission on Civil Disorders (the Kerner Commission) imputed the riots to "white racism," to a societal structure and to attitudes and mores premised on white superordination and black subordination. The legal proscription of slavery, disfranchisement, and segregation, the corruption of vagrancy and indebtedness laws to perpetuate bondage and debt peonage, lynchings and other deadly expressions of white people's animosity toward black people, white exclusiveness in residential neighborhoods, politics, the labor movement, schools, and recreational facilities, the urban race riots of the World War I era— all these, the Kerner Commission asserted, attested to the existence of America's caste society with its proclivity for violence. Moreover, the Commission added, racial separation, despite the enactment of civil rights laws, was growing, not decreasing. With the continuing migration of Southern blacks to the metropolises of the North, and with the accelerating flight of frightened whites to the suburbs, two worlds were ever emerging in the United States, one white, one black.

[36] See especially the California Governor's [McCone] Commission on the Los Angeles Riots, *Violence in the City—An End or a Beginning?* (Los Angeles: n.pub., 1965); *Report of the National Advisory Commission on Civil Disorders* (Washington: Government Printing Office, 1968); National Commission on the Causes and Prevention of Violence, *To Establish Justice, To Insure Domestic Tranquility* (Washington: Government Printing Office, 1969).

Because of the racial violence of the 1960's, scholars and other observers began to rediscover the fact of the World War I riots. Urban race riots were not new, they said; there was a history of such violence in America. But were these riots similar in origins, ecology, and participants to the more recent urban conflagrations? Was Chicago in 1919, for example, similar to Harlem, Rochester, Watts, Newark, and Detroit forty-five years later?

"Get whitey," cried out black men and women in the 1960's as they firebombed white-owned shops in black ghettos. Yet the objects of these angry attacks were symbols, not real people; they were whitey's property, not whitey himself. The white lady marksman in the suburbs could not point to actual examples of black assaults and invasions as justification for her fears. In Chicago in 1919, however, blacks actually assaulted whites, not just their property, and sometimes they killed them; and whites were even more violent in their attacks on blacks. Waged not primarily for psychic gratification, but waged over such gut-level issues as jobs and a place to live, the Chicago riot pitted people of one race against those of another. Many black people died in the disorders of the 1960's, but they did not die at the hands of white rioters; they usually fell as a result of bullets fired by the police. Whites also died in the riots of the 1960's, but these whites were not marauders who had invaded the black belt in search of victims; they were ordinarily policemen and firemen who had been dispatched to the scenes of violence to suppress mobs and extinguish fires. Self-defense was the byword in Chicago in 1919, but there were no invaders to defend against in the 1960's. Black people in the 1960's judged their actions to be "justifiable retaliation" against faceless white oppression. "I clean the white man's dirt all the time," recalled a cleaning lady during the 1964 Harlem riot. But when she got home Saturday night, during the apogee of the violence, "something happened to me." She went onto the roof, "but hearing the guns I felt like something was crawling in me, like the whole damn world was no good, and the little kids and the big ones and all of us was going to get killed because we don't know what to do. And I see the cops are white and I was crying. Dear God, I am crying! And I took this pop bottle and it was empty and I threw it down on the cops, and I was crying and laughing." [37]

But there are certain similarities between the riots of World War I and the outbursts of the 1960's. Both sets of riots occurred during periods of rising expectations on the part of black people. During World War I black men and women threatened the nation's accommodative race system of white supremacy and black inferiority as they had not done since the years of Reconstruction. Whites had long been hostile to the aspirations of black people, and this hostility deepened as a half-million Southern blacks migrated to the North. There, in overcrowded metropolises like Chicago, blacks met in bitter competition with whites over access to employment, housing, political power, and facilities for education, transportation, and recreation. Having migrated in anticipation of a better life for themselves and their children, and having fought in a war that purportedly would make the world safe for democracy, black people entered the year 1919 with aspirations for a more equitable share in both the nation's democracy and its wealth. But racial tension mounted, and eventually violence erupted, as these aspirations collided with the general white determination to reaffirm the black people's prewar status on the bottom rung of the nation's racial ladder.

In the 1960's, too, the expectations of black men and women reached heights unhoped for in recent years. The civil

[37] August Meier and Elliott Rudwick, *From Plantation to Ghetto* (N.Y.: Hill and Wang, 1966), 247–51; Meier and Rudwick, "Black Violence in the 20th Century: A Study in Rhetoric and Retaliation," in National Commission on the Causes and Prevention of Violence, *Violence in America,* prepared under the direction of Hugh Davis Graham and Ted Robert Gurr (N.Y.: Signet edition, 1969), 384–87; Joseph Boskin, "Violence in the Ghettos: A Consensus of Attitudes," *New Mexico Quarterly,* XXXVII (Winter 1968), 317–34; *Time,* LXXXIV (July 31, 1964), 11.

rights movement, the Freedom March on Washington in 1963, federal laws guaranteeing equal access to public accommodations and assuring the right to vote, Supreme Court decisions sympathetic to racial equality—these events seemed to offer hope of a better life, one that would make black people conscious agents of their own destinies. Integration was the promise of the civil rights movement, but it did not deliver on this promise, especially in the urban North. There, in the mid-1960's, the public schools were more segregated than they had been ten years before. The same was true of housing. The unemployment rate for blacks was still much higher than that for whites, while the rate for black teenagers was astronomical; and the increases in black wages in the 1960's, though notable, were far outstripped by the increases in white wages. "The Second Reconstruction," muttered disconsolate blacks, had been as dismal a failure as the first. "The Blackman in America," declared a black revolutionary, "must realize that integration of the Black and white races in the U.S. will never work. He must realize that he is not a citizen denied his rights but a colonized captive held in colonial bondage inside the U.S." Clearly, as one observer noted in the mid-1960's, "the revolution of rising expectations had become the revolution of rising frustrations." [38]

It was this frustration, augmented by the opportunism of looters to enrich themselves, that gave birth to the violent impulse to destroy the visible signs of white authority in urban black belt areas. Later, rioters and black militants justified the riots as insurrections and rebellions, as indeed they probably were to some. "We're men now," said one. "We won't take any more from Whitey." "We won," added another. "We won because we made the world pay attention to us." [39]

The riots of World War I resemble those of the 1960's in

[38] John H. Bracey, Jr., August Meier, and Elliott Rudwick (eds.), *Black Nationalism in America* (Indianapolis: Bobbs-Merrill, 1970), 514; see also Victor H. Bernstein, "Why Negroes Are Still Angry," *Redbook Magazine*, CXXVII (July 1966), 54 ff.
[39] See Boskin, "Violence in the Ghettos," 330–32.

other ways as well. Both groups of riots erupted during periods of war and international unrest. Indeed, war, throughout American history, has provided a setting conducive to racial violence. Draft and labor riots between the races broke out frequently during the Civil War. In 1917 there were race riots in Houston and East St. Louis. The year of the Red Summer was 1919, the first year of peace after one of the most disruptive wars in history and also a year of worldwide anxiety and disorder. Race riots engulfed Detroit and Harlem in 1943, during World War II. And most of the riots of the 1960's were contemporaneous with the military violence in Vietnam. Generative of rapid social and economic change, wars also seem to stimulate a generalized climate of violence, which, like the ghetto-based "subculture of violence," itself a promoter of riots, fosters an acceptance of violence as normal in everyday life.[40] It is significant, too, that in both eras the riots occurred in clusters, giving credence to the "contagion phenomenon" thesis held by certain students of violence.[41]

Also, virtually every riot erupted in the summer, when the weather was hot and uncomfortable, and when many people were restless and susceptible to the commission of acts of violence. In addition, the preponderance of the rioters of both races were teenagers and young adults, typically unattached males with fewer inhibitions and responsibilities than their elders. And in both periods of widespread rioting, blacks advocated retaliatory violence. Finally, an indispensable element in these riots was an attitude of derision and contempt for the police, and an almost utter disbelief in the willingness and ability of the police to deal justly with black people. Feeling thus, it was a short step for black people to rationalize the

[40] Grimshaw, "Study in Social Violence," 180; Bernard F. Robinson, "War and Race Conflicts in the United States," *Phylon,* IV (4th Quarter 1943), 311–27; Marvin E. Wolfgang and Franco Ferracuti, *The Subculture of Violence: Towards an Integrated Theory in Criminology* (N.Y., London: Tavistock Publications, 1967), *passim.*

[41] Richard Maxwell Brown, "Historical Patterns of Violence in America," in *Violence in America,* 55, 76n.

use of violence. Certainly this was true in Chicago in 1919, and it was also abundantly evident in the 1960's. White policemen in Harlem, James Baldwin wrote in 1960, cannot possibly understand "the lives led by the people they swagger about in two's and three's controlling. Their very presence is an insult, and it would be, even if they spent the entire day feeding gumdrops to children. They represent the force of the white world." A white judge and former police chief could do no less than concur with Baldwin. "The Negro citizen," stated George Edwards, "sees the police officer in blue coat, with white face, as the representative of the white man's law who for nearly 300 years enforced the laws—first of slavery and next of legally sanctioned segregation." The "historic function" of the police, he added, "has been 'keeping the Negro in his place'. . . ." [42]

When the Kerner Commission indicted white racism for being "essentially responsible for the explosive mixture which has been accumulating in our cities since the end of World War II," it alluded specifically to "pervasive discrimination and segregation" and to the "black migration and white exodus." [43] All these contributed to "the massive and growing concentration of impoverished Negroes in our major cities. . . ." In these "teeming racial ghettos," moreover, "segregation and poverty have intersected to destroy opportunity and hope and to enforce failure." Most whites, on the other hand, "have prospered to a degree unparalleled in the history of civilization." Thus emerged the two worlds to which the Kerner Commission referred. The importance of this concept in understanding the Chicago race riot of 1919 is that these processes leading to the virtual physical isolation of blacks from whites in cities were just beginning to gain momentum in the World War I era. Racial segregation, of

[42] Both Baldwin and Edwards quoted in *Civil Rights Digest,* II (Fall 1969), 27, 31.

[43] *Report of the National Advisory Commission on Civil Disorders,* 91–93.

course, had always existed to some degree in Chicago. As Allan H. Spear has noted, Chicago had its black ghetto in 1915, even before the migration of tens of thousands of Southern blacks to the city. Thus "the period between 1915 and 1920 was more a time of continuity than of change"; and, indeed, Spear has added, "in many significant ways, remarkably little had changed since 1920 as well." [44] In terms of the essential character of the institutions serving the ghetto and of the fundamental nature of the white resistance to black expansion outside the ghetto, Spear's observation might be an accurate one. But can one doubt that the increase of Chicago's black population from 110,000 in 1920, itself an increase of 148 per cent over 1910, to well over 800,000 in 1960 presented immense possibilities for change, some of it of the most profound nature? In 1920 Chicago had just one black ghetto, on the South Side. Now it has two, with a large concentration of blacks on the West Side as well as on the South. Furthermore, in 1920 the federal census listed 4.1 per cent of Chicago's population as being of the Negro race; in 1960, the figure was over 23 per cent.[45]

These statistics for Chicago, as well as population figures for the nation's other metropolises, provide insights vital to an understanding of the evolution of urban racial violence in the United States. The fact that Chicago's black belt abutted on neighborhoods of Irish- and Polish-Americans and other ethnic groups which were violently antiblack, and not just rhetorically so, was mirrored in the ecology of the 1919 riot. It was clear that the origins of the violence were imbedded deep in the competing social, economic, and political structures of the neighborhoods east and west of Wentworth Avenue. In Chicago in 1919 contacts between blacks and whites tended

[44] Spear, *Black Chicago,* 129–30, 223–29.
[45] U. S. Department of Commerce, Bureau of the Census, *14th Census of the United States, 1920* (Washington: Government Printing Office, 1922), III, 274; Bureau of the Census, *Statistical Abstract of the United States, 1967* (Washington: Government Printing Office, 1967), 22.

to be charged with animosity and hostility—but they were contacts nevertheless. By the 1930's and 1940's, however, interracial contacts had diminished, as black people were increasingly isolated in Chicago and other American cities. The racial violence of these years reflected this change. "New-style" riots like those of the 1960's erupted in Harlem in 1935 and again in 1943, with angry blacks demolishing symbols of white authority. Yet, as August Meier and Elliott Rudwick have demonstrated, it was the Detroit race riot of 1943 that marked a transition between the "old-style" and the "new." For while the retaliation of black people against white aggression precipitated the bloodshed, "the Negro mobs' major attention was directed toward destroying and looting white-owned business in the Negro ghetto, and . . . most of the Negroes who were killed were shot by white policemen. . . ." [46]

By the 1960's, with the emergence of America's two worlds of black and white, the new-style riot had definitely arrived. Unparalleled in American history had been the exodus of Southern blacks to Northern cities in the decades from 1910 to the advent of World War II; but this migration paled beside that of subsequent decades. Each decade since 1940 has matched or even exceeded the figure for the entire thirty-year period, 1910–1940. Millions of people poured into inner-city areas; and, aided by the demolition of slums through urban renewal and the Supreme Court's decision that restrictive covenants were legally unenforcable, the vast ghettos continued to expand. By the 1960's, urban black voters in the North were able to elect mayors from their own race, and it was evident that before long black people would constitute a majority in numerous cities. "Indeed," as Meier and Rudwick point out, "compared to the enormous ghettos of today, the Negro residential areas of the World War I period were mere enclaves." No white person with any sanity would invade

[46] Meier and Rudwick, "Black Violence in the 20th Century," 385–387; Meier and Rudwick, *From Plantation to Ghetto*, 247–51.

such massive black belts to commit violence against black people; even in earlier riots hostile whites had been hesitant about entering any areas but isolated black neighborhoods and the peripheries of the ghetto. More important, though, as these scholars have also noted, the massive ghettos "provide a relatively safe place for the destruction and looting of white-owned property. . . ." In such hostile territory, police and soldiers find it difficult if not impossible to protect property from destruction.[47]

What the future holds regarding race relations in America nobody knows. With examples like the Chicago race riot of 1919, the nation's unhappy history of the relations between black and white people is frightening enough to survey. There have been predictions, of course, including the disturbing one made in the 1830's by the prescient Alexis de Tocqueville. "If ever America undergoes great revolutions," he wrote, "they will be brought about by the presence of the black race on the soil of the United States; that is to say, they will owe their origin, not to the equality, but to the inequality of condition." [48] Whether Tocqueville is correct only time can tell, but one thing is evident. The optimist cannot take solace in the past.

[47] Meier and Rudwick, "Black Violence in the 20th Century," 386–387.

[48] Alexis de Tocqueville, *Democracy in America* (N.Y.: Vintage edition, 1964), II, 270.

Essay on Sources

MANY CHICAGOANS, both black and white, were eager to cooperate in interviews. Some spun spurious tales, others repeated rumors that had been current during the riot, and one Irish bailiff even claimed that he had killed a dozen blacks himself. Truly helpful, however, were a handful of people. Mrs. Alfreda Duster not only gave graciously of her time recalling her memories of wartime race relations, she also put me in touch with Mr. John Turner Harris, a man who was clinging to the same raft as Eugene Williams when the riot started, and she made available the unpublished memoirs of her mother, Mrs. Ida B. Wells-Barnett. My interview with Mr. Harris, of course, was invaluable, and I am deeply grateful to him for his candor and cooperation. Also valuable were the recollections of Mr. Chester Wilkins, formerly Chief Red Cap at the Illinois Central Station, Mr. A. L. Jackson, secretary during World War I of the Wabash Avenue YMCA, and Miss Lillian Herstein, labor organizer, member of the Women's Trade Union League, and teacher at Chicago's predominantly black Wendell Phillips High School.

Fruitful starting points for historians using the National Archives to study black history or race relations are: Paul Lewinson (comp.), *A Guide to Documents in the National Archives: For Negro Studies* (Washington: American Council of Learned Societies, 1947); and James R. Mock, "The National Archives with Respect to the Records of the Negro," *Journal of Negro History,* XXIII (January 1938), 49–56. Easily one of the most valuable archival sources for this study is located at the Federal Records Center in Suitland, Maryland. The Records of the Federal Mediation and Conciliation Service (RG 280) contain information without which historians cannot really deal with the labor unrest of this period. To use these records, the scholar should first consult an elaborate card file index at the National Archives in Washington, D.C. Catalogued in several different ways (according to the industry involved, the location of the industry, the name of the conciliator, the chronology of the labor disputes), the file indicates a case number for each strike, threatened strike, or lockout in which the government mediated. With these numbers, the scholar may then order the appropriate case file at the Suitland building. The material dealing with the Chicago stockyards and its troubled race relations is massive, including not only correspondence and investigations but also thousands of typescript pages of verbatim testimony by workers, union officials, and representatives of the packers. Other pertinent records at Suitland are those of the U. S. Railroad Administration (RG 14), with material on segregation in railroad employment and transportation; the U. S. Food Administration (RG 4), which maintained a Negro Press Section; the National War Labor Board (RG 2);

and the Veterans Administration (RG 244), which under a different title had a Negro Division headed by N. R. A. Crossland during World War I.

In Washington's National Archives historians researching into the causes of racial violence should consult the General Records of the Labor Department (RG 174); particularly helpful for this study were the Labor Department papers dealing with the wartime migration, the Chicago and East St. Louis riots, the Division of Negro Economics, Chicago's black community, and employment conditions, nationally and in Chicago. The General Records of the Justice Department (RG 60) contain the Glasser Files with their investigations of radicalism during and after World War I. Also in the Glasser Files are eyewitness reports by military personnel of various riots, including Chicago's upheaval; these are useful, though not always accurate because of the proclivity of some military men for seeing radicals as the instigators of every disturbance. In the Records of the War Labor Policies Board (RG 1) is a folder of correspondence between Felix Frankfurter of the Board and Dr. George E. Haynes of the Division of Negro Economics; also in these records are data regarding the U. S. Employment Service and the "Recruiting of Labor." Disappointingly sparse for black history, and indeed for almost any kind of study, are the Records of the U. S. Employment Service (RG 183) and of the U. S. Housing Corporation (RG 3). Emmett J. Scott, special assistant to the Secretary of War, left little evidence of his work in the Records of the Adjutant General's Office (RG 94) and only scattered other materials in the Records of the Office of the Secretary of War (RG 107); his personal papers at the Soper Library, Morgan State College, Baltimore, likewise reflect next to nothing about his activities in behalf of black troops.

Insufficiently appreciated by historians have been the research materials uncovered and preserved by the Works Progress Administration of the 1930's. Two monuments of the WPA's work stand ready for use in Chicago, "The Negro in Illinois" and the Foreign Language Press Survey. Located at the George Cleveland Hall Branch of the Chicago Public Library, "The Negro in Illinois" project occupies but a pair of filing cabinets; these, however, are filled with newspaper clippings, notes on interviews, and brief histories of black civic groups, businesses, fraternities, and churches. The Foreign Language Press Survey, organized by the WPA in 1936, resulted in the production of 120,000 typewritten sheets of information translated from the newspapers of twenty-two foreign-language groups. Located in the original at the University of Chicago's Harper Library and on microfilm at the Chicago Public Library, the Survey's materials reveal a great deal not only about the attitudes that these groups held on a variety of subjects but also about their contributions to Chicago's political, economic, and social life.

Since the riot was a blot on Chicago's reputation and a source of shame, few people seemed to want to write about it in their private letters. As a result, manuscript collections are usually more valuable for auxiliary information than for direct references to the riot. The papers of two members of the Chicago Commission (Victor F. Lawson and Julius Rosenwald) do have miscellaneous materials dealing with the investigation into the riot; and since the Commission's files of correspondence, questionnaires, transcripts of conferences, and records of interviews were later destroyed in a fire, along with the apparently invaluable research records of the Chicago Urban League, these fragments are significant. Even though the personal papers of only two of the Commission's thirteen members have been preserved, the historian can gain some idea of the Commission's operations from the Chicago Commission on Race Relations Papers, which Francis Shepardson, the vice chairman, deposited in the Illinois State Archives in Springfield.

Labor leaders and other Chicagoans concerned with organizing the stockyards generally bequeathed their personal papers to the Chicago Historical Society. The papers of Mary

McDowell of the settlement house back-of-the-yards are extremely useful for labor conflict in the stockyards in 1904, though they are sparse for the subsequent years. Helpful, too, are the papers of John Fitzpatrick of the Chicago Federation of Labor, Agnes Nestor of the glovemakers' union and the Women's Trade Union League, and Victor Olander of the Illinois Federation of Labor. Also at the Chicago Historical Society, but unfortunately of little use for a study of the riot, are the manuscript collections of such civic organizations as the Citizens' Association of Chicago and Municipal Voters' League, the Hyde Park Protective Association, and the United Charities of Chicago. Like the Chicago Historical Society, the University of Illinois, Chicago Circle, has done an admirable job of collecting the papers of civic and social welfare organizations—for example, the Wabash Avenue YMCA, the Juvenile Protective Association, the Phyllis Wheatley Association, the Immigrants' Protective League, the Chicago Urban League, Travelers Aid Society, League of Women Voters, and the Chicago Women's Club. Dealing primarily with the years after 1919, however, these collections proved to be of minor assistance in identifying and appraising the causes of the riot. Of some value for an understanding of the Chicago Urban League's efforts to help the migrants adjust to urban-industrial life were the papers at the Chicago Circle campus of Arthur T. Aldis, a realtor and member of the executive board of the local Urban League.

Two other major Chicago depositories of manuscript collections are the Newberry Library and the University of Chicago. At the Newberry are the Victor F. Lawson Papers, containing a mimeographed draft copy of the Chicago Commission's findings, which in some ways is more honest than the published report. Also at the Newberry, but disappointing, are the papers of Carter Harrison II, mayor of Chicago just prior to Mayor William H. Thompson, and Graham Taylor, a prominent social worker and civic leader in the city. Included in the Julius Rosenwald Papers at the University of Chicago are the minutes of the Commission's meetings. In addition, this collection is the most authoritative source of information about the financing of Chicago's social service agencies, especially the Urban League. Also helpful are the Charles Merriam Papers. A political scientist at the University of Chicago and an active political foe of Mayor Thompson, Merriam was also the teacher of Harold F. Gosnell, author of *Negro Politicians: The Rise of Negro Politics in Chicago*. Gosnell's notes for the book, including election statistics giving the black vote for the city over the decades, are in the Merriam Papers. In the Frank O. Lowden Papers are the governor's reactions to the work of the Chicago Commission, but little else. Lowden's daughter, however, Mrs. C. Phillip Miller of Chicago, made her mother's diary available to me, and in it were quotable reactions to the race riot. Also at the University of Chicago, but of limited value, are the Grace and Edith Abbott Papers, outlining the work of these two pioneering scholars in the academic discipline of professional social work.

Although the papers of the Chicago branch of the NAACP were destroyed in 1959, the organization locally was rather weak in 1919 and its records doubtless would have reflected its inactivity. The records of the national office, however, are most useful indeed for a study of racial violence during the wartime era. Kept in two locations, at the offices of the Middle Atlantic branch of the NAACP's Youth Division in Washington and at the Library of Congress, the NAACP Papers include board minutes, reports of officers, investigations of lynchings and the migration, records relating to the publishing of the *Crisis,* and materials dealing with black labor and the NAACP's political lobbying. Moreover, the papers at the Youth Division deal amost exclusively with the postwar racial violence, with an abundance of clippings, first-hand investigations by Walter White, John R. Shilladay, and Herbert J. Seligmann, affidavits of riot victims, and correspondence relating to the victims' legal problems.

Historians using the Library of Congress for the study of

black history or race relations should read "Sources of Negro History in the Manuscript Division of the Library of Congress," by Thomas P. Martin in *Journal of Negro History,* XIX (January 1934), 72–76; and John McDonough, "Manuscript Resources for the Study of Negro Life and History," *Quarterly Journal of the Library of Congress,* XXVI (July 1969), 126–48. Especially valuable for the migration are the Carter G. Woodson Papers. Woodson, founder and longtime guiding spirit of the Association for the Study of Negro Life and History, was for years the foremost collector of primary source materials relating to the history of black people in the United States; and among his papers are scores of letters written by Southern blacks to the *Chicago Defender,* Chicago Urban League, and Olivet Baptist Church, describing conditions in the South and requesting answers to their questions about schools, housing conditions, and the availability of jobs. Also at the Library of Congress are the papers of Booker T. Washington, Arthur B. Spingarn, and Robert H. and Mary Church Terrell.

Except for occasional illuminating letters, the following collections were singularly disappointing for this study: Frank Walsh Papers, New York Public Library; the Raymond Robins Papers, American Federation of Labor Papers, John R. Commons Papers, and William G. Haan Papers, all at the State Historical Society of Wisconsin; Frank Morrison Letterbooks in AFL-CIO Headquarters, Washington, D.C.; Samuel Gompers Letterbooks, Library of Congress; Arthur J. Smith newspaper clippings files, Morgan State College; Charles S. Johnson Papers, Amistad Research Center, Fisk University; and in the Moorland Collection, Howard University, the papers of Joel Spingarn, Archibald Grimke, and Mary Church Terrell.

This bibliographical essay is supposed to be merely suggestive, and thus no attempt has been made to list all of the secondary sources and the other primary sources used in this study. For that information, the reader should consult the footnotes.

Newspapers are perhaps the most fruitful source of information about the Chicago race riot. A clear picture of the city's growing interracial tension may be seen by studying Chicago's newspapers for the wartime years preceding the riot and for a period of several months after the bloodshed had subsided. Chicago newspapers used in this manner are the *Daily Tribune, Daily News, Daily Journal, Herald-Examiner,* and *Daily Drovers Journal.* Two significant black newspapers are Chicago's *Defender* and *Broad Ax.* The *Chicago Whip,* which commenced publication just two months prior to the riot, is a militant "New Negro" newspaper. Scattered issues of Chicago's first black newspaper, the *Conservator,* are available on microfilm at the Kansas State Historical Society in Topeka. Three other representative black newspapers are the *New York Age, Washington Bee,* and *Cleveland Gazette.* The most authoritative and informative members of Chicago's labor press are *The New Majority* of the Chicago Federation of Labor and the Illinois Federation's *Weekly News Letter.* Regional and national newspapers helped to provide reactions to Chicago's race relations and insights into the shattered state of race relations throughout the country; helpful in this way were the *New York Times, Milwaukee Journal, St. Louis Globe-Democrat, Omaha Daily Bee, Washington Post, Dallas Morning News, Nashville Tennessean, San Antonio Express, Memphis Commercial Appeal, Charleston News and Courier, New Orleans Times-Picayune,* and *Arkansas Gazette.*

Many national periodicals displayed their anxiety about the deterioration of race relations in 1919, and pertinent articles, though too often second-hand, appeared frequently.

For accurate and insightful reporting, the most noteworthy periodical is the *Survey. Charities,* its predecessor, is likewise important. For labor organization, particularly in the stockyards, see the magazine of the Women's Trade Union League, *Life and Labor.* The most informative black periodical is the *Crisis. Opportunity,* even though not introduced until 1923, and *The Southern Workman* are also helpful. For Chicago's black community, see *The Champion Magazine,* a short-lived periodical, copies of which are in the Moorland Collection. Outstanding individual articles are discussed under the specialized headings.

BIBLIOGRAPHIES:

A necessary starting point for any study of black people in the United States is Monroe N. Work's *A Bibliography of the Negro in Africa and America* (N.Y.: H. W. Wilson, 1928). Work compiled a massive list of pertinent literature published before 1928. Being concerned with quantity in his bibliography, he failed to disregard some useless material, and he even listed nonexistent items; but it is worth a few false leads to discover sources that otherwise might not come to one's attention. Recent supplements are Elizabeth W. Miller (comp.), *The Negro in America: A Bibliography* (Cambridge: Harvard University Press, 1966); and Erwin K. Welsch, *The Negro in the United States: A Research Guide* (Bloomington: Indiana University Press, 1965). The student should check also the extensive bibliographies in Charles S. Johnson, *The Negro in American Civilization* (N.Y.: Henry Holt, 1930); and John Hope Franklin, *From Slavery to Freedom* (N.Y.: Knopf, 1967). A further useful reference source is Monroe Work (ed.), *Negro Year Book* (Tuskegee Institute, Alabama: Negro Year Book Co.).

RACIAL VIOLENCE AND THE CHICAGO RIOT:

Until recently, few social scientists have investigated the origins of racial violence; fewer still have outlined them in terms understandable to anyone but fellow sociologists and psychologists. Of special value to the historian, however, are H. O. Dahlke's concise article, "Race and Minority Riots—A Study in the Typology of Violence," *Social Forces,* XXX (May 1952), 419–25; and Allen D. Grimshaw, "A Study in Social Violence: Urban Race Riots in the United States" (unpublished Ph.D. dissertation, University of Pennsylvania, 1959). Grimshaw has also written several articles based on his dissertation, and these are cited in Chapters I and VIII. A helpful conceptual framework for understanding such "hostile outbursts" as race riots is Neil J. Smelser, *Theory of Collective Behavior* (N.Y.: Free Press, 1962). Robert E. Park, a pioneering sociologist working in the field of race relations, is still well worth reading; see especially his *Race and Culture* (Glencoe, Illinois: Free Press, 1950). A classic in the field of social conflict is Georg Simmel, *Conflict and The Web of Group-Affiliations* (Glencoe: Free Press, 1955). Certain of Simmel's conclusions have been altered in *The Functions of Social Conflict* (Glencoe: Free Press, 1956), by Lewis A. Coser. Pertinent for its analysis of black people as scapegoats and primary objects of aggression is Leonard Berkowitz, *Aggression: A Social Psychological Analysis* (N.Y.: McGraw-Hill, 1962). Recently scholars have compiled collections of articles on racial violence; among the most comprehensive of these are The Academy of Political Science, *Proceedings,* XXIX (July 1968), *passim;* Shalom Endleman (comp.), *Violence in the Streets* (Chicago: Quadrangle, 1968); "Patterns of Violence," *Annals,* CCCLXIV (March 1966), *passim;* and National Commission on the Cause and Prevention of Violence, *Violence in America,* prepared under the direction of Hugh Davis Graham and Ted Robert Gurr (N.Y.: Signet edition, 1969).

Indispensable for an appreciation of the suspicious and violence-prone atmosphere of 1919 are John Higham, *Strangers in the Land: Patterns of American Nativism, 1860–1925* (New Brunswick: Rutgers University Press, 1955); Robert K. Murray, *The Red Scare: A Study in National Hysteria, 1919–1920* (Minneapolis: University of Minnesota Press, 1955); and William Preston, Jr., *Aliens and Dissenters: Federal Suppression of Radicals, 1902–1933* (Cambridge: Harvard University Press, 1963). Although the more recent account of the "Red Summer" is Arthur I. Waskow's *From Race Riot to Sit-In* (Garden City, N.Y.: Doubleday & Co., 1966), in many ways the more thorough study is still Herbert J. Seligmann's *The Negro Faces America* (N.Y.: Harper & Bros., 1920). Waskow's study is descriptive rather than analytical, and it deals more with postriot than with pre-riot events; rather than explaining why the Chicago riot erupted, for example, he tells how the Chicago Commission on Race Relations proceeded to investigate the causes of the violence.

Most attempts to explain the Chicago riot have parroted the report of the Chicago Commission, *The Negro in Chicago* (Chicago: University of Chicago Press, 1922). This is understandable. The Commission's research was penetrating and its report honest. For example, the Commission resisted efforts by Governor Frank O. Lowden to change one of its findings regarding the mentality of black people. Citing Army intelligence tests and contending that the intelligence of black people was still below that of "the race which furnished . . . Aristotle more than 2000 years ago," Lowden wrote that he was "not persuaded that the Commission acted upon sufficient evidence when it found that negroes have not 'inferior mentality.' . . ." But the Commission was not as thorough in certain areas as it could have been, most notably in the area of labor, where it failed to convey the interracial conflict over unionization and the seething labor unrest that punctuated the atmosphere in 1919. The report is also weak in its coverage of politics and the "New Negro." Many of its explanations, moreover, are based on post-riot events and evidence. Several significant investigations of the riot supplement the Commission's report. The findings of the coroner are Peter Hoffman (comp.), *The Race Riots: Biennial* [Cook County Coroner's] *Report* (Chicago: n.pub., n.d.). Valuable, too, are the reports of Carl Sandburg, who as a young newspaper reporter wrote *The Chicago Race Riots* (N.Y.: Harcourt, Brace & Howe, 1919); and of an NAACP official, Walter White, "Chicago and Its Eight Reasons," *Crisis,* XVIII (October 1919), 293–97. Organized labor's view of the causes of the racial bloodshed is Harrison George, *Chicago Race Riots* (Chicago: Great Western Publishing Co., 1919); and that of black economic radicals is represented by articles in *The Messenger,* II (September 1919), 11 ff. Disappointing because of its superficiality is Guido Dobbert, "A History of the Chicago Race Riot of 1919" (unpublished A.M. thesis, University of Chicago, 1957).

CHICAGO'S BLACK COMMUNITY:

Throughout the twentieth century Chicago's black community has been the living laboratory for scholars from the University of Chicago, and one of the results has been a series of excellent surveys. Perhaps the best account, and one which is also in many ways the most comprehensive study of any ghetto, is St. Clair Drake and Horace R. Cayton, *Black Metropolis: A Study of Negro Life in a Northern City* (N.Y.: Harcourt, Brace, 1945). The community has also had a very excellent history written about it: Allan H. Spear's *Black Chicago: The Making of a Negro Ghetto, 1890–1920* (Chicago: University of Chicago Press, 1967). Earlier and much sketchier studies are Fannie Barrier Williams, "Social Bonds in the 'Black Belt' of Chicago," *Charities,* XV (October 7, 1905), 40–44; R. R. Wright, Jr., "The Negro in Chicago," *Southern Workman,* XXXV (October 1906), 553–56; and Louise de K. Bowen, *The Colored People of Chicago* (Chicago: Juvenile Protective Association, 1913). At the height of the migration Junius B. Wood's research in the black belt was published as *The Negro in Chicago* (Chicago: Chicago Daily News, *ca.* 1916). Essential to an appreciation of the ominous state of race relations in the spring of 1919 is a speech by A. L. Jackson which was reprinted as "Chicago's Negro Problem," City Club of Chicago *Bulletin,* XII (March 17, 1919), 75–76. A useful tool for placing Chicago's black businessmen in proper perspective is a directory of notable black people: Ford S. Black, *Black's Blue Book* (Chicago: Ford S. Black, 1917). Also helpful are "A Review of Colored Chicago," *Champion Magazine,* I (March 1917), 336–49; Frederic H. H. Robb (ed.), *The Negro in Chicago, 1779–1929* (Chicago: Washington Intercollegiate Club of Chicago, 1929); the entire issue of *Opportunity,* VII (March 1929); "Colored Chicago," *Crisis,* X (September 1915), 234–42; Franck L. Schoell, "La 'Ceinture Noire' de Chicago," *Revue de Paris,* II (March-April 1920), 410–28; and John H. Taitt (ed.), *The Souvenir of Negro Progress, 1779–1925* (Chicago: De Saible Association, 1925). As the black community continued to expand after the war, numerous researchers flocked to study it. Immediately following the riot, Howard Gold and Byron K. Armstrong discussed, but with little insight, race relations in Chicago in *A Preliminary Study of Inter-Racial Conditions in Chicago* (N.Y.: Home Missions Council, 1920).

MIGRATION:

By far the best source of information about the inducements to migrate and the various means by which the migration was carried out are the letters of the migrants themselves: Emmett J. Scott (comp.), "Letters of Negro Migrants of 1916–1918," *Journal of Negro History,* IV (July 1919), 290–340; and Scott, "Additional Letters of Negro Migrants of 1916–1918," in *ibid.* (October 1919), 412–65. The adjustment of the newly arrived migrants is well portrayed in Arvarh E. Strickland, *History of the Chicago Urban League* (Urbana: University of Illinois Press, 1966). Perhaps the most competent investigation of the migration, based on field trips throughout the South, is Emmett J. Scott, *Negro Migration during the War* (N.Y.: Oxford University Press, 1920). Extensive field research is also reflected in Department of Labor, Division of Negro Economics, *Negro Migration in 1916–17* (Washington: Government Printing Office, 1919). Other studies are the thoroughly readable but impressionistic *Anyplace But Here* by Arna Bontemps and Jack Conroy (N.Y.: Hill and Wang, 1966); Henderson H. Donald, "The Negro Migration of 1916–1918," *Journal of Negro History,* VI (October 1921), 383–498; Louise V. Kennedy, *The Negro Peasant Turns Cityward* (N.Y.: Columbia University Press, 1930); Louise V. Kennedy and Frank A. Ross, *A Bibliography of Negro Migration* (N.Y.: Columbia University Press, 1934); Carter G. Woodson, *A Century of Negro Migration* (Washington: Association for the Study of Negro Life and History, 1918); and Thomas J. Woofter, *Negro Migration* (N.Y.: W. D. Gray, 1920). In order really to understand the magnitude of the adjustment caused by the migration, the historian needs to know not only about the new and strange conditions in the city but also about the environment that the migrants had left behind. An excellent source for this information is Charles S. Johnson *The Shadow of the Plantation* (Chicago: Phoenix Books of University of Chicago Press, 1966).

HOUSING:

Two notable summaries of the evolution and social problems of Northern black belts, the primary example in each of which is Chicago, are Robert C. Weaver, *The Negro Ghetto* (N.Y.: Harcourt, Brace, 1948); and E. W. Burgess, "Residential Segregation in American Cities," *Annals,* CXL (November 1928), 105–15. For pertinent demographic studies, see Chapter V (footnote 9). Comprehensive premigration investigation of the housing for Chicago's black people are A. P. Comstock, "Chicago's Housing Conditions," VI: "The Problem of the Negro," *American Journal of Sociology,* XVIII (September 1912), 241–57; Monroe N. Work, "Negro Real Estate Holders of Chicago" (unpublished M.A. thesis, University of Chicago, 1903); and S. P. Breckenridge, "The Color Line in the Housing Problem," *Survey,* XXIX (February 1, 1913), 575–76. For insights into the quality and sanitation of this housing, see H. L. Harris, "Negro Mortality Rates in Chicago," *Social Service Review,* I (March 1927), 58–77. A classic in American sociology and invaluable to this study is E. Franklin Frazier's *The Negro Family in Chicago* (Chicago: University of Chicago Press, 1932), especially the portions dealing with living conditions in the different zones of housing for different classes of black people. *The Inter-Racial Situation in Chicago* (Chicago: Interchurch World Movement, n.d.) contains useful facts about the rash of racial bombings in 1918–1919. C. S. Duke, a black engineer, offered solutions to the housing problem in *The Housing Situation and the Colored People of Chicago* (Chicago: n.pub., 1919). Issues of the Chicago Real Estate Board *Bulletin* recommending the restriction of black expansion were essential to gauging the opposition of white realtors to the "invasion."

POLITICS:

A noteworthy investigation of black people as an urban political power is Harold F. Gosnell's *Negro Politicians* (Chicago: University of Chicago Press, 1935). Important appraisals of black political potency before the migration are G. W. Ellis, "The Negro in the Chicago Primary," *Independent,* LXXII (April 25, 1912), 890–91; and Ellis, "The Chicago Negro in Law and Politics," *Champion Magazine,* I (March 1917), 349 ff. The Municipal Voter's League's *Annual Preliminary Report* (no imprints) is available for scattered years in the Chicago Historical Society, and is an excellent guide to the qualifications of the black aldermen. Also available at the Chicago Historical Society are copies of *The Republican,* the wildly partisan newspaper published by supporters of Mayor Thompson.

Thompson's alliance with the black belt has never been more than superficially examined. Yet several articles are of some assistance: George Schottenhamel, "How Big Bill Thompson Won Control of Chicago," *Journal of the Illinois State Historical Society,* XLV (Spring 1952), 30–49; G. F. Robinson, Jr., "The Negro in Politics in Chicago," *Journal of Negro History,* XVII (April 1932) 180–229; Ralph J. Bunche, "The Thompson-Negro Alliance," *Opportunity,* VII (March 1929), 78–80; John M. Allswang "The Chicago Negro Voter and the Democratic Consensus: A Case Study, 1918–1936," *Journal of the Illinois State Historical Society,* LX (Summer 1967), 145–75; and Harold F. Gosnell, "The Chicago Black Belt as a Political Battleground," *American Journal of Sociology,* XXXIX (November 1933), 329–41. Two highly useful masters' theses are Joseph A. Logsdon, "The Rev. Archibald J. Carey and the Negro in Chicago Politics" (unpublished M. A. thesis, University of Chicago, 1961); and George C. Hoffman, "Big Bill Thompson of Chicago, His Mayoral Campaigns and Voting Strength" (unpublished M.A. thesis, University of Chicago, 1956).

The most insightful survey of black labor, even though it is sometimes inaccurate in its presentation of evidence, is Sterling D. Spero and Abram L. Harris, *The Black Worker* (N.Y.: Atheneum edition, 1968). Other discussions of black workers which touch on the interracial labor tension in Chicago are H. R. Cayton and G. S. Mitchell, *Black Workers and the New Unions* (Chapel Hill: University of North Carolina Press, 1939); and H. R. Northrup, *Organized Labor and the Negro* (N.Y.: Harper, 1944).

Three excellent studies examining the wartime tension in the stockyards are Alma Herbst, *The Negro in the Slaughtering and Meat-Packing Industry in Chicago* (Boston: Houghton Mifflin, 1932); Edna Louise Clark, "History of the Controversy in the Slaughtering and Meat Packing Industries in Chicago" (unpublished M.A. thesis, University of Chicago, 1922); and David Brody, *The Butcher Workmen: A Study of Unionization* (Cambridge: Harvard University Press, 1964). See also William M. Tuttle, Jr., "Some Strikebreakers' Observations of Industrial Warfare," *Labor History,* VII (Spring 1966), 193–96; and Tuttle, "Labor Conflict and Racial Violence: The Black Worker in Chicago, 1894–1919," in *ibid.,* X (Summer 1969), 408–32. There are, in addition, numerous contemporary articles about efforts to organize the stockyards workers: A. Kaztauskis, "From Lithuania to the Chicago Stockyards," *Independent,* LVII (August 4, 1904), 241–48; Ernest Poole, "The Meat Strike," in *ibid.* (July 28, 1904), 179–84; John R. Commons, "Labor Conditions in Meat Packing and the Recent Strike," *Quarterly Journal of Economics,* XIX (November 1904), 1–32; R. R. Wright, Jr., "The Negro in Times of Industrial Unrest," *Charities,* XV (October 7, 1905), 69–73; and W. Z. Foster, "How Life Has Been Brought into the Stockyards," *Life and Labor,* VIII (April 1918), 63–72. A history of Judge Alschuler's mediations is in *Monthly Labor Review,* XI (July 1920), 101–5.

Demobilization was a period of anxiety for black workers, as several studies well indicate; see Department of Labor, Division of Negro Economics, *The Negro at Work during the War and during Reconstruction* (Washington: Government Printing Office, 1921); J. W. Johnson, "Changing Status of Negro Labor," National Conference of Social Work, *Proceedings, 1918,* 383–88; G. E. Haynes, "Negro Labor and the New Order," in *ibid., 1919,* 531–38; F. B. Washington, "Reconstruction and the Colored Women," *Life and Labor,* VIII (January 1919), 3–7; W. L. Evans, "The Negro in Chicago Industries," *Opportunity,* I (February 1923), 15–16; and Graham Taylor, "An Epidemic of Strikes in Chicago," *Survey,* XLII (August 2, 1919), 645–46. Particularly helpful for the story of black labor in Chicago are two other works: R. R. Wright, Jr., "The Industrial Condition of Negroes in Chicago" (unpublished D.B. thesis, University of Chicago, 1901); and Charles S. Johnson, "How the Negro Fits in Northern Industry," *Industrial Psychology,* I (June 1926), 399–412.

An influential article dealing with the distrust black workers had of the labor movement is Booker T. Washington's "The Negro and the Labor Unions," *Atlantic Monthly,* CXI (June 1913), 755–67. Several other articles also reveal this deep apprehension, two of the best of which are Kelly Miller, "The Negro as a Workingman," *American Mercury,* VI (November 1925), and John P. Frey, "Attempts to Organize Negro Workers," *American Federationist,* XXXVI (March 1929), 296–305.

THE NEW NEGRO AND MILITANT SELF-DEFENSE:

Superb beginning points for a study of the "New Negro" are, first, a contemporary statement, Alain Locke (ed.), *The New Negro* (N.Y.: Atheneum edition, 1968); and, second, an intellectual history, August Meier's *Negro Thought in America, 1880–1915* (Ann Arbor: University of Michigan Press, 1963). Also illuminating are Rayford Logan (ed.), *The New Negro Thirty Years Afterward* (Washington: Howard University Press, 1955); Robert T. Kerlin, *The Voice of the Negro, 1919* (N.Y.: E. P. Dutton, 1920); E. Franklin Frazier, "New Currents of Thought among the Colored People of America" (unpublished M.A. thesis, Clark University, 1920); Loraine R. Green, "The Rise of Race-Consciousness in the American Negro" (unpublished M.A. thesis, University of Chicago, 1919); and W. O. Brown, "The Nature of Race Consciousness," *Social Forces,* X (October 1931), 90–97. Several good articles discuss the ascendancy of the New Negro attitudes and leaders after Booker T. Washington's death: E. Franklin Frazier, "The American Negro's New Leaders," *Current History,* XXVIII (April 1928), 56–59; V. F. Calverton, "The New Negro," in *ibid.,* XXIII (February 1926), 694–98; and H. M. Bond, "Negro Leadership since Washington," *South Atlantic Quarterly,* XXIV (April 1925), 115–30. A sketchy exposition of the activities of Chicago's New Negroes is Carroll Binder's *Chicago and the New Negro* (Chicago: Chicago Daily News, 1927); perhaps more suggestive are the words of one of Chicago's New Negroes in William M. Tuttle, Jr. (ed.), "Views of a Negro during 'the Red Summer' of 1919," *Journal of Negro History,* LI (July 1966), 209–18.

Two articles by W. E. B. Du Bois are significant because they point up the New Negro's acute resentment of the contradiction between the ideals for which the black troops were fighting and the manner in which the Army discriminated against them: "An Essay toward a History of the Black Men in the Great War," *Crisis,* XVIII (June 1919), 63–87; and "Documents of the War," in *ibid.* (May 1919), 16–21. Of the several general accounts of black troops, the most thorough and accurate is Emmett J. Scott, *Scott's Official History of the American Negro in the World War* (Chicago: Homewood Press, 1919). A little-known contribution to an appreciation of the war's impact on an individual black soldier is an obscure volume, *With "Old Eph" in the Army* (Baltimore: H. E. Houck, 1919), by W. H. Jordan. Also useful is "The American Negro in World Wars I and II," *Journal of Negro Education,* XII (Summer 1943), 263–584. Chicago's black troops recorded some of their experiences in *Heroes of 1918* (no imprint), in the stacks of the Library of Congress; and in a series of articles by the 8th Regiment's chaplain, William S. Braddan, in the May-June 1919, issues of the *Chicago Broad Ax.* A white officer with the 8th, Warner A. Ross, wrote a patronizing account, *My Colored Battalion* (Chicago: Warner A. Ross, 1920).

If, as Robert E. Park and Robert T. Kerlin have asserted, the literature of black people, and especially their poetry, is a "transcript" of their lives, then the literary outpouring of the postwar period is an exceedingly valuable source. Park commends the "New Negro" poetry in "Negro Race Consciousness as Reflected in Race Literature," *American Review,* I (September-October 1923), 505–17. N. I. White, on the other hand, criticizes it because it is too harsh on white people: "Racial Feeling in Negro Poetry," *South Atlantic Quarterly,* XXI (January 1922), 14–29. A more complete study of the subject is R. C. Barton, *Race Consciousness and the American Negro* (Copenhagen: Nørrebros Central Printing, 1934); also significant are Robert A. Bone's *The Negro Novel in America* (New Haven: Yale University Press, 1958); and John Hope Franklin, "The New Negro History," *Journal of Negro History,* XLII (April 1957), 89–97.

MISCELLANY:

Since so few organizations in 1919 expressed concern about the troubled state of race relations in the United States, it is a relatively easy task to isolate the ones that did. The annual reports, bulletins, special studies, and other publications of these groups were thus a key source of data for this study. Practically any historian working in the twentieth century fields of urban history, race relations, or social reform will find valuable the publications of Chicago's many settlement houses, the Juvenile Protective Association, Women's Trade Union League, Chicago Community Trust, National Conference of Social Work (*Proceedings*), Chicago Committee of Fifteen, Chicago Crime Commission, NAACP, National and Chicago Urban League, Citizens' Association of Chicago, and Municipal Voter's League.

Index

Abbott, Robert S., 172, 197. *See also Chicago Defender*

Abyssinians, *see* Star Order of Ethiopia

Acme Packing Company, 130

Adams, Henry, 78

Africa, 225, 227

African Methodist Episcopal Church: on Lowden and East St. Louis, 231, 232

African Methodist Episcopal Sunday School Convention, 137

Alabama, 94, 231; and migration, 78–81 *passim*, 85, 86; and labor agents, 87–88

Alschuler, Judge Samuel: as U.S. Administrator for Adjustment of Labor Differences in Certain Packing House Industries, 126, 133–34

Amalgamated Clothing Workers, 144

Amalgamated Meat Cutters and Butcher Workmen of North America (AMCBW): in Chicago stockyards, 114–56 *passim;* and black workers, 115–56 *passim*

AMCBW, Local 651 (black) of, 136, 151; and petition to Wilson, 135

American Car and Foundry Company: labor violence at, 139

American Federation of Labor: and black members, viii; racially exclusionist policies of, 111, 125, 142–56 *passim;* federal charters of, 125, 144; blacks' attitudes toward, 145–56 *passim. See also* names of individual unions of; Gompers; segregation

American Legion, 186, 247

American Protective Association, 199

American Railway Union, 112

American Unity Labor Union, 152

Anderson, Louis B., 189, 190, 194, 197; on fire "back-of-the-yards," 61; Municipal Voters' League on, 196; and Thompson, 196; and black constituents, 196

Angelus Apartments: during Chicago riot, 41

antiradicalism: in U.S. in 1919, 17–21. *See also* Red Scare

"Appeal of White Women to American Humanity," 251

Argo, Illinois: labor violence at, 137–38, 140. *See also* Corn Products Refinery

Arkansas: and migration, 78, 85. *See also* Elaine, Arkansas, race riot

Arkansas Gazette (Little Rock), 247

Armour, J. Ogden, 61, 150; on strikebreakers, 118

Armour and Company, 60, 101, 117, 129, 151; Chicago blacks on, 153. *See also* Chicago meatpackers

Army, U.S., 260; in Washington race riot, 30; in Omaha race riot, 245; in Elaine race riot, 247. *See also* National Guard; Illinois National Guard

Association for the Study of Negro Life and History, 223

athletic clubs, 4, 32–33; in Chicago riot, 32–33, 33n.; and racial hostility, 103; and assaults on blacks, 199, 201n.; and political intimidation, 199–200, 201. *See also* Ragen Colts

Atlanta, Georgia, 91, 92; race riot of 1906, 11, 212

Attorney General, U.S.: and black radicalism, 227–28

Austin, William B.: and house bombing, 158–59

Baker, Newton D.: and Washington race riot, 30

Baker, Ray Stannard: on migrants, 94; on Chicago's labor consciousness, 141